Ravel Studies

Demonstrating the vibrant nature of current research on Maurice Ravel, one of the most significant figures in twentieth-century French music, a team of distinguished international scholars provides new interdisciplinary perspectives and insights. Through historical, critical, and analytical means, the volume reveals the symbiotic relationships between Ravel's music and aesthetic, cultural, literary, gender, performance-based, and medical studies. While the chapters progress from French aesthetic–literary association, including with Colette and Proust, to more extended disciplinary couplings, with American history, jazz, dance, and neurology, the organization is relatively free to enable other thematic links to emerge. The volume presents a refreshing variety of scholarly approaches to Ravel and his music, set within broad contexts and current musicological debates. In a Ravelian spirit, it is intended that the essays will serve collectively as a model for expanding the agendas of other composer-based studies.

DEBORAH MAWER is Professor of Music within the Lancaster Institute for the Contemporary Arts at Lancaster University. Her books include *The Ballets of Maurice Ravel: Creation and Interpretation* (2006), *Darius Milhaud: Modality and Structure in Music of the 1920s* (1997), and *The Cambridge Companion to Ravel* (2000). Her articles and reviews on varied topics have appeared in the *Journal of the Royal Musical Association*, *Twentieth-Century Music*, *Music & Letters*, *Opera Quarterly*, *Music Theory Online*, and the *British Journal of Music Education*, as well as in essay collections on French music.

Ravel Studies

EDITED BY
Deborah Mawer

CAMBRIDGE UNIVERSITY PRESS
Cambridge, New York, Melbourne, Madrid, Cape Town, Singapore,
São Paulo, Delhi, Dubai, Tokyo, Mexico City

Cambridge University Press
The Edinburgh Building, Cambridge CB2 8RU, UK

Published in the United States of America by Cambridge University Press, New York

www.cambridge.org
Information on this title: www.cambridge.org/9780521886970

© Cambridge University Press 2010

First published 2010

Printed in the United Kingdom at the University Press, Cambridge

A catalogue record for this publication is available from the British Library

Library of Congress Cataloguing in Publication data
Ravel studies / [edited by] Deborah Mawer.
    p.   cm.
  Includes bibliographical references and index.
  ISBN 978-0-521-88697-0 (hardback)
  1. Ravel, Maurice, 1875–1937 – Criticism and interpretation.   I. Mawer, Deborah, 1961–
  II. Title.
  ML410.R23R38 2010
  780.92–dc22
  2010026363

ISBN 978-0-521-88697-0 Hardback

Contents

Plates

Tables

Contributors

Erik Baeck (MD; Fellow, American Academy of Neurology) is Honorary Chief in the Department of Neurology at the Algemeen Centrum Ziekenhuis, Antwerp (ACZA) in Belgium. He has longstanding interests in musicology, having been a prizewinner of the International Competition for Young Conductors at Besançon in 1963, and having conducted works of Ravel. His musicological publications range from articles in journals such as *Nachrichten zur Mahler-Forschung* and *Revue de musicologie*, through to monographs on *Peter Benoit: een pathografie van leven, werk en persoonlijkheid* (2000) and *André Cluytens: itinéraire d'un chef d'orchestre* (2009).

David Epstein (1930–2002), formerly Professor in Music at the Massachusetts Institute of Technology (MIT), was a distinguished international figure in music theory and analysis. He is best remembered for his influential texts: *Beyond Orpheus: Studies in Musical Structure* (1979) and *Shaping Time: Music, the Brain, and Performance* (1995; winner of the Deems Taylor Award from the American Society of Composers, Authors, and Publishers). Long-time Music Director of the MIT Symphony Orchestra, he was a guest conductor with the Boston Symphony Orchestra, Royal Philharmonic Orchestra, Bavarian Radio Symphony Orchestra, Jerusalem Orchestra, and Berlin Radio Orchestra, as well as founding conductor of the New Orchestra of Boston; in 2003 he was awarded posthumously the prestigious Max Rudolph Award by the Conductors Guild.

Nicholas Gebhardt is Lecturer in American Studies at Lancaster University, with interests in intellectual contexts including American social and cultural history, American studies, sound arts, and popular music studies. He worked previously in radio broadcasting as Music Director of 2SER-FM in Sydney. His publications include *Going for Jazz: Musical Practices and American Ideology* (2001), and articles on Michel Chion and Ajay Heble; he is currently completing a book called *Music is Our Business: The Rise of the Popular Musician in American Culture, 1882–1929*.

Steven Huebner holds the James McGill Chair in the Schulich School of Music at McGill University, Montreal, where his research focuses on French and Italian music. He is the author of *The Operas of Charles Gounod* (1990) and *French Opera at the Fin de Siècle: Wagnerism, Nationalism, and Style* (1999; winner of the Prix Opus 2000). His articles and reviews have appeared in *19th-Century Music*, *Journal of the American Musicological Society*, *Cambridge Opera Journal*, *Music & Letters*, and *Journal of the Royal Musical Association*; he is currently preparing a cycle of essays about Ravel.

Stephanie Jordan is Research Professor in Dance at Roehampton University, London. A former dancer, musician, and dance critic, she is the author of *Striding Out: Aspects of Contemporary and New Dance in Britain* (1992) and *Moving Music: Dialogues with Music in Twentieth-century Ballet* (2000; awarded the 2001 Special Citation of the Dance Perspectives Foundation, New York); she is sole or joint editor of five other volumes. Her monograph *Stravinsky Dances: Re-visions across a Century* (2007) examines recent choreographic productions and rereadings of the Stravinsky legacy as well as early settings of his work.

Emily Kilpatrick is a freelance musicologist and pianist based in London. Her published articles include 'Into the Woods: Re-telling the Wartime Fairytales of Ravel', *Musical Times* (2008), 'Jangling in Symmetrical Sounds: Maurice Ravel as Storyteller and Poet', *Journal of Music Research Online* (2009), '*L'Enfant et les sortilèges*: fantaisie lyrique, poésie musicale', *Quodlibet* (2009), and 'The Carbonne Copy: Tracing the Première of *L'Heure espagnole*', *Revue de musicologie* (2009). She is also a highly regarded vocal accompanist and piano duo partner; with Roy Howat she has recorded Fauré's piano duets (*Belle Epoque: A Portrait of Gabriel Fauré*, 2009).

Deborah Mawer is Professor of Music within the Lancaster Institute for the Contemporary Arts at Lancaster University. Her books include *The Ballets of Maurice Ravel: Creation and Interpretation* (2006), *Darius Milhaud: Modality and Structure in Music of the 1920s* (1997), and *The Cambridge Companion to Ravel* (Cambridge University Press, 2000); her articles and reviews on varied topics have appeared in the *Journal of the Royal Musical Association*, *Twentieth-Century Music*, *Music & Letters*, *Opera Quarterly*, *Music Theory Online*, and the *British Journal of Music Education*, as well as in essay collections on French music.

Michael J. Puri is Assistant Professor of Music Theory at the University of Virginia, where his research interests include critical theory, hermeneutics, and the music of Wagner, Ravel, and Debussy. His articles and reviews have appeared in *19th-Century Music*, *Music & Letters*, and *Notes*; his article on Ravel's dandyism, published in the *Journal of the American Musicological Society*, received the 2008 Alfred Einstein Award. He has recently finished a book entitled *Decadent Dialectics: Memory, Sublimation, and Desire in the Music of Maurice Ravel* (forthcoming).

Lloyd Whitesell is Associate Professor of Music History in the Schulich School of Music at McGill University, Montreal. He has published articles on Maurice Ravel, Benjamin Britten, film music, minimalism, modern tonalities, and the anxiety of influence. An essay collection which he co-edited, *Queer Episodes in Music and Modern Identity* (2002) that included his essay on 'Ravel's Way', won the 2002 Philip Brett Award for excellence in gay and lesbian musicology. He is the author of a monograph on *The Music of Joni Mitchell* (2008).

Acknowledgements

This book has been some time in gestation and there are many individuals whose generosity and support it is my pleasure to acknowledge. The very first contributor to this volume was the late David Epstein, formerly of the Massachusetts Institute of Technology, who was a most enthusiastic supporter of the idea from the outset. It is, therefore, highly fitting to be able to complete and present his final musicological essay with the kind permission of his family. Much gratitude is due to all the contributors who have given freely of their time and expertise to secure this volume, and to the many libraries and associated research institutions. For undertaking the major task of setting all the music examples with both expertise and enthusiasm, I wish to offer special thanks to Adam Greig, a highly dedicated doctoral student at Lancaster University. At Cambridge University Press, warm thanks are also extended to Vicki Cooper and her supportive staff, especially to Pat Harper for her perceptive copyediting. Other more specific acknowledgements are given in the footnotes.

Crucially this project could not have been brought to fruition without financial assistance from various organizations. I am very grateful for an award from the Trustees of the journal *Music & Letters*, which contributed significantly to the costs of setting the various music examples, especially those presented in tribute to David Epstein. Equally, I am appreciative of funding from the National Teaching Fellowship Scheme (NTFS 2008), awarded to acknowledge and promote research-led teaching and learning, as well as from Lancaster University. Both these sources have assisted with the costs involved in clearing music permissions and in acquiring photographic illustrations.

Copyright musical materials are reproduced as follows.

Excerpts from the *Sonatine* ('Modéré', 'Mouvement de menuet'), © Editions Durand, 1905; *Daphnis et Chloé*, ballet score, © Editions Durand, 1913; *La Valse*, orchestral score, © Editions Durand, 1921; *L'Enfant et les sortilèges*, © Editions Durand, 1925; *Sonate pour violon et piano*, © Editions Durand, 1927; Concerto pour la main gauche, © Editions Durand, 1931; Concerto pour piano et orchestre, © Editions Durand, 1932, are reproduced by kind permission of Durand-Salabert-Eschig (Universal Music Publishing Group).

Excerpts from *A la manière de... Borodine*, © A. Z. Mathot, 1914, Salabert, are reproduced by permission of Durand-Salabert-Eschig (Universal Music Publishing Group).

The excerpt from *Alborada del gracioso*, orchestral score, © Editions Max Eschig, 1923, renewed 1970, is also reproduced by permission of Durand-Salabert-Eschig (Universal Music Publishing Group).

The excerpt from Billy Mayerl, 'Marigold', © Keith Prowse Music Publishing, 1927, is reproduced by kind permission of KPM Music, London.

The excerpt from George Gershwin, 'Summertime' (*Porgy and Bess*®), music and lyrics by George Gershwin, Du Bose Heyward, and Dorothy Heyward and Ira Gershwin, © 1935 (renewed 1962) Chappell & Co. Inc., Warner/Chappell North America Ltd, is reproduced by permission of Faber Music Ltd. All rights reserved.

Note on the text

With the exception of specific literary contexts, materials are presented in English translation within the main text and, for verification purposes, in French within the footnotes (and in the case of Chapter 1, by Steven Huebner, also within a substantial appendix). Unless otherwise stated, translations have been undertaken by the author of the chapter. For previously published English translations, the French original is not supplied.

Musical references employ a mixture of bar numbers and rehearsal figures depending on the available editions of a work. Generally, bar numbers are used for piano or chamber music scores and rehearsal marks (Figures) are used for full orchestral or staged work scores. Consequently, a shorthand system has been devised for orchestral references: Fig. 1^{-1} refers to the bar preceding rehearsal figure 1; Fig. 1 denotes the full bar with this label attached; Fig. 1^{+1} refers to the bar following rehearsal figure 1.

In musical discussion, the sign '/', as in F/F$\sharp$, indicates a simultaneity, and, dependent upon context, sometimes the specific notion of modal 'mixture': the presence of alternative pitches used in a flexible, inflected manner. Separation of pitches by commas indicates a neutral listing, such as for scalic components. Separation of pitches by means of '–' denotes a voice-leading progression: a directed linear motion from one pitch to another. Minor chords within a harmonic progression are indicated by lower-case Roman numerals, as in the expression 'G: ii–V–I' (within a tonality of G major); or by the qualification 'm', as in the expression C$\sharp$–A$\sharp^7$–D$\sharp$m–F$\sharp$m. Finally, the chordal symbol 'ø', as in D$\sharp^{ø7}$, denotes a half-diminished seventh construction (i.e. D$\sharp$, F$\sharp$, A, C$\sharp$).

Unless otherwise marked, music examples which involve transposing instruments (such as David Epstein's reduced orchestral scores) are presented at sounding pitch.

Introduction: the growth of Ravel studies

Deborah Mawer

The last few years have seen a pleasing expansion in research on Maurice Ravel (1875–1937), one of the most significant figures within French musical culture in the first half of the twentieth century. This trend may be attributable in part, perhaps, to the success of *The Cambridge Companion to Ravel* in 2000, which itself sought to stimulate fresh interest in the composer by supplementing a core of eminent Ravel scholars with a group of experts from related French music studies.

According to the Société des auteurs, compositeurs, et éditeurs de musique (SACEM), which collects composers' royalties, Ravel's estate earns more than that of any other French musician; similarly, Ravel remains for his main publisher, Durand-Salabert-Eschig (Universal Music Publishing Group), amongst its best sellers. Although back in copyright within France until 2022, as a consequence of a previous temporary lapse across the mid 1980s to mid 1990s, Ravel's music is available to scholars and students from a range of American and European publishing houses, in original and subsequent editions. In the United States, these publishers include Dover Publications with its album collections and miniature scores,[1] together with Schirmer, and the Alfred Masterwork Editions.[2] Within Europe, G. Henle Verlag has produced some of the piano repertory in an Urtext edition,[3] and of particular scholarly note is the New Urtext Edition of the piano works edited by Roger Nichols for Edition Peters, London.[4]

Equally, despite current economic challenges, the market for recordings of Ravel's music has been buoyant, with many strong catalogue additions since

[1] See, for instance, Arbie Orenstein (ed.), *Maurice Ravel Songs 1896–1914* (New York: Dover Publications, 1990); and, in miniature score, Maurice Ravel, *La Valse* (New York: Dover Publications, 1997, reprinted 2004), or *Daphnis et Chloé*, Suite No. 2 (New York: Dover Publications, 1999).

[2] For examples, see Maurice Ravel, *Jeux d'eau*, ed. Robert Casadesus (New York: Schirmer [Great Performer's Edition], 1985); or Maurice Ravel, *Gaspard de la nuit*, ed. Nancy Bricard (Los Angeles: Alfred Masterwork Edition, 1990, second edition, 2003).

[3] See, for instance, Maurice Ravel, *Miroirs*, ed. Peter Jost (Munich: Henle Urtext Edition [HN842], 2008).

[4] This complete collection of piano music, undertaken in the early to mid 1990s, remains available: *Pavane pour une infante défunte, Jeux d'eau, Sonatine, Miroirs, Gaspard de la nuit, Ma mère l'Oye, Valses nobles, Le Tombeau de Couperin*, plus an *Album of Shorter Pieces* (including *A la manière de…* and *Menuet sur le nom d'Haydn*).

the year 2000. It is worth highlighting the major undertaking by Claudio Abbado and the London Symphony Orchestra to record the complete orchestral works, the CD of that name released in 2002,[5] and a subsequent recording of the complete ballet music for *Daphnis et Chloé* conducted by Myung-Whun Chung with the Orchestre philharmonique de Radio France.[6] In a parallel move, 2007 saw the launch of a *Complete Piano Works* by Artur Pizarro, including in its first volume the *Miroirs*, *Gaspard de la nuit*, and *La Valse*;[7] while 2009 witnessed Sir Simon Rattle's acclaimed recording of *L'Enfant et les sortilèges*, coupled with the complete ballet music for *Ma mère l'Oye*.[8]

Within the academic world we have seen a notable engagement with Ravel on both sides of the Atlantic, resulting in high-profile articles, dedicated monographs, and more occasional essays within collected volumes on a variety of themes. Often the focus has been upon individual works of Ravel, sometimes reapproached via interdisciplinary means or used as a catalyst for wider-ranging musicological issues. Special attention may be drawn to two contrasting articles that appeared consecutively in a single issue of the *Journal of the American Musicological Society* late in 1999, which undoubtedly gave a boost to Ravel scholarship and confirmed the legitimacy of such enquiry: Carolyn Abbate's 'Outside Ravel's Tomb', which considered Ravel's *Le Tombeau de Couperin* in the context of historical and philosophical notions of machines and animated objects, and Steven Baur's 'Ravel's "Russian" Period', on the composer's early octatonicism.[9]

There has been a discernible increase in high-quality doctorates on Ravel, especially in the United States and Australia, which augurs very well for the future health of Ravel studies.[10] And together with the welcome arrival of this new generation of researchers has occurred a necessary consolidation of essential reference material on Ravel. The substantial, largely rewritten, entry on Ravel by Barbara Kelly was published in the second edition of *The New Grove Dictionary of Music and Musicians*, accessible within an updatable online resource.[11] In the United States, the timely reprint of Arbie Orenstein's

---

[5] Ravel, *Complete Orchestral Works*, Claudio Abbado/London Symphony Orchestra and Chorus (Deutsche Grammophon 000289 469 3542 2 [2002]).

[6] Ravel, *Daphnis et Chloé*, Myung-Whun Chung/Orchestre philharmonique and choir of Radio France (Deutsche Grammophon 000289 477 5706 1 [2006]).

[7] Artur Pizarro, *Complete Piano Works of Maurice Ravel*, vol. I (Linn Records CKD290 [2007]).

[8] Ravel, *L'Enfant et les sortilèges*, Simon Rattle/Berlin Philharmonic (EMI Classics 5099926419725 [2009]).

[9] Carolyn Abbate, 'Outside Ravel's Tomb', and Steven Baur, 'Ravel's "Russian" Period: Octatonicism in His Early Works, 1893–1908', *Journal of the American Musicological Society*, 52/3 (1999) 465–530 and 531–92.

[10] Among others, we may note Elisabeth Winnecke (University of Vienna, 2000), Eddy Kwong Mei Chong (University of Rochester, 2002), Gurminder Bhogal (University of Chicago, 2004), Michael J. Puri (Yale University, 2004), and Emily Kilpatrick (University of Adelaide, 2008).

[11] Barbara L. Kelly, 'Ravel, (Joseph) Maurice', in Deane L. Root (ed.), *Grove Music*

invaluable sourcebook *A Ravel Reader* was followed by Stephen Zank's most useful survey of conducted research.[12] In France, the long-term commitment to the *Cahiers Maurice Ravel* has continued, with significant input from Michel Delahaye, and also from Marcel Marnat, Philippe Rodriguez, Jean Roy, and Orenstein.[13]

Upon this basis, selected themes may be identified, without any claims to comprehensiveness. An analytical trajectory is ongoing, with a wealth of articles on harmony, style, and rhythm presented in a dedicated volume of *Ostinato rigore* (2006),[14] as well as those which have appeared in *Musurgia*.[15] Specific mention should be made of Peter Kaminsky's analytical contribution, including his pursuit of music–text relations.[16] Performance-related analysis of Ravel's piano music has received notable treatment by Yvonne Loriod-Messiaen,[17] Daphne Leong, David Korevaar,[18] and Roy Howat.[19] In extending Ravel research into the domain of film studies, we may highlight Julie Brown's insightful article 'Listening to Ravel'.[20] Chiming with Simon Rattle's recording project and with interests in music–text relations, Ravel's preoccupation with childhood fantasy has been further explored recently by Steven Huebner and by

Online: www.oxfordmusiconline.com/public/ (accessed 10 October 2009).

[12] Arbie Orenstein (ed.), *A Ravel Reader: Correspondence, Articles, Interviews* (New York: Columbia University Press, 1990; reprinted [with minor corrections] New York: Dover Publications, 2003); Stephen Zank, *Maurice Ravel: A Guide to Research* (New York: Routledge, 2005).

[13] Volume 7 was issued in 2000, with volume 12 scheduled for 2009; originally produced under the auspices of the Fondation Maurice Ravel, the *Cahiers Maurice Ravel* has since 2004 been published by Atlantica-Séguier and edited by Michel Delahaye.

[14] Jean-Claude Teboul (ed.), *Ostinato rigore: revue internationale d'études musicales*, 24 (2006): *Maurice Ravel*.

[15] Henri Gonnard, 'Maurice Ravel, *Le Tombeau de Couperin*: approche analytique de la fugue', *Musurgia: analyse et pratique musicales*, 8/2 (2001), 49–58; and Carine Perret, 'Le Romanticisme ravélien, un héritage choisi', *Musurgia*, 13/2 (2006), 17–32.

[16] Peter Kaminsky's essay 'Vocal Music and the Lures of Exoticism and Irony', in Deborah Mawer (ed.), *The Cambridge Companion to Ravel* (Cambridge University Press, 2000), 162–87, was accompanied by a more overtly analytical cousin: 'Of Princesses, Children, Dreams and Isomorphisms: Text–Music Transformation in Ravel's Vocal Works', *Music Analysis*,

19/1 (2000), 29–68. See too Kaminsky, 'Ravel's Late Music and the Problem of "Polytonality"', *Music Theory Spectrum*, 26/2 (2004), 237–64, which perhaps balances Steven Baur's article.

[17] Olivier Messiaen and Yvonne Loriod-Messiaen, *Ravel: analyses des œuvres pour piano de Maurice Ravel* (Paris: Durand, 2004).

[18] Daphne Leong and David Korevaar, 'The Performer's Voice: Performance and Analysis in Ravel's *Concerto pour la main gauche*', *Music Theory Online*, 11/3 (2005): http://mto.societymusictheory.org/issues/mto.05.11.3/mto.05.11.3.leong_Korevaar.html

[19] Founded on his essay 'Ravel and the Piano', in Mawer (ed.), *The Cambridge Companion to Ravel*, 71–96, chapters in Roy Howat's *The Art of French Piano Music: Debussy, Ravel, Fauré, Chabrier* (New Haven and London: Yale University Press, 2009) analyse aspects of *Gaspard de la nuit*, *Le Tombeau de Couperin*, and 'Alborada del gracioso'. See too Roy Howat, 'Modernization: From Chabrier and Fauré to Debussy and Ravel', in Richard Langham Smith and Caroline Potter (eds.), *French Music since Berlioz* (Aldershot: Ashgate, 2006), 197–221.

[20] Julie A. Brown, 'Listening to Ravel, Watching *Un coeur en hiver*: Cinematic Subjectivity and the Music-Film', *Twentieth-Century Music*, 1/2 (2004), 253–75.

Emily Kilpatrick.[21] Larger questions of the complex relationship between Ravel the man and Ravel the musician, and between his private and public personas, underpinned Benjamin Ivry's thought-provoking biography *Maurice Ravel: A Life*, published in 2000,[22] and have subsequently been taken up by others.[23]

Arguably one work more than any other has served to stimulate high-level enquiry in recent years: Ravel's masterly ballet *Daphnis et Chloé* (completed not long before World War I) including its associated visual art and balletic dimensions. (The contender for second position would likely be *La Valse*.) This trajectory was surely given initial impetus by Lawrence Kramer in an essay on exoticism in *Daphnis* within his influential book *Classical Music and Postmodern Knowledge* of the mid-1990s.[24] A selective list would acknowledge the detailed probing of the ballet's elusive origins by Simon Morrison; the melodic, rhythmic, and symbolic uses of ornamental arabesque pursued by Gurminder Bhogal; and Ravel's strategies of self-portraiture and concealment in *Daphnis et Chloé*, as proposed by Michael Puri.[25] My own contribution on the creative and interpretative perspectives of Ravel's ballets extended outwards from *Daphnis* and the Ballets russes, while the work has also proved a significant force behind Puri's new full-length study of Ravel, directed by the conceptual agenda of 'decadent dialectics'.[26]

Aim and summary of chapters

This field of research is not, however, saturated. Although the treatment of Ravel's music has suffered traditionally from a certain conservatism, implicit

[21] Steven Huebner, 'Ravel's Child: Magic and Moral Development', in Susan Boynton and Roe-Min Kok (eds.), *Musical Childhoods and the Cultures of Youth* (Middletown, CT: Wesleyan University Press, 2006), 69–88; Emily Kilpatrick, 'Into the Woods: Re-telling the Wartime Fairytales of Ravel', *Musical Times*, 149 (2008), 57–66, and 'Jangling in Symmetrical Sounds: Maurice Ravel as Storyteller and Poet', *Journal of Music Research Online*, 1 (2009), 1–19: http://journal.mca.org.au (accessed 12 October 2009).

[22] Benjamin Ivry, *Maurice Ravel: A Life* (New York: Welcome Rain, 2000, reprinted 2003).

[23] See for instance Lloyd Whitesell, 'Ravel's Way', in Sophie Fuller and Lloyd Whitesell (eds.), *Queer Episodes in Music and Modern Identity* (Urbana and Chicago: University of Illinois Press, 2002), 49–78; and Steven Huebner, 'Maurice Ravel: Private Life, Public Works', in Jolanta T. Pekacz (ed.),

Musical Biography: Towards New Paradigms (Aldershot: Ashgate, 2006), 69–87.

[24] Lawrence Kramer, 'Consuming the Exotic: Ravel's *Daphnis et Chloé*', in his *Classical Music and Postmodern Knowledge* (Berkeley: University of California Press, 1995), 201–25.

[25] Simon Morrison, 'The Origins of *Daphnis et Chloé* (1912)', *19th-Century Music*, 28/1 (2004), 50–76; Gurminder Bhogal, 'Debussy's Arabesque and Ravel's *Daphnis et Chloé* (1912)', *Twentieth-Century Music*, 3/2 (2006), 171–99; Michael J. Puri, 'Dandy, Interrupted: Sublimation, Repression, and Self-Portraiture in Maurice Ravel's *Daphnis et Chloé* (1909–12)', in *Journal of the American Musicological Society*, 60/2 (2007), 317–72.

[26] Deborah Mawer, *The Ballets of Maurice Ravel: Creation and Interpretation* (Aldershot: Ashgate, 2006); Michael J. Puri, *Decadent Dialectics: Memory, Sublimation, and Desire in the Music of Maurice Ravel* (Oxford University Press, forthcoming).

within the developments outlined above is a strengthening strand of inter-disciplinarity, one crucial to a vibrant, forward-looking musicology. Several years on from *The Cambridge Companion to Ravel*, this observation became the main *raison d'être* for a new multi-authored volume. Thus *Ravel Studies* aims to celebrate and explore further the potential benefits of interdisciplinary perspectives as a way of progressing core research on Ravel – the artist himself, his music, and his cultural contexts – as well as contributing substantially to broader musicological debate.

To this end, *Ravel Studies* presents a rich variety of approaches and content. Methodological approaches range from the historical and source-based, through the analytical (still maintaining accessibility, often in conjunction with an extra-musical dimension), to the critical and hermeneutic. Frequently the essays partake of one, or more of these means. Similarly, the interdisciplinary content operates in diverse ways. Even within music, there are of course many (interacting) subdisciplines, so that in *Ravel Studies* the composer's music is assessed in the light of performance studies from a conductor's stance, and in relation to aspects of early jazz. Interdisciplinarity involves music academics extending their terms of reference to those of 'music-plus': for instance, considering how association with aesthetics, literature, cultural or gender issues may enhance our understanding of Ravel's art. In a sense, this notion of interdisciplinarity follows on from and develops Ravel's own example, as witnessed in his song setting and operatic or balletic endeavours (all genres which are discussed in this volume). Equally, we may perceive more multidisciplinary content where Ravel and his music are viewed from alternative disciplinary positions: specifically, those of an American historian, a dance scholar, and a neurologist. In brief, the topics addressed include Ravel's aesthetic quest for perfection; associations between the composer and Colette, and Proust; Ravel the dandy, and questions of sexuality; the composer's relationship with American culture, embracing jazz; the conducting and choreographing of Ravel's music; understanding the composer's final illness and its creative implications.

To support the continued growth of Ravel scholarship, with the exception of the editor the contributors to *Ravel Studies* do not duplicate those of *The Cambridge Companion to Ravel*. All have strong academic credentials: the majority are internationally established figures who have published previously on Ravel, but a minority are early-career scholars chosen to recognize and reflect the new blood and increasing interest in Ravel studies. In keeping with the interdisciplinary pursuit, yet despite never being strictly collaborative, some authors' essays do nevertheless 'speak' to each other. Although contributors hail from the United States, Canada, Australia, and Europe (with two each from McGill University and Lancaster University), the prominence of North American representation in *Ravel Studies* is congruent with North America being such a thriving hub of current activity.

Various orderings of the chapters are possible, but the following archlike structure is offered as perhaps the most plausible and coherent. The collection opens with Steven Huebner's Chapter 1 on 'Ravel's perfection', which provides, simultaneously, a point of departure and context for the chapters that follow (especially 2, 3, and 4) and a sense of summation of Ravel's quest, achievement, and legacy. (This chapter could also function well as a conclusion to the volume.) While concerned primarily with early French perceptions of Ravel's aesthetic, the chapter probes relations between (neo) classicism, artistry, and artisanship (or 'craft') in both music and literature, drawing perhaps unexpected parallels with the (paradoxical) symbolism of Stéphane Mallarmé and, particularly, the creative ambience of his poetic descendant, Paul Valéry. An Appendix offers a valuable resource on contemporary French criticism. In Chapter 2, Emily Kilpatrick's contribution on *L'Enfant et les sortilèges* maintains the interest in source study and musico-literary comparison, within an *opéra-ballet* context, specifically between Ravel and the celebrated Colette. (Kilpatrick is also sensitive to artisanship in this context.) An examination of archival manuscript correspondence between the two figures enables a fresh perspective on the creative process and artistic collaboration, and the close-knit nature of music–text relations in *L'Enfant* itself is equally apparent.

Michael Puri (Chapter 3) uses Marcel Proust's preoccupation with memory – a means both of reanimating the past and creating anew – to provide an apt model for Ravel's reanimations: both of pastiche in *A la manière de…* and more fundamentally in the 'Introduction' of *Daphnis et Chloé*, which Puri interweaves analytically with the famous 'madeleine' scene from Proust's epic novel *A la recherche du temps perdu*. Lastly in this first group of chapters, Lloyd Whitesell (Chapter 4) expands the agenda explicitly through to gender studies, whilst continuing the interest in aesthetics and literature (combined with the image of the dandy registered in Chapter 1). The ways in which Ravel's persona did not conform to social norms are summarized and related to personal 'tunings' advocated by the sociologist Henning Bech. In turn, this ploy is tested in hermeneutic analytical readings of varied music written by Ravel before World War I: the exotic song cycle *Shéhérazade*, the grotesque *Gaspard de la nuit*, together with *Jeux d'eau* and *Valses nobles et sentimentales*. Sexual desire is seen as handled through guarding private space, withholding erotic fulfilment, and engaging in teasing and evasion.

The second half of the volume comprises two pairs of chapters, followed by a final, single chapter. In chapters 5 and 6, two Lancaster University authors offer connected perspectives on Ravel, America, and jazz: 'Crossing borders' I and II. Little has so far been written about the historical context for, and significance of, Ravel's North American tour, a niche filled by the historian Nicholas Gebhardt in Chapter 5. He sees Ravel's experience in terms of an evolution of tours undertaken by European virtuoso performers in the later nineteenth century, and within a growing American consciousness of modernism itself. Questions about the artist resurface, and about the balancing of freedom and autonomy against commercialism and entertainment. An Appendix gives a detailed summary of Ravel's tour itinerary. Ravel's writings published on his tour are the cue for my own Chapter 6, examining two interconnected relationships: firstly, between Ravel's theory of early jazz and historical actualities in America and France; secondly, between his theory and practice, mainly across the Sonata for Violin and Piano and piano concertos. In the former relationship, close correspondences are accompanied by some 'transformation'; in the latter, theorized transformative processes are closely played out, amid untheorized correspondences between Ravel's music and potential sources. Ravel's engagement with jazz is well informed, Gallicized, and personalized.

Performance studies acts as the connector for the next pair of chapters. In Chapter 7, the late David Epstein uses his dual experience as a conductor and music theorist to probe the importance of tempo in interpreting and performing *La Valse* appropriately. He argues against overly rushed renditions of the climax which succumb to the dictates of theatricality and commercialism over those of the music. A detailed analysis blends elements from music theory, European culture and literature (thus relating to earlier chapters), performers' testimony, and, if more implicitly, cognitive perception. The danceability of Ravel's music is the subject of Stephanie Jordan's 'choreomusical' analysis in Chapter 8, explored through the *Sonatine* and three movements from *Miroirs*, which are unified and reinterpreted in Richard Alston's dance piece, *Shimmer*. Performers' testimony similarly informs this essay (which links with Chapter 2 not only in its balletic connection, but also in its exploitation of primary sources – a choreographer, a pianist, and dancers).

Finally, the neurologist Erik Baeck (Chapter 9) presents within musicological literature an authoritative, but readable account of Ravel's terminal illness, including the arguments for and against its possible impact on his late *œuvre* (from *Boléro* onwards),[27] which has been restricted previously to medical circles. Divergent contemporary accounts are drawn upon, more recent relevant developments in neurological science are outlined, and comparisons are made with other famous artists who suffered brain disorders that affected their creativity.

---

[27] See L. Amaducci, E. Grassi, and F. Boller, 'Maurice Ravel and Right-Hemisphere Musical Creativity: Influence of Disease on His Last Musical Works?', *European Journal of Neurology*, 9 (2002), 75–82; Erik Baeck, 'The Terminal Illness and Last Compositions of Maurice Ravel', in Julien Bogousslavsky and François Boller (eds.), *Neurological Disorders in Famous Artists*, Frontiers of Neurology and Neuroscience, vol. 19 (Basle: Karger, 2005), 132–40.

This book may be read in various ways: from working through the chapters in the given order, through to the more likely scenario of dipping into essays of individual interest. While the chapters progress generally from music's association with aesthetic and literary matters to more extended disciplinary couplings, or groupings, the organization is relatively free so that other thematic links may emerge. Different trajectories have unexpected meeting points. Consequently, in any given chapter, selected cross-references have been added to identify further discussions of a piece or concept in other chapters, citing, where applicable, the heading under which they appear. Such intersections may be approached from complementary points of view, reflecting the lively plurality of current debate. Beyond this, larger-scale groupings may be signalled: Ravel's aesthetic and aestheticism (chapters 1, 3, and 4); neoclassicism (1 and 3); music and literature (1, 2, 3, and 4); reception study (1, 2, 5, 7, and 9); analytical studies (3, 4, 6, 7, and 8); studies of one main composition: *L'Enfant*, *La Valse*, and Alston's *Shimmer* – combining *Sonatine* and *Miroirs* (2, 7, and 8, respectively); music–text genres (2 and 4); piano repertory (3 and 8); primary sources and ballet (2 and 8); American perspectives (5 and 6); performance studies (7 and 8); beginnings, endings, and legacy (1 and 9).

So a range of themes may be pursued, and Ravel's music is represented across most genres – orchestral and instrumental music, in addition to those mentioned above. Nevertheless, coverage is not designed to be comprehensive. Some areas are left relatively untouched, ripe for future research: for example, beyond useful work conducted by Orenstein (and despite Ravel's destruction of material to conceal his compositional toil), there is considerable scope for developing music manuscript and sketch studies, as well as a case for substantial methodological analyses of Ravel's œuvre, especially once music copyright restrictions are lifted.

Ravel Studies aims to attract a wide readership: it is pitched primarily at academics in musicology and music theory/analysis, other music professionals, and postgraduate students; but it should also appeal to those in other arts that relate to the disciplines of contributors. Additionally, it is intended to be readable by interested undergraduates, concertgoers, and general enthusiasts of French music.

In a Ravelian spirit, it is hoped that these essays may serve collectively as a model for expanding the agendas of other composer-based studies.

1 Ravel's perfection

Steven Huebner

Carlo Caballero's recent monograph on Gabriel Fauré's aesthetics enriches criticism not only by positioning its subject against a wide background of French musical thought, but also by encouraging further thinking.[1] Caballero touches briefly upon the construct of perfection to illustrate Fauré's understanding of sincerity as an aesthetic attribute. 'Sincerity is a never-ending effort to create one's soul as it is,' once wrote the critic and editor Jacques Rivière, and Caballero continues this thought by equating Fauré's commitment to sincerity with an almost spiritual striving for perfection.[2] Maurice Ravel puts in an appearance as a foil, a composer who had little use for framing his work as either spiritual endeavour or completion of the self.[3] Ravel generally disparaged the manipulation of sincerity in value judgements, notes Caballero, while he concomitantly upheld compositional technique as a 'means to beauty and perfection'.[4] Thus, even as an ancillary point, perfection appears in Caballero's account as an unstable term – touching upon ethics and the psychology of the artist when applied to Fauré, and upon aesthetics for Ravel.

Despite, or perhaps because of, such ambiguities, perfection as a criterion in reception and criticism has received very little systematic reflection in writing on music, or even the arts in general. Caballero's only direct quotation of Fauré's own use of the word both underlines its multivalence and suggests some reasons for this musicological reticence: 'To express what you have within you with sincerity and in the clearest and most *perfect* terms possible would always seem to me the summit of art.'[5] Here Fauré seems to mean something a bit different from the Rivière-derived idea of completing the self inasmuch as he emphasizes manner of presentation over substance, perfection as

An early version of this chapter was presented at the annual meeting of the American Musicological Society, Washington DC (October 2005).

[1] Carlo Caballero, *Fauré and French Musical Aesthetics* (Cambridge University Press, 2001).
[2] *Ibid.*, 34.
[3] *Ibid.*, 33–4. On this general point see Steven Huebner, 'Maurice Ravel: Private Life, Public Works', in Jolanta T. Pekacz (ed.), *Musical Biography: Towards New Paradigms* (Aldershot: Ashgate, 2006), 69–87.
[4] Caballero, *Fauré*, 34.
[5] Letter from Fauré to Mme de Chaumont-Quitry (summer 1899), cited by Caballero, *Fauré*, 18. 'Exprimer ce que l'on a en soi avec sincérité et dans les termes les plus clairs et les plus *parfaits* me semblera toujours le comble de l'art.'

a means rather than an end. But, more important, 'perfect' in this instance may be read either as a synonym for 'best' or as 'best under the circumstances' (as implied by 'most perfect terms *possible*'). Is 'possible' in this formulation to be understood in an absolute or a relative sense? Moreover, strictly speaking the expression 'most perfect' would seem dubious against a view of perfection as a unique and absolute state. Now, to measure Fauré against such rigorous standards of expression would not be quite fair. After all, he might simply have sought an inflated way of saying 'excellent' – that which exhibits a high degree of accomplishment – without implying uniqueness (as would be suggested had he used the word 'best' *tout court*). This usage is a commonplace of everyday conversation, where 'perfect' often functions as a synonym for 'outstanding' or 'very good', as, say, in a description of the weather as 'perfect'. When the critic Emile Vuillermoz wrote in his well-known general history of music that Debussy combined his respect for national tradition with a 'métier parfait',[6] he meant ostensibly that Debussy had a superb command of his craft. Vuillermoz could just as well have written 'métier formidable', 'métier exceptionnel', or some comparable superlative. In short, 'perfection' has often been deployed with little self-consciousness, and even less controversy or critical scrutiny. On the one hand, generic superlatives by themselves rarely produce aesthetic categories amenable to criticism. On the other, better-honed manipulations of the word risk engaging philosophical speculation at the expense of real critical insight into music.

For all their vagueness, the words 'perfect' and 'perfection' have agglomerated with eyebrow-raising frequency around Ravel's music in reviews, biographies, and critical studies from his day to ours. This is perhaps to be expected from an *œuvre* generally regarded as excellent, indeed a corpus where critics have identified few artistic failures so that Ravel's very consistency encourages an evaluation as perfect-as-excellent. But the ubiquity of the term as applied to Ravel begs the question of whether it represents some other cultural work or critical orientation. In short, why 'perfect', and why so often? Before I show that the cultural roots for this critical vocabulary are manifold and that they provide a window on Ravel's aesthetics, I would suggest that perfection has become associated with Ravel as a discursive practice in which some musicians unconsciously follow the lead of others without apprehending fully why the word springs so easily to mind. To inject an anecdotal note, I recently asked a fine pianist why he enjoys playing Ravel. He responded that 'every note seems in the right place and perfect' – spoken as if this were the gospel truth immanent in the notes themselves. This remark reminded me of the composer Georges Auric's preface to a commemorative volume celebrating the centenary of Ravel's birth: '[Ravel] puts together the least significant

---

[6] Emile Vuillermoz, *Histoire de la musique*,
revised edition (Paris: Fayard, 1973), 378.

passage with infallible lucidity […] not one chord that isn't in its proper position, not one note forgotten'.[7] On the face of it, it would seem that many other composers might be characterized in the same way; indeed, one might make a credible case that aesthetic success for a wide range of music involves convincing the listener of the appropriateness of means to ends. The utter coincidence of these remarks by Auric and my pianist friend – both bordering on clichés – might merely reflect this general critical orientation. More probably it reflects a habit of thought particular to Ravel within our musical culture that warrants closer examination.

The rhetoric of perfection

First the case for salience. Any merely statistical survey of vocabulary applied to French composers in this period would be a dubious proposition at best, if only for its insensitivity to context and nuance. The appendix to this chapter, therefore, provides a representative anthology of passages from music criticism where Ravel's perfection comes into play, broad-ranging but certainly not exhaustive. It starts with Ravel's own remarks, on the premise that his criticism and testimony had a role to play in the development of a critical vocabulary around his work. 'Quelques réflexions sur la musique' (see excerpt *1*) was appended to a short autobiographical sketch that he dictated to his friend, the composer and critic Alexis Roland-Manuel. After establishing the terms 'conscience de l'artiste' – which I take in the sense of artistic conscientiousness and/or artistic conscience – and 'sincérité', Ravel observes that the second term has little value if not accompanied by the first. A healthy artistic conscience demands the development of the skilled craftsman, and, consequently, 'my goal is technical perfection', writes Ravel. 'I can strive towards this forever because I'm assured of never attaining it.' At his famous lecture on 'Contemporary Music' given at the Rice Institute on 7 April 1928 (*2*), Ravel spoke of his own compositional strategy as a 'process of elimination' which entailed a rigorous effort towards 'perfection'. An interview in *La Revue musicale* from March 1931 (*3*) also suggests a striving for economy of means in that Ravel equates 'sincerity' with 'imperfection' and works that are 'loquacious'. In another contemporary interview (*4*), we read that 'What Mozart wrote for the delectation of our ears is perfect' and that Saint-Saëns also achieved perfection, but to a 'lesser degree': another manifestation of perfection as a relative condition. Beethoven, on the other hand, despite

---

[7] Georges Auric, 'Le Centenaire de Maurice Ravel', in *Maurice Ravel 1875–1975* (Paris: Société des auteurs, compositeurs, et éditeurs de musique, 1975): 'agençant la moindre page avec une infaillible lucidité […] pas un accord qui ne soit à son exacte place, pas une note oubliée'.

striving towards the same ideal, falls short because he 'dramatizes and glori-fies himself'. Perfection becomes attached to 'purity' and 'absolute beauty' with reference to Mozart's music (5), contrasted here with that of Beethoven and Berlioz, the latter an instinctual but technically inferior artist. And in a late interview of May 1932 (6), Mozart once again earns praise as 'the most perfect of all', a model for those who would seek immutable aesthetic values and a paragon for those with a neoclassical orientation.

Staying in the classical/neoclassical vein, we continue with the views of Ravel's critics and associates. In his obituary for the composer (7), the music-ologist Jacques-Gabriel Prod'homme praises Ravel's search for 'perfection in form' in the same breath as noting his dislike of Romantic effusion, character-istics that combine to produce 'a traditional classical character'. Adhering to the spirit of *L'Action française*, the newspaper for which he wrote, Dominique Sordet celebrates the national roots of Ravel and his art (8): 'the direct off-spring of eighteenth-century *clavecinistes*, a classical artist, enemy of over-wrought emotion [and ...] zealous about formal perfection'. Sordet continues with a familiar description of Ravel as a man who is 'somewhat dry and tak-ing only one thing really seriously, his art; month after month shaping works out of difficult and recalcitrant raw material'. In his book on French piano music (9), the pianist Alfred Cortot also emphasizes national character when he writes of a 'luminous technique, the accents of material perfection', typical of great French art. Meanwhile, in 'Pour Ravel' (10), the writer André Suarès (one of the four pillars of *La Nouvelle Revue française*, along with Paul Valéry, Paul Claudel, and André Gide) ties his characterization of Ravel as exemplary of French taste to his 'perfection of taste and style'.

Like Prod'homme and Sordet, Louis Aguettant, in his history of piano music (11), associates perfection with classicism, but strikes a different note from them by actually casting doubt on Ravel's classical tendencies. The composer's taste for 'paradox, surprise, the unexpected' all fall short of the higher order of 'the perfectly natural, the supreme fluency of the classics'. Instead, Aguettant argues that Ravel's perfection occurs at the level of a mini-aturist by reminding his readers of Ravel's 'obsession with detail [and ...] for the small perfect object'. Writing in *La Rose rouge* (12), Jean Bouchor, a literary intellectual associated with Les Six, evaluates Ravel's 'science' or technical knowledge as an example of 'perfect taste', but goes on to critique this by arguing that 'perfection does not move the heart of man'. Beethoven's technique might have been poor and of uncertain taste, Bouchor claims, but his emotional world was a godsend to humanity. According to the critic and editor of *La Revue musicale* Robert Bernard, commenting within his book on modern French music (13), Ravel's music is 'all surface', but a 'sur-face of perfection' characterized by elegance of workmanship. In a review from the time of the premiere of *L'Enfant et les sortilèges* (14), even Ravel's friend Roland-Manuel suggests that perfection produced an obstacle against self-renewal. He describes perfection as limiting and Ravel as 'a prisoner' who pounded violently against his enclosure at the end of *La Valse*. (For a detailed discussion of the close of *La Valse*, see Chapter 7, under 'The idea of destruction'.)

In the final paragraphs of his later, magisterial biography of 1938 (*15*), however, Roland-Manuel endorses Ravel's perfection as technical mastery, suggesting that his genius lay in the combination of taste and *métier*, and (like Sordet, Cortot, and Suarès) tying this to a French sensibility that resolutely resists 'thinking through music'. In his homage (*16*), the composer Louis Aubert understands Ravel's perfection as a product of incessant research into the hidden reaches of his art and cites Ravel's questions about harp scoring as an example. In a later history of music (*17*), the critic Emile Vuillermoz champions Ravel's mechanical perfection, the product of painstaking labour never felt in the final result and worthy of tributes to skill rather than Stravinsky's disdain. Arthur Hoerée groups perfection together with Ravel's innate elegance in an article within the 1925 dedicated issue of *La Revue musicale* (*18*), imagining a homology between frilly cuffs and the composer's creative muse. Finally, according to Ravel's friend Léon-Paul Fargue in his tribute 'Autour de Ravel' (*19*), his 'preoccupation with perfection' was the result of a highly developed artistic conscience (here we come full circle to Ravel's own remarks in excerpt *1*) that could only sanction works that were 'finished and polished to a supreme degree'. Secret exigencies pressing relentlessly upon an acutely receptive creative spirit gave Ravel the appearance of a dry gentleman, hard to approach, meticulous, and cold.

Philosophical adumbrations

Unsurprisingly, a survey of these critical applications of perfection to Ravel's music does not give an impression of consistency. On the one hand, some writers do little to dispel the basic ambiguity between perfect-as-excellent and perfect as a culturally more meaningful term. When, for example, Prod'homme (*7*) comments that Ravel's art may be characterized by its 'quest for perfection of form', might he not mean simply that Ravel gives special and expert attention to the parameter of form? On the other hand, leitmotives of integrity, craft, and national character do circulate through many of these writings and would seem to suggest a substratum of common denominators.

One place to look for such denominators would be in the Western philosophical tradition itself. Perfection has been put to many philosophical uses, more in metaphysics and ethics than in aesthetics. In a survey published across 1979–81,[8] the Polish philosopher Wladyslaw Tatarkiewicz underscored how Aristotle's tripartite definition has buttressed the term over time: (1) perfect is that which is complete, that is, which is not missing anything and which cannot sustain elimination of any of its parts; (2) perfect is that which is the best of its kind, for which it is impossible to conceive of a better example; (3) perfect is that which fulfils its goals, its intentional object. Tatarkiewicz noted that the first of these concepts 'is fairly well subsumed within the second'.[9] Here it is important to understand the completeness of the first definition in a broad sense as implying not only material form but also a fullness of expression. Aristotle's third definition opens a window to a more utilitarian view by addressing purposes: objects may not be the best of their kind according to a set of prescribed ideals of form and content, but may attain perfection by functioning as they were intended. Concepts allied variously to this threefold description in the history of philosophy include the idea of finality implicit in the integrity of the perfect; the characterization of perfection as an absolute state, even a divine one; the notion of perfection as purity, understood as something conceived or executed according to a single principle; and the related idea of perfection as harmony, a consensus that unites divergent elements.

Aristotle's third definition was rearticulated to accommodate specifically aesthetic purposes (for example the production of sensory pleasure) in reflections upon the relationship between beauty and perfection that would later preoccupy aestheticians. The eighteenth-century German philosopher Alexander Baumgarten (1714–62) was especially influential in attaching perfection to the beautiful and to the production of pleasure, while his teacher Christian Wolff (1679–1754) described moral beauty of the soul as a kind of ethical perfection that also caused pleasure.[10] Edmund Burke (1729–97), not surprisingly, proved instrumental in a paradigm shift by holding that beauty did not depend upon the attributes conventionally associated with perfection, for example the optimal arrangement of materials with a particular aesthetic goal or various theories of ideal proportions. In his view, the sensory experience of imperfection was not dissonant with true beauty inasmuch as imperfection was the expression of melancholy or suffering that might produce its own aesthetic charm.[11]

---

[8] Wladyslaw Tatarkiewicz, 'Perfection: The Term and the Concept', *Dialectics and Humanism*, 6/4 (1979), 5–10; 'Paradoxes of Perfection', *Dialectics and Humanism* 7/1 (1980), 77–80; 'Perfection in the Sciences', *Dialectics and Humanism*, 7/2 (1980), 137–9; 'Aesthetic Perfection', *Dialectics and Humanism* 7/4 (1980), 145–53; 'Ontological and Theological Perfection', *Dialectics and Humanism*, 8/1 (1980), 187–92; 'On Perfection', *Dialectics and Humanism*, 8/2 (1981), 11–12.

[9] Tatarkiewicz, 'Perfection: The Term and the Concept', 7.
[10] Robert E. Norton, *The Beautiful Soul: Aesthetic Morality in the Eighteenth Century* (Ithaca, NY: Cornell University Press, 1995), 80–7.
[11] René Vinçon, 'Perfection (esth.)', in André Jacob (ed.), *Encyclopédie philosophique universelle*, 4 vols. (Paris: Presses universitaires de France, 1990), vol. II, 1907.

Immanuel Kant (1724–1804) also disassociated perfection from the judgement of taste by dismissing Baumgarten's perfectionist view of beauty (the harmony of an object's properties with its underlying concept): 'the judgment of taste is an aesthetical judgment, i.e. such as rests on subjective grounds, the determining ground of which cannot be a concept'.[12] In short, Kant prioritizes 'feeling' over 'understanding' in aesthetic judgement. Perfection is entirely dependent upon 'understanding', though Kant goes on to distinguish between a free beauty untainted by the representation of purposes and an inferior, dependent beauty, say the distinction between beautiful flowers (or 'music phantasies [i.e. pieces without any theme] and in fact all music without words') and a building or a horse. In the latter cases, purposes become constraints in artistic production and distractions in aesthetic judgements, difficult, but not impossible, to ignore in apprehensions of beauty. Given the subsequent resonance of Kant's thought, which often informed musical reflections of German Romantic letters, it is not surprising that perfection had a much smaller place in discussions of aesthetics in the nineteenth century than it had before.

Although my witnesses to Ravel's perfection wrote as musicians and critics, and not as philosophers, the formal thinking about aesthetics all too briefly outlined here suggests a subtext beneath these variegated surface expressions that is related to certain fundamental premises which the composer himself frequently articulated. In his vociferous opposition to authenticity and inspiration as criteria for creation and value judgement, Ravel went so far as to remark once that there is 'something humiliating' in being thought of merely as a sincere artist. As a corollary, he also censured the use of 'spontaneity' as a criterion in critical discourse.[13] In our archaeological dig around the word 'perfection', its revalorization as a criterion of aesthetic judgement (whatever its use in specific examples) would seem consonant with a critique of the absolute primacy of feeling – and here I suggest Ravel's 'sincerity' as a synonym for 'feeling' – over understanding. When Cortot implies (9) that a Kantian subordination of 'understanding' did not take root solidly in France, he does so with an obvious intent of appropriating Ravel (and his *perfection matérielle*) for a nationalist cause as exemplary of cultural difference. In tandem, critical discourse by, and around, Ravel implicating perfection also became part of an implied programme to clear a distinct aesthetic space in the shadow of such French contemporaries as Vincent d'Indy and Debussy. The former sought to define national difference by underlining the inseparability of ethics from aesthetics.[14] Consequently, d'Indy's emphasis on

[12] Immanuel Kant, *The Critique of Judgment*, trans. J. H. Bertrand (Amherst, NY: Prometheus Books, 2000; orig. published 1892), 79.

[13] Maurice Ravel, 'Mes souvenirs d'enfant paresseux', *La Petite Gironde* (12 July 1931), 1.
[14] For elaboration of this point, see Steven Huebner, 'Striptease as Ideology',

craft, normally a criterion much valued by Ravel, appeared to Ravel more like dogma and slavish intellectualism uninflected by genuine artistic sensibility (which he understood as different from 'sincerity').[15] Differentiation from Debussy became even more urgent because Ravel had so much in common with him: suspicion of the mixture of ethics and aesthetics, love of symbolist poetry, culturally progressive inclinations, critique of Beethoven, Wagner, and Berlioz, and use of Spanish music as a resource, to name just a few shared orientations. But Ravel did not share Debussy's privileging of nature in the creative process, nor his advocacy of music as a language of feeling unfettered by past syntactical practice.

Artist and artisan

Nature, of course, need not be inimical to discourses of perfection. With little regard for Kantian purposive purposelessness, the twentieth-century philosopher Lucien Rudrauf once identified manifold realizations of perfection in nature with implicit reference to Artistotle's third definition, praising ecosystems and adaptable organisms that had produced stability through change across thousands of generations.[16] Rudrauf described different criteria for aesthetic perfection: 'formal structures: spacio-metric or chrono-metric, visual or auditory [...] it stems from a knowledge both sensitive and rational'.[17] (Pointing specifically to the perfection of Ravel's form, Prod'homme and Sordet (excerpts 7 and 8) implicitly shared this line of thinking, and, in a different vein, Rudrauf's entwinement of rationality and sensitivity mirrors the linkage that Ravel himself made – if we assimilate sensitivity with artistic sensibility.)

Perfection in the arts, Rudrauf also noted, is often judged according to an ideal type derived *a posteriori* (Aristotle's second definition), yet posited as an antecedent to reality, almost as an article of faith. This is a natural human impulse, but evaluations of perfection, particularly as they relate to manner of execution instead of considerations of beauty (or, put in Aristotle's terms, the identification of 'that which is complete') sit best in relation to 'the art forms of the hand crafts [where] one may exact the highest degree of technical

Nineteenth-Century Music Review, 1/2 (2005), 3–25; 'Le Hollandais fantôme: Ideology and Dramaturgy in *L'Etranger*', in Manuela Schwartz and Myriam Chimènes (eds.), *Vincent d'Indy et son temps* (Liège: Mardaga, 2006), 263–81; 'Vincent d'Indy et le "drame sacré": de *Parsifal* à *La Légende de Saint Christophe*', in Jean-Christophe Branger and Alban Ramaut (eds.), *Opéra et religion sous la IIIe*

République (Saint-Etienne: Publications de l'Université de Saint-Etienne, 2006), 227–55.

15   A good example of Ravel's response to a merely intellectualized craft is his critique of Witkowski's Second Symphony in Arbie Orenstein (ed.), *Maurice Ravel: lettres, écrits, entretiens* (Paris: Flammarion, 1989), 296.

16   Lucien Rudrauf, 'Perfection', *Journal of Aesthetics and Art Criticism*, 23 (1964), 123–30.

17   *Ibid.*, 126.

perfection – in jewellery, for example, and in engraving where the cutting follows a rule so clearly defined and so rigorously systemized that the least deviation from and the least departure from the drawing are felt as intolerably bad work by every amateur'.[18] Rudrauf's suggestion of the heightened amenability of discourses of perfection to an artisan's work certainly rhymes with one important way in which Ravel himself used the word (*1*) and, in a larger sense, with his anti-Romantic orientation and his critique of those who set too much store by 'sincerity'. For Emile Vuillermoz (*17*), Stravinsky's epithet of the 'Swiss clockmaker' made for an unintended compliment: a tribute to the perfection of the artisan who effortlessly regulated the tiny cogwheels of his work (think of Rudrauf's 'spacio-metric or chrono-metric' structures). Ravel's close friend the poet Léon-Paul Fargue once wrote a brief essay entitled 'Artisans d'art' wherein he argued that the terms 'artist' and 'artisan' were coextensive. Division of the two was an artificial creation of 'the bad part of the seventeenth century', namely academies and academicians who created abstract principles deracinated from reality.[19] Fargue's essay is of a piece with his more general celebration in his poetry of working-class Paris, a celebration with which Ravel sympathized.[20] Fargue (*19*) claims that Ravel welcomed comparisons of his art to artisanship, 'to make, and to make well [… to] bear the mark of perfection'. The language of Aubert's reminiscence (*16*) also sustains an artisan's perspective, but now more like Aristotle's third definition relating to fulfilment of purposes. So too, Ravel explores the technical possibilities of all the instruments in his quest for new sounds. More generally, as far as Ravel's reputation goes, there is a side of the master-orchestrator trope that hints of technological *savoir-faire*, a rational command of the machine that is the modern orchestra.

But orchestration is, of course, also an art. When Ravel himself conflates artist with artisan (excerpt *1*) he does so in a way that points to a paradox of the conflation as it relates to perfection (and without Fargue's populist slant).[21] First, he says that artistic conscience impels the artist to be 'a good craftsman', which means a striving for technical perfection. But then he confesses that he will never attain this goal. Modesty, of course. But, in addition, following Rudrauf's terms, perfection is easier to identify in the artisan's world of conformity with specific models than in the artist's world of conformity to more nebulous ideal types where (to adopt Ravel's terms) 'sensibility' plays an important role. Put another way – now after Aristotle's first

---

[18] *Ibid.*, 128.
[19] Léon-Paul Fargue, *Lanterne magique* (Marseilles: R. Laffont, 1944), 128–36: 130.
[20] For testimony of their like-mindedness and attraction to popular culture, see André Beucler's reminiscences of conversations between Fargue and Ravel, in Roger Nichols (ed.), *Ravel Remembered* (New York: Norton, 1987), 150–6.
[21] For a specific perspective on the artistic–artisanal dialectic in comparing Ravel and Colette, see Chapter 2, under 'The enchantress and the illusionist'.

definition – 'completeness' means something different for the artist than for the artisan. Conformity to ideal types became especially difficult to evaluate in Ravel's world of rapidly evolving musical syntax at the beginning of the twentieth century. Ravel refers approvingly to Schoenberg's work (3) as avoiding the 'imperfections' of sincerity, but, in praising both its originality and its adherence to newly invented constraints his vocabulary here does not suit craft objects. He does appear to suggest (5) that Berlioz was not enough of an artisan because he lacked basic skills. Yet Ravel's nuancing of this view on other occasions drew it increasingly into the realm of more-difficult-to-measure sensibility, where, for example, Berlioz's shortcomings lay in his putative inability to 'feel' the harmonies for his melodies as he heard them (not to mention his propensity to wear sincerity on his sleeve).[22] That Ravel's ideal types were icons from a more distant past produced a bridge between perfection and a classicizing orientation (reflected more or less strongly in excerpts 7, 8, 9, and 10). Mozart's music (excerpts 4, 5, and 6) becomes an ideal of perfection, a perfection unattainable almost by definition because of the cultural prestige surrounding it and the difficulties of identifying what form emulation might take, without pastiche, in a climate of rapidly changing musical language. And Ravel's understanding of Mozart's perfection – his 'completeness' – surely transcended 'mere' craft values because of his appreciation of Mozart's marriage between technique and sensibility, a marriage difficult to describe and, consequently, a chimerical goal.

What was truly classic to one critic was not always so to another, a polemic that could also shift Ravel's perfection back into the artisan's field of activity. Aguettant (11) argues that Ravel himself is not classical in a full understanding of the word because of his inclination to preciousness, unusual effects, and surprises. In a critical orientation that betrays an understanding of the classical as serene, magisterial, and lofty, Ravel's perfection becomes that of the anonymous makers of finely wrought Tanagra figurines, instead of being comparable with the life-sized statuary of the great sculptor Phidias. Bouchor (12) pushes this way of thinking much further by making a distinction between perfection and 'the great concept'. For Roland-Manuel (14), Ravel's perfection before *La Valse* was serene enough, but emotionally limiting, a view echoed obliquely in the characterization by Bernard (13) of Ravel's art as a perfection of surfaces. This is a point that Bernard develops more fully elsewhere in his essay – and in a way with which Bouchor would certainly have agreed – by holding that Ravel's music did not display a dialectic between joy and sorrow which was the mark of great art. To transcend romanticism, one had partially to absorb Romantic tendencies, just as the

---

[22] M.-D. Calvocoressi, 'Maurice Ravel on Berlioz', *Daily Telegraph* (12 January 1929).

Romantics themselves had assimilated classical elements without fully eradicating them. Classical art moves listeners, says Bernard, because of an implicit duality at its core that Ravel did not exploit. Ravel's avoidance of tragic undertones exemplified his shortcomings and flattened his music to brilliant and polished surfaces.

By drawing a sharp distinction between depth and surface, Bernard follows a well-trodden path of post-Kantian and German Romantic aesthetics. Surface perfection becomes a denial of depth – an impoverishment to critics like Bernard and Bouchor. From a Ravelian perspective, by contrast, such denial became a liberation from music infused with 'sincerity', a rupture from a discourse that (in the words of a recent analysis of German romanticism) 'emerged […] to glorify a kind of "deep" subjectivity that thwarted the inquiries of reason' and had a 'capacity to expand the subject's sense of inner space beyond the limits prescribed by Enlightenment rationalism'.[23] Without naming his target explicitly, Vladimir Jankélévitch once countered Bernard's position by writing that 'Ravel is profound precisely because he is superficial: the quintessential example of clear depth, that of Vermeer and Terborch, a depth constituted entirely by precision.'[24] And by ingenuousness, Jankélévitch continues, citing the innocence and candour of children as paradigmatic of the kind of depth he means. Their every word, every gesture is significant and gives cause for wonder without recourse to metaphors favouring richness of texture and limitless inner worlds. By extension, so might the surface of an artwork.[25] And by extension also, we might add, Ravel's marked propensity to orchestrate piano compositions or enjoy mimetic effects in *L'Heure espagnole* and *Histoires naturelles* is a manifestation of the same processes.[26] What you see is what you get: surfaces themselves teem with thousands of details, precisely regulated for sensory enjoyment – and to which a discourse of perfection symbiotically became attached.

Crystal towers

I want now to burrow deeper into the cultural background to the association of Ravel's music with perfection by returning to his suspicion of instinct, sincerity, spontaneity, and glorification of the subject. In this, he was a

[23] Holly Watkins, 'From the Mine to the Shrine: The Critical Origins of Musical Depth', *19th-Century Music*, 27 (2004), 179–207: 181.

[24] Vladimir Jankélévitch, *Ravel*, ed. Jean-Michel Nectoux, third edition (Paris: Editions du Seuil, 1995), 176–7. 'Ravel sera profond justement parce que superficiel: c'est le type même de la profondeur limpide, celle de Vermeer et de Terborch, celle qui tient tout entière dans la précision.'

[25] For a recent and compelling articulation of this point of view see Carolyn Abbate, 'Outside Ravel's Tomb', *Journal of the American Musicological Society*, 52/3 (1999), 465–530.

[26] See Steven Huebner, '*Laughter*: In Ravel's Time', *Cambridge Opera Journal*, 18 (2006), 225–46.

committed reader of Charles Baudelaire (1821–67). Among the highest manifestations of feeling for the Romantic artist were expressions of affinity with
Nature, the fruit of rare and sublime experiences, of suffering and joy – and
such expressions were not granted to mere bourgeois temperaments. 'Nature
is always there, she beckons and loves; / Bury yourself in her breast that she
opens for you', writes Alphonse de Lamartine (1790–1869) in 'Le Vallon'.[27]
But Baudelaire was (famously) *not* a nature poet – one of his great paradigm
shifts celebrated the urban environment as a space for poetic epiphany – and
he had little use for Romantic reverence of the natural world. As he noted
ironically on one occasion to a correspondent: 'I have even always thought
that in Nature, flourishing and replenished, there was something brazen
and distressing.'[28] Nature deceives, and claims for the naturalness of art also
deceive, a standpoint which Baudelaire combined with a keen eye for human
evil. Romantic affirmations of truth grounded in nature became particularly
suspect in the face of the transitory, fleeting experience of modern city life.[29]
In 'Rêve parisien', Baudelaire imagines an urban utopia:

> *I banished irregular vegetation from these spectacles,*
> *And, a painter proud of my genius,*
> *I savoured in my painting*
> *The intoxicating monotony*
> *Of metal, marble and water.*
> *[…]*
> *There were extraordinary rocks*
> *And magic cascades, there were*
> *Giant mirrors that dazzled*
> *With all their reflections.*[30]

The 'intoxicating monotony' of symmetrical or repeating structures sup-
plants the irregularities of nature. With this hint of aesthetic trends that
would emerge many years later – perhaps futurism, perhaps *Boléro*, perhaps
minimalist art beyond – Baudelaire (as usual) impresses with his modernist
premonitions. The world set as a counterpoise to chaotic nature becomes a
paradis artificiel with hard edges and brilliant reflecting surfaces: mirrors,
Miroirs. Clean lines and replicating patterns admit a certain kind of perfection: one of compliance to formal archetypes or the production of exact
mimesis, Jankélévitch's 'depth' produced by precision. Even taking words

[27] Alphonse de Lamartine, 'Le Vallon' (lines
49–50), available at www.toutelapoesie.com/
poemes/lamartine/le_vallon.htm (accessed
15 October 2009): 'Mais la nature est là qui
t'invite et qui t'aime; / Plonge-toi dans son
sein qu'elle t'ouvre toujours'.
[28] Cited by F. W. Leakey, *Baudelaire and
Nature* (Manchester University Press,
1969), 122: 'J'ai même toujours pensé
qu'il y avait dans la *Nature*, florissante

et rajeunie, quelque chose d'impudent et
d'affligeant.'
[29] Articulated by Charles Baudelaire in
the chapter 'La Modernité' from *Le Peintre
de la vie moderne*, in *Œuvres complètes*,
Claude Pichois (ed.), 2 vols. (Paris: Gallimard
[Bibliothèque de la Pléiade], 1975–6), vol. II,
694–700.
[30] Baudelaire, *Les Fleurs du mal*, in
Œuvres complètes, vol. I, 101–2 (lines 7–12;

such as 'hard' and 'sharp' by themselves, the link to precision, and beyond to perfection, seems more direct than along the amorphous tangles of 'irregular vegetation'. In vocabulary that sounds like a distant echo of Baudelaire – but now taking on the aspect of a nightmare – Roland-Manuel (*14*) wrote of Ravel's 'walls of granite, towers of crystal and diamonds' as metaphors for the perfection within which Ravel had become trapped.

When Ravel himself said to M.-D. Calvocoressi, 'I can be artificial by nature', he implied artifice as a primary condition of self-identification and value judgement set against a construct of the natural world that provided difficult-to-articulate aesthetic fulfilment.[31] In the Baudelairean creative world, a privileging of artifice led to heightened self-consciousness during the act of writing itself. This entailed greater attention to the surface element of style – and especially the evaluation of style on its own merits – than had obtained in views of poetry that extolled an egress of a lyrical and artistic temperament as it responded to nature. 'Imagine if French were a dead language', wrote Baudelaire, '[…] which authors would teachers and linguists at that time pick to learn about the principles and attributes of the French language? Would it be, I ask you, those caught up in shambles of sentiment?'[32] Because of their stylistic faults, Baudelaire holds that these works would be the least intelligible, the least translatable. Paul Valéry (1871–1945) endorsed this orientation many years later by distinguishing between an 'auteur' and an 'écrivain': without style, all the intelligence and cultural sophistication in the world would prevent the 'auteur' from becoming an 'écrivain'.[33] 'Style, not sincerity, is the essential', would remark Oscar Wilde (1854–1900),[34] whose thinking partakes more generally of the literary tradition that I am discussing. Such valorizations of style have a bearing on perfection if one understands the operation of constraints as a fundamental element of style, or more precisely, to follow Leonard Meyer, the replication of patterning within a set of constraints.[35] For Valéry, constraints were the essence of art, the marble

29–32): 'J'avais banni de ces spectacles / Le végétal irrégulier, / Et, peintre fier de mon génie, / Je savourais dans mon tableau / L'enivrante monotonie / Du métal, du marbre et de l'eau. […] C'étaient des pierres inouïes / Et des flots magiques; c'étaient / D'immenses glaces éblouies / Par tout ce qu'elles reflétaient.'

[31]   Michel-Dimitri Calvocoressi, *Music and Ballet* (London: Faber and Faber, 1934; reprinted 1978), 51.

[32]   Baudelaire, *Sur mes contemporains: Théophile Gautier*, in *Œuvres complètes*, vol. II, 151. 'Figurez-vous, je vous prie, la langue française à l'état de langue morte […] Dans quels auteurs supposez-vous que les

professeurs, les linguistes d'alors, puiseront la connaissance des principes et des grâces de la langue française? Sera-ce, je vous prie, dans les capharnaüms du sentiment ou de ce que vous appelez le sentiment?'

[33]   Paul Valéry, 'Pensée et art français', in *Œuvres*, Jean Hytier (ed.), 2 vols. (Paris: Gallimard [Bibliothèque de la Pléiade], 1957–60), vol. II, 105–33.

[34]   Quoted from Oscar Wilde, 'Phrases and Philosophies for the Use of the Young' (1894), Project Gutenberg, www.readeasily.com/oscar-wilde/00206/index.php (accessed 10 June 2008).

[35]   This is the basic premise of Leonard B. Meyer, *Style and Music: Theory, History,*

that assured permanence over productions of mere clay: 'The requirements of strict prosody are the artifice that confers upon natural language the quality of resistant material.'[36] Here Valéry reconfigures Baudelaire's hard surfaces and Roland-Manuel's crystal towers into language itself. Constraints suggest greater or lesser degrees of conformity to a culturally conditioned set of practices. Now, when André Suarès (*10*) noted that Ravel 'touches a kind of perfection in taste and style' and Arthur Hoerée (*18*) wrote of a style that 'was innate elegance, imaginative richness, and perfection', neither was perhaps thinking of constraints (or crystal towers) in penning these phrases. Understanding the vocabulary of perfection here entails a broad focus: to assert that 'style' (however nebulously defined) was one of Ravel's strong suits can imply an understanding of its inherent perfectibility.

For poets in the symbolist tradition, Baudelaire, Mallarmé, and Valéry (as well as the novelist Gustave Flaubert), this perfectibility was a matter of hard work, endless self-examination and revision. 'MM Alfred de Musset and Alphonse de Lamartine would not have been among our company, had they lived in our day. They did not have enough will power and self-discipline,' wrote Baudelaire.[37] Contrast this with Lamartine's assertion: 'To create is beautiful, but to correct, to spoil remains impoverished and shallow; it is the work of bricklayers and not of artists.'[38] Thus we return to the issue of artisanship and art, now from the angle of literary history instead of philosophical models. Although they did not of course think of themselves as artisans, the symbolists nonetheless did absorb artisanal values. Sordet's remark (*8*) that Ravel 'worked month after month with recalcitrant materials' (to produce works that exhibited perfect form) reads as something Valéry himself might have said with reference to his own poetry. 'Perfection. C'est travail,' he once wrote.[39] His famous struggles with chimerical *poésie pure*, poems whose only referents were themselves, posit a kind of abstract perfection that was a formidable challenge indeed.

Wilde neatly described the *l'art pour l'art* idea of the text as a closed system: 'Art finds her own perfection within, and not outside of, herself. She is not to be judged by any external standard of resemblance.'[40] From this

and Ideology (Philadelphia: University of Pennsylvania Press, 1989).

[36] Paul Valéry, 'Au sujet d'Adonis', in *Œuvres*, vol. I, 480. 'Les exigences d'une stricte prosodie sont l'artifice qui confère au langage naturel les qualités d'une matière résistante.'

[37] Baudelaire, 'Etudes sur Poe', in *Œuvres complètes*, vol. II, 247–337: 274. 'MM Alfred de Musset et Alphonse de Lamartine n'eussent pas été de ses amis, s'il avait vécu parmi nous. Ils n'ont pas assez de volonté et ne sont pas assez maîtres d'eux-mêmes.'

[38] Excerpt from a letter cited by Arthur Tilley, 'Lamartine's *Méditations poétiques*', *Modern Language Review*, 26 (1931), 288–314: 302: 'Créer c'est beau, mais corriger, gâter, reste pauvre et plat, c'est l'œuvre des maçons et non pas des artistes.'

[39] Paul Valéry, *Cahiers*, Judith Robinson-Valéry (ed.), 2 vols. (Paris: Gallimard, 1988–9), vol. II, 1011.

[40] Oscar Wilde, *The Decay of Lying*: *Collected Works of Oscar Wilde* (Ware, Hertfordshire: Wordsworth Editions, 1997), 933.

position the pleasure of writing itself and the posture of the writer as more calculated than inspired required no additional justification. And what could be more calculated than a lie? Ravel once played up the rupture between artist and nature by observing that 'the lie, taken as the power to create illusion, is the only thing that makes man superior to animals; and, if it has something to do with art, the only way that an artist is superior to other men'.[41] Be it informed by magic or lies, calculation engendered different metaphors for the creative process (consonant with how perfection became associated with Ravel) than an allegory fostered by nature-based thinking that (in music) prioritized a kind of organic germination or 'composing out' of motives, or the florid and tangled realization of sparse fundamental structures. Edgar Allan Poe (1809–49) posited a famous alternative in 'The Philosophy of Composition', and Ravel repeatedly endorsed the admiration that Baudelaire, Mallarmé, and Valéry all exhibited toward the American writer's approach.[42] Baudelaire's introduction to his translation – 'let us look backstage, in the workshop, the laboratory, the internal mechanism' ('voyons la coulisse, l'atelier, le laboratoire, le mécanisme intérieur') – speaks volumes about what exactly he admired. Poe's goal in the essay is to recreate the genesis of his famous poem 'The Raven'. After eliminating both Truth and Passion, Poe settles on Beauty as the sole province of poetry and notes that 'Beauty [is not] a quality, as is supposed, but an effect […] it is an obvious rule of Art that effects should be made to spring from direct causes – that objects should be attained through means best adapted for their attainment.'[43] First he decides that he needs a short refrain, because artistic 'piquancy' lay in situating the refrain in ever-changing contexts. Too long a refrain would be a distraction. Moreover, the refrain needs to encourage monotone delivery, a kind of anchor in a changing field of effects. Yet it also needs to be sonorous. Hence the choice of the word 'Nevermore'. The next step lies in finding a rational pretext for the continuous use of one word as a refrain, which falls to a 'non-reasoning creature capable of speech' – not a parrot, but a raven in keeping with the gloomy tone. Note how considerations of form and sonority precede those of meaning. The essay and the construction of the poem continue with a description of how poetic metres were chosen, where Poe identifies his primary concern as achieving originality by an unusual combination of patterns sanctioned by tradition, 'by no means', he adds, 'a matter, as some suppose, of impulse or intuition'. And so he continues, privileging logic and sonority at every turn, and, at the end almost as an afterthought, writing of the quality of

---

[41] Ravel, 'Mes souvenirs d'enfant paresseux', 1.
[42] For a fuller appreciation of the influence of Poe on Ravel, see Michel Duchesneau, 'Maurice Ravel et Edgar Allan Poe: une théorie poétique appliquée', *Ostinato rigore*, 24 (2005), 7–24; Steven Huebner, 'Ravel's

Poetics: Literary Currents, Classical Takes' (forthcoming).
[43] The text of 'The Philosophy of Composition' that I cite is at http://xroads. virginia.edu/~HYPER/poe/composition. html (accessed 8 June 2008).

'suggestiveness' to be added as a necessary ingredient to impart 'richness' to the chain of effects.

Roland-Manuel (*15*) mirrors Poe's mastery by describing Ravel as 'a man completely absorbed by the rules of his game, having neglected nothing in order to play it to perfection'. An important turn of phrase here is the identification of the game as 'his' game, the sense that, just like Poe, Ravel lays out the parameters and goals anew with each work. Later in the same passage Roland-Manuel remarks that Ravel subordinates meaning (one might extend this to 'feeling') to sonority: 'For Ravel, just as for any musician in the authentic French line, the proper duty of a composer is not to "think through music", which means exactly nothing, but to order sounds "in a manner agreeable to the ear".' And he adds, with a more symbolist touch: 'it is up to the work to resonate in spiritual realms'. In short, the machinist Ravel remains preoccupied by pulleys and trapdoors. Poe's adoption of a language of mechanistic purposefulness suggests that individual poems or pieces either work properly or do not, in the vein of Aristotle's third definition of perfection relating to functional goals. *Boléro* might be thought of as a *tour de force* that 'works', much like the 'Nevermore' refrain. Valéry once praised 'the quest after mechanical prowess': a rigour that led to a kind of perfection which he contrasted with the desire to 'appear spontaneous […] and unlimited in resources and depth'.[44] The surface/depth metaphor appears again. The illusionist Ravel whom I quoted earlier might have added: lies either succeed or are uncovered. 'Art is meant to correct nature's imperfections. Art is a beautiful lie. The most interesting thing in art is to try to overcome difficulties. My teacher in composition was Edgar Allan Poe':[45] Ravel initiates this sequence of remarks to a Spanish newspaper by referring explicitly to art's ability to correct 'imperfections' – that is, to achieve perfection through both cunning and calculation ('Art is a beautiful lie') and through the overcoming of difficulties, the mark of a real stylist.

Perfection and character

Bound up with Ravel's attraction to symbolist writers, we might consider finally the man himself: in particular, the aura or myths around him that undoubtedly contributed to perceptions of perfection that persisted well beyond his lifespan. This is certainly the sense of Fargue's remark (*19*) that

[44] Valéry, *Cahiers*, vol. II, 1166: 'à la recherche des moyens mécaniques […] le désir de sembler spontanée […] illimité en resources et en profondeur'.
[45] André Révész, 'The Great Musician Maurice Ravel Talks about His Art', in Arbie Orenstein (ed.), *A Ravel Reader: Correspondence, Articles, Interviews* (New York: Columbia University Press, 1990; reprinted [with minor corrections] New York: Dover Publications, 2003), 431–5: 433.

an artistic conscience preoccupied with perfection produced an aloof exterior. When Hoerée (*18*) suggests that Ravel gave the impression of having been born with 'frilly cuffs', creating an aristocratic demeanour that exuded 'innate elegance', he evokes Ravel's much-remarked-upon dandified public image.[46] The dandy in classic French descriptions by Jules Barbey d'Aurevilly (1808–89) and Baudelaire focuses upon outward elegance and avoids external signs of emotion.[47] He cultivates indifference. He understands the distinction between originality and eccentricity. Too little of the former was bourgeois, too much of the latter bohemian. According to Barbey d'Aurevilly the dandy achieved originality by at once respecting and chafing against the rules of society, suggesting the achievement of personal style within a set of sanctioned constraints – a point of view, we might add, not unlike that advocated by Poe in 'The Philosophy of Composition'. Spontaneity was as much a negative value in his comportment as in Ravel's discussions of composition, most memorably when the composer equated spontaneity with sincerity, as mere 'chatter'.[48] By contrast, the dandy's surfaces were very studied indeed, a kind of impassivity that seems homologous to Roland-Manuel's characterization (*14*) of perfection as a hard, impenetrable surface, those 'towers of crystal and diamonds'. (For more on Ravel and the dandy, see especially, Chapter 4.)

In a certain respect, the dandy's image does not harmonize very well with that of the artisan's workmanship. But, as I mentioned earlier, to understand workmanship in a symbolist vein is to consider creation as a process of unending refinement in shaping *poésie pure*: writing that Valéry equated with perfection in the sense of a complex object where the parts (phonemes, words, phrases) existed in a complex web of interrelationships regulated by etymology, phonetics, and analogical language. Valéry's great mentor, of course, was Stéphane Mallarmé (1842–98), much admired by Ravel too, whose 'will to perfection' Valéry associated explicitly with the fully integrated idea of *poésie pure*.[49] Much as Ravel excoriated Massenet, Valéry contrasted the facile verbosity of Emile Zola and Alphonse Daudet with Mallarmé's work: 'small, unusual poems, strange and obscure' and of vastly greater influence than acres of realist novels.[50] Quantity was irrelevant. Mallarmé had no apologies to make for the slender corpus of his works, each poem wrung from intense labour.

[46] For a recent discussion, see Michael J. Puri, 'Dandy, Interrupted: Sublimation, Repression, and Self-Portraiture in Maurice Ravel's *Daphnis et Chloé* (1909–1912)', *Journal of the American Musicological Society*, 60/2 (2007), 317–72.

[47] Two excellent studies of the dandy in culture are: Ellen Moers, *The Dandy: Brummell to Beerbohm* (London: Secker and Warburg, 1960) and Michel Lemaire, *Le Dandysme de Baudelaire à Mallarmé* (Montreal: Les Presses de l'Université de Montréal, 1978).

[48] Ravel, 'Mes souvenirs d'enfant paresseux', 1.

[49] Valéry, *Cahiers*, vol. II, 1137.

[50] *Ibid.*, 1117: 'ses rares, petits poèmes bizarres et obscurs'.

By the standards of the times, Ravel wrote relatively little music in his career. That this could occasion criticism in the music culture of his day seems amply suggested by the opinion of his near contemporary Camille Saint-Saëns (1835–1921), who argued that facility was a mark of excellence. Thus Jules Massenet (1842–1912), a composer in whom Saint-Saëns usually found much to critique, did achieve greatness as an artist precisely because he was prolific: 'The artist who produces little, if he has talent, might well be interesting; but he will never be a great artist.'[51] Even Ravel himself at times felt self-conscious about this, a stance which is evidenced in a letter to the musician Claude Delvincourt in which he remarked: 'I have failed in my life […] I am not one of the great composers. All the great [composers] have produced enormously. There is everything in their work; the best and the worst, but there is always quantity. But I have written relatively very little […] I did my work slowly, drop by drop.'[52] Among generations of critics – and as with Mallarmé – the construct of perfection as an exigent master has always been his best defence.

Appendix: Anthology of critical writings

Ravel himself

1   On s'est plu parfois à me prêter des opinions, fort paradoxales en apparence, sur le mensonge de l'art et les dangers de la sincérité. Le fait est que je me refuse simplement mais absolument à confondre la *conscience* de l'artiste, qui est une chose, avec sa *sincérité*, qui en est une autre. La seconde n'est d'aucun prix si la première ne l'aide pas à se manifester. Cette conscience exige que nous développions en nous le bon ouvrier. Mon objectif est donc la perfection technique. Je puis y tendre sans cesse, puisque je suis assuré de ne jamais l'atteindre. L'important est d'en approcher toujours davantage.

> Maurice Ravel, 'Quelques réflexions sur la musique [1928]', in Roland-Manuel, 'Lettres de Maurice Ravel et documents inédits', *Revue de musicologie*, 38 (1956), 49–53: 53

2   When the first stroke of a work has been written, and the process of elimination begun, the severe effort toward perfection proceeds by means almost intangible, seemingly directed by currents of inner forces, so intimate and intricate in character as to defy all analysis.

> Maurice Ravel, *Contemporary Music*, Rice Institute Pamphlet 15/2 (1928), 131–45: 142

---

[51] Camille Saint-Saëns, *Ecole buissonnière: notes et souvenirs* (Paris: Pierre Lafitte, 1924), 273. 'L'artiste qui produit peu, s'il a du mérite, pourra être un artiste intéressant; il ne sera jamais un grand artiste.'

[52] Cited by Victor Seroff, *Maurice Ravel* (Freeport, NY: Books for Libraries Press, 1953), 207.

3   J'ai beaucoup d'amitié pour l'école de Schoenberg: ce sont à la fois des romantiques et des sévères. Des romantiques parce qu'ils veulent toujours briser de 'vieilles tables'. Des sévères par les nouvelles lois qu'ils s'imposent et parce qu'ils savent se méfier de la haïssable sincérité, mère des œuvres loquaces et imparfaites.

> [Uncredited], 'Entretien avec Ravel', *La Revue musicale*, 12 (March 1931),
> 193–4: 193

4   Ce que Mozart a écrit pour le plaisir de l'oreille est parfait, à mon sens, et même Saint-Saëns a atteint cet objectif, encore qu'à un niveau bien inférieur. Beethoven, en revanche, en fait de trop, dramatise et se glorifie lui-même, si bien qu'il n'atteint pas son objectif.

> [Uncredited], 'Une visite chez Maurice Ravel', *De Telegraaf* (31 March
> 1931), in Arbie Orenstein (ed.), *Maurice Ravel: lettres, écrits, entretiens*
> (Paris: Flammarion, 1989), 360–3: 361

5   Mozart, c'est la beauté absolue, la pureté parfaite. La musique serait morte avec lui, morte de consomption ou de cette pureté-là, si nous n'avions eu Beethoven qui était sourd. Et ce qu'on en admire le plus, c'est l'injouable *Neuvième*. Après cela nous vint Berlioz. Berlioz, c'est le génie qui sut toute chose d'instinct, sauf ce que tout élève du Conservatoire réussit en un tour de main: mettre une bonne basse sur une valse.

> José Bruyr, 'Un entretien avec Maurice Ravel', *Le Guide du concert*, 18
> (16 October 1931), 39–41: 41

6   Mon maître préféré? En ai-je un?… En tout cas, j'estime que Mozart demeure au plus parfait de tous […] Sa grande leçon, aujourd'hui, c'est qu'il nous aide à nous *débarrasser de la musique*, à n'écouter que nous-mêmes et le fonds éternel, à oublier ce qui nous précède immédiatement: ainsi le retour actuel aux formes pures, ce néo-classicisme – appelez-le comme vous voudrez – m'enchante, en un certain sens.

> Nino Frank, 'Maurice Ravel entre deux trains', *Candide* (5 May 1932)

Friends and critics

7   L'art de Ravel, précis et féerique, discret, pudique, c'est-à-dire ennemi des effusions romantiques, se confère, par ces qualités mêmes, et aussi par la recherche de la perfection dans la forme – malgré des outrances peut-être voulues – un caractère classique, traditionnel, qui explique l'étonnante fortune qu'il a rencontrée dès longtemps dans des pays plus musicaux que le nôtre où ses œuvres représentent, à côté de celles de Debussy, ce qu'il y a de plus hautement original dans notre art moderne.

> J.-G. Prod'homme, 'Maurice Ravel (1875–1937)', *Le Courrier du centre*
> (8 January 1938)

8   Il achève en tout cas d'éclairer le génie de son auteur, musicien français, héritier direct des clavecinistes français du XVIIIe siècle, artiste classique, ennemi du pathétique, des effusions et des confidences, mais habile à manier l'artifice, jaloux de perfection formelle, plus cérébral et sensuel qu'émotif et sensible; ironique détaché, lucide, paradoxal, un peu sec, ne prenant au fond qu'une chose au sérieux, son art; travaillant des mois et des mois une matière rebelle et difficile qu'il livre au public le jour seulement où elle est ajustée à la forme de son exigeante fantaisie.

> Dominique Sordet, 'Festival Maurice Ravel', *L'Action française* (22 January 1932)

9   On a souvent abusé, et quelquefois dans un sens péjoratif, de la qualification: art français, pensée française. Mais en trouverait-on une autre pour définir ce précieux alliage d'intelligence et de sensibilité, de pondération et de hardiesse, d'instinct et de réflexion representé par l'ensemble de la production que nous venons de parcourir et dont le *Tombeau de Couperin*, momentanément, forme l'aboutissement rayonnant? Et cette technique lumineuse, cet accent de perfection matérielle, – dont nous ne songeons même plus à tirer vanité, tant nous sommes habitués depuis des siècles à voir les artistes de chez nous en revêtir les moindres productions de l'esprit – ne sont-ce pas là des privilèges que nous puissions revendiquer pleinement?

> Alfred Cortot, *La Musique française de piano* (Paris: Presse Universitaire de France, 1948), 291

10   La musique française n'a sans doute pas connu de plus belle époque, si ce n'est sous la Renaissance, au siècle des Valois. Le charme et la beauté de la forme en sont des témoins infaillibles. De Vincent d'Indy à Debussy, ou de Fauré à Poulenc, une foule d'auteurs savent écrire, les uns avec une force originale, les autres avec un rare agrément. Entre tous, Maurice Ravel touche à une sorte de perfection dans le goût et le style. S'il y a, désormais, un style français en musique, Ravel y est pour beaucoup.

> André Suarès, 'Pour Ravel', *La Revue musicale*, 6 (April 1925 [special issue]), 3–8: 8

11   Est-il un classique au sens complet du mot? Non, peut-être pas au même degré que Fauré, par exemple. Il y a chez lui une pente vers la préciosité, une recherche continuelle du rare, le goût du paradoxe, de la surprise, de l'imprévu. Tout cela est extrêmement piquant, délicieux même chez un tel artiste, mais non pas d'un ordre aussi élevé que le naturel parfait, l'aisance souveraine des classiques. Dans ce sens, il faut noter aussi l'extrême recherche du détail, un certain goût de la miniature, de la petite chose parfaite. Un petit poème peut être sans prix; les figurines de Tanagra sont souvent exquises; tout de même, ne les mettons pas pour autant au rang des cavaliers et des déesses de Phidias.

> Louis Aguettant, *La Musique de piano: des origines à Ravel* (Paris: Albin Michel, 1954), 428

12   Une pagode est charmante, en principe. Mais il y a trop de pagodes dans l'œuvre de Ravel, et je pense au mot de Degas critiquant une composition de Gustave Moreau: 'Que ces dieux ont donc des chaînes de montres!' Trop de pagodes: trop de sonnailles; trop de clochettes qui tintinnabulent; trop de technique, trop de virtuosité! Je sais le reproche très injuste fait trop souvent à ceux qui eurent un métier impeccable […] La science de M Ravel est d'un goût parfait et sa sensibilité française ne commet certes pas de fautes de goût: mais cela même est une erreur, car la perfection ne touche pas le cœur de l'homme. La peur de se tromper paralyse le cerveau des musiciens modernes. La technique d'un Beethoven est pauvre et d'un goût pas toujours très sûr, mais l'émotion beethovenienne est un bienfait pour l'humanité […] et puisque maintenant nous connaissons la technique incomparable des musiciens modernes, puisque nous avons des chefs d'orchestre comme Monteux et Rhené-Baton, des pianistes comme Viñes et Pierre Lucas – c'est-à-dire le moyen d'exprimer, n'allons-nous pas voir enfin M Ravel, au lieu de tricoter à l'ombre du tombeau de

Couperin et de rester le plus grand des petits maîtres, nous donner tout ce que nous attendons de la musique française moderne, non seulement la réalisation parfaite, mais la grande conception?

>   Jean Bouchor, 'Chronique musicale: Maurice Ravel ou le Diable dans la
>   Pagode', *La Rose rouge* (26 June 1919)

13   Or, Ravel a réduit cette part d'inconscient à son extrême minimum, ôtant par là même l'émotion tragique de son œuvre. La musique de Ravel est toute en surface; cette surface est d'une perfection, d'une somptuosité de matière, d'une élégance de facture et de pensée, d'une complexité telles que, à un point de vue strictement réceptive, il est insensé de déplorer cette lacune.

>   Robert Bernard, *Les Tendances de la musique française moderne: cours
>   d'esthétique* (Paris: Durand et Fils, 1930), 85

14   Partout ailleurs, ce ne sont que portes sans issues, murailles de granit, tours de cristal et de diamant.

Prisonnier de sa même perfection, parvenu à l'époque climatérique où les grands créateurs sont obligés de se reformer sous peine de se redire, Ravel a connu la nécessité de mépriser des acquisitions si patiemment réunies et si précieuses; de prendre, à cinquante ans, le bâton du pèlerin pour courir de nouveau la chance des aventures […]

Déjà *La Valse* trahissait chez Ravel la venue du démon de midi. Une sourde violence s'est insinuée dans son art. Nous le voyons composer ses charmes avec moins de détachement et tenir ses gageures avec moins de sérénité.

>   Roland-Manuel, *L'Enfant et les sortilèges* [review], *Revue Pleyel* (February 1926)

15   Voici donc un homme tout occupé des règles de son jeu, qui n'a rien négligé afin de le jouer en perfection, et qui raisonnait de son art comme s'il eût été le maître des puissances qui le gouvernaient à son insu. Le génie de l'espèce musicale opérait en lui avec une infaillibilité souveraine, secrètement attendu et fidèlement servi par le plus beau métier du monde.

On s'est parfois autorisé de l'attitude de Ravel devant l'œuvre à faire pour diminuer la portée de son message, comme si l'artiste ne disait pas toujours plus de choses qu'il n'en exprime; comme si l'homme ne se dépassait pas toujours dans l'acte qui l'engage tout entier!

Ce n'est pas à Ravel qu'il faut demander des œuvres où le sentiment s'exagère sans cesse dans la véhémence de son expression […] Pour un Ravel, comme pour tout musicien d'authentique lignée française, l'office propre du compositeur n'est pas et ne peut pas être de 'penser en musique', ce qui ne veut exactement rien dire, mais d'ordonner les sons 'd'une manière agréable à l'oreille'. Cet ordre atteint par le sensible et dans le sensible, il reste à l'œuvre de retentir dans le spirituel.

Telle est la loi de Ravel. Elle ne prétend pas à la nouveauté: le classicisme la suppose et la réussite lui suffit.

>   Roland-Manuel, *Ravel* (originally entitled *A la gloire de… Ravel*, Paris: Editions
>   de la Nouvelle revue critique, 1938; reprinted Mémoire du livre: 2000), 184–5

16   Souvent, au plus tard de la soirée où nous étions réunis en famille, un coup de sonnette inattendu nous faisait dresser l'oreille, et quelqu'un proclamait aussitôt 'Tiens! voilà Ravel.' Il venait, par exemple, étudier telle ou telle combinaison d'écriture de la harpe, instrument dont jouait une de mes sœurs.

Ce sera en effet chez lui, autant par curiosité d'esprit que par volonté de perfection, un souci constant de pénétrer jusque dans leurs secrets les plus cachés, les divers éléments de son art. Point d'instrument dont il n'ait usé avec une connaissance totale de toutes ses ressources.

> Louis Aubert, 'Souvenir', *La Revue musicale*, 19 (December 1938 [special issue]), 206–7

17   Dès lors, le jeune pionnier put se consacrer librement à sa mission d'explorateur, prospectant avec méthode des zones inconnues du mystérieux pays des sons. Sa vie, étrangement préservée de tout orage passionnel, sera désormais remplie par un labeur lent et minutieux d'ajusteur de précision, engrenant, la loupe à l'œil, les minuscules roues dentées de ses chefs-d'œuvres dont la perfection mécanique ne sent jamais l'effort. Car, en traitant dédaigneusement Ravel d' 'horloger suisse', Stravinsky n'a fait que rendre, malgré lui, un magnifique hommage à la maîtrise artisanale qui assure tant de solidité, d'équilibre et d'aisance à son style éblouissant.

> Emile Vuillermoz, *Histoire de la musique* (Paris: Fayard, 1949), 384

18   N'a-t-on pas dit de Buffon qu'il 'mettait' ses manchettes pour écrire? C'était sa façon de se mettre dans 'l'état littéraire' qui n'a pas de correspondant en musique, celle-ci n'ayant pas de langue véhiculaire. Mais on pourrait dire de Ravel qu'il est 'né' avec des manchettes et que sa plume est le râteau précieux préposé à la toilette du plus féerique des jardins, tant son style est élégance innée, richesse imaginative et perfection.

> Arthur Hoerée, 'Les Mélodies et l'œuvre lyrique', *La Revue musicale*,
> 6 (April 1925 [special issue]), 46–64: 63–4

19   [...] les œuvres de Ravel. Aucun ratage, aucune médiocrité, aucune courtisanerie, pas de morceaux de commande, pas de musique 'de salon, de bar ou de sentimentalité mondaine'. Des œuvres, au sens le plus parfait du terme [...]

Un des traits les plus frappants de ce curieux Pyrénéen fut le souci de la perfection. Cet homme foncièrement intelligent, varié, précis, savant comme personne et dont la facilité était proverbiale, avait le caractère et les qualités d'un artisan. Aucune comparaison ne lui allait aussi directement au cœur. Il aimait faire et bien faire: tout ce qui sortit de son cerveau, quelles que soient les réserves sur l'inspiration que puissent formuler les censeurs ou les critiques, porte la marque de la perfection, d'une certaine perfection. Il savait qu'on peut dire d'une chose, d'un poème, d'un roman, d'une toile, d'un jardin, d'un amour ou d'une cérémonie, que ces événements ou ces drames sont 'finis', pour employer une expression d'atelier. Et sa passion fut d'offrir au public des œuvres finies, polies jusqu'au degré suprême.

Cette haute conscience professionnelle ne se rencontre plus de nos jours qu'à de très rares intervalles. Le souci de bien faire, de contenter les exigences les plus secrètes d'un esprit constamment en éveil, donnait à Ravel l'aspect d'un gentilhomme un peu sec, difficilement abordable, méticuleux et froid.

> Léon-Paul Fargue, 'Autour de Ravel', in Colette et al., *Maurice Ravel par*
> *quelques-uns de ses familiers* (Paris: Editions du tambourinaire, 1939),
> 153–61: 158–60

2 Enchantments and illusions: recasting the creation of *L'Enfant et les sortilèges*

Emily Kilpatrick

Across the first quarter of the twentieth century, a spirit of interdisciplinary collaboration shaped French artistic practice decisively. Consider the extraordinary example of *Parade* (1917), composed by Erik Satie to a scenario by Jean Cocteau, with costume and set designs by Pablo Picasso, and choreography by Léonide Massine. Yet, despite the excited conversations in the bistros of Montmartre and despite *Parade* and the Ballets russes, successful collaborations between composers and writers of stature remained surprisingly rare in the so-called 'ville lumière'. *L'Enfant et les sortilèges* (The Child and the Enchantments) was thus almost unique in pairing the then most acclaimed living composer in France, Maurice Ravel, with Sidonie-Gabrielle Colette (1873–1954), equally acknowledged as one of the finest writers of her generation.[1] Moreover, it was not for an adaptation of an existing work that they came together (as was the case with Debussy's *Pelléas et Mélisande* and Ravel's *L'Heure espagnole*, both based on successful plays), but for an *opéra-ballet* set to a new, purpose-written libretto.

Welcomed enthusiastically at its 1925 Monte Carlo premiere, *L'Enfant* received a more turbulent reception in critical Paris a year later. Nevertheless, as a collaborative enterprise, the work was generally deemed a success. 'How well [the exquisite score] is matched to the delicious fantasy of Mme Colette's libretto!' wrote André Corneau of the Monte Carlo production,[2] while of the Parisian reprise Raymond Balliman asserted:

> To treat this original and delicate subject, M Ravel was the best of choices – one could say the only one possible. The Ravel–Colette collaboration seems to have been ordained by the order of things, and in listening to the work it is impossible to conceive any other possible musical setting than Ravel's […] The union of poetry and music is such that it is impossible to separate the collaborators.[3]

[1] The choreographic involvement in *L'Enfant* of the rising star George Balanchine (1904–83), ballet-master for the Ballets russes from January 1925, may also be noted. For more on Balanchine, see Chapter 8.

[2] André Corneau, '*L'Enfant et les sortilèges*' [review], *Journal de Monaco* (24 March 1925), 4: 'comme [la ravissante partition] convient à

la délicieuse fantaisie du livret de la façon de Mme Colette!'

[3] Raymond Balliman, '*L'Enfant et les sortilèges*' [review], *Lyrica* (February 1926), 693: 'Pour traiter cet original et délicat sujet, M Ravel était le mieux désigné, le seul pourrait-on dire. La collaboration Colette–Ravel devait être car elle semble dans l'ordre des choses, et en entendant l'œuvre, on

Nobody remarked, in 1926, that this artistic pairing was perhaps a surprising one, comprising a librettist famously flamboyant and a composer just as famously discreet (*pudique*). Across the decades since the premiere, however (and despite Balliman's words), this seeming disparity has come to loom large. Set beside the dearth of documented communication in the nine years between the work's conception and premiere (1916–25), it has given rise to an assumption that there was little or no truly 'collaborative' process in the preparation of *L'Enfant*: writer and musician remain as oddly assorted as the fox-trotting teapots, waltzing frogs, and lumbering armchairs of their creation.

The point of departure here has long been Colette's 1939 reflection upon the creation of *L'Enfant*: the essay 'Un salon en 1900'. The salon of which Colette wrote was that of Marguerite de Saint-Marceaux where, as Gabriel Fauré and André Messager improvised outrageous spoofs on Wagner's operas and the Prince de Polignac sat and sketched, Ravel, 'perhaps secretly shy', kept his distance: 'I don't remember any particular conversation with him, no surge of friendship'.[4] But then in 1916, Jacques Rouché, director of the Opéra Garnier, approached Colette with a commission for a libretto of a 'fairy-ballet':

> I still cannot explain how I, who work slowly and painfully, was able to give him *L'Enfant et les sortilèges* in less than eight days… He liked my little poem, and suggested several composers whose names I accepted as politely as I could.
>
> 'But', said Rouché after a silence, 'if I suggested Ravel to you?'
>
> I was startled out of my politeness and the expression of my enthusiasm left nothing to be desired.
>
> 'We mustn't kid ourselves', said Rouché, 'it could take a long time, even assuming Ravel accepts…'
>
> He accepted. It took a long time. He disappeared with my libretto and we heard nothing more of Ravel, nor of *L'Enfant*… Where did Ravel work? *Was* he working? I was not then familiar with what the creation of a new work demanded of him, the slow frenzy that possessed him and held him isolate, careless of the days and hours. The war took Ravel, consigning his name to hermetic silence, and I fell out of the habit of thinking of *L'Enfant*. Five years passed. The completed work and its author emerged from silence, escaping from the blue, nyctalopic gaze of his confidants, his Siamese cats. But Ravel did not treat me with any privilege, neither explaining anything nor granting me an early hearing. He seemed to concern himself only with the duo of the two Cats, demanding gravely if I minded whether he replaced 'mouaô' with 'mouain', or perhaps it was the other way around.[5]

---

ne peut se figurer une autre musique que celle de Maurice Ravel […] L'union du poème et de la musique est telle qu'on ne peut séparer les collaborateurs.'
4 Colette, 'Un salon en 1900', in *Journal à rebours, Œuvres*, Claude Pichois (ed.), 4 vols. (Paris: Gallimard [Bibliothèque de la Pléiade], 1984–2001), vol. IV, 164–8: 165–6. 'Peut-être secrètement timide […] Je n'ai à me rappeler aucun entretien particulier

avec lui, aucun abandon amical.' The essay was first published as 'Un salon de musique en 1900', in Colette et al., *Maurice Ravel par quelques-uns de ses familiers* (Paris: Editions du tambourinaire, 1939), 115–24.
5 Colette, 'Un salon en 1900', 166–7:

> Vint le jour où M Rouché me demanda un livret de féerie-ballet pour l'Opéra. Je ne m'explique pas encore comment je lui

'Un salon en 1900' is our only authorial reflection on the genesis of this *féerie-ballet* that was to become a *fantaisie lyrique*. Yet in strictly documentary terms it is, as we will see, an abbreviated and inflected history; from a great fiction writer we should perhaps expect no less. A more holistic view of the collaboration and a clearer understanding of 'Un salon en 1900' emerge if we re-examine the sources that surround *L'Enfant*, juxtaposing well-known with previously unpublished correspondence and viewing both against Ravel's and Colette's writings on the creative process. Questions of personality and the minutiae of authorship have long pervaded discussions of this most intriguing of collaborations. Beyond these, however, is the richer field of artistic and collaborative philosophy and practice, wherein lie the structural and conceptual roots of *L'Enfant*.

Creating an *opéra-ballet*: titles, forms, and the collaborative process

On 22 March 1916, a pneumatique arrived in Jacques Rouché's office, sent from the rue Jouffroy d'Abbans in the seventeenth arrondissement of Paris: 'Cher Monsieur, I've finished. I've sorted out the last third – changed it, rather – and I'd like to know if you share Sidi's [Henri de Jouvenel's] good opinion of the *Ballet pour ma fille*. Would you telephone me? Believe me amicably yours, Colette de Jouvenel.'[6]

Here, at the beginning of our history, we find the first elision in Colette's published account, for the first composer approached about the then *Ballet*

donnai, moi qui travaille avec lenteur et peine, *L'Enfant et les sortilèges* en moins de huit jours… Il aima mon petit poème, et suggéra des compositeurs dont j'accueillis les noms aussi poliment que je pus.

'Mais, dit Rouché après un silence, si je vous proposais Ravel?'

Je sortis bruyamment de ma politesse, et l'expression de mon espoir ne ménagea plus rien.

'Il ne faut pas nous dissimuler, ajouta Rouché, que cela peut être long, en admettant que Ravel accepte…'

Il accepta. Ça fut long. Il emporta mon livret, et nous n'entendîmes plus parler de Ravel, ni de *L'Enfant*… Où travaillait Ravel? Travaillait-il? Je n'étais point au fait de ce qu'exigeait de lui la création d'une œuvre, de la lente frénésie qui le possédait et le tenait isolé, insoucieux des jours et des heures. La guerre prit Ravel, fit sur son nom un silence hermétique, et je perdis l'habitude de penser à *L'Enfant et*

les sortilèges. Cinq ans passèrent. L'œuvre achevée et son auteur sortirent du silence, échappèrent à l'œil nyctalope et bleu des chats du Siam, confidents de Ravel. Mais celui-ci ne me traita pas en personne privilégiée, ne consentit pour moi à aucun commentaire, aucune audition prématurée. Il parut seulement se soucier du 'duo miaulé' entre les deux Chats, et me demanda gravement si je ne voyais pas d'inconvénient à ce qu'il remplaçât 'mouaô' par 'mouain', ou bien l'inverse.

6 Pneumatique with date postmarked, Fonds Rouché 406, Colette de Jouvenel (1)/ LAS [autograph letter], Bibliothèque-musée de l'Opéra (Bm-O), Paris: 'Cher Monsieur / J'ai fini. J'ai arrangé le dernier tiers, changé, plutôt – et je voudrais savoir si vous partagez la bonne opinion qu'a Sidi du "Ballet pour ma Fille". Voulez-vous me téléphoner? Croyez-moi amicalement vôtre / Colette de Jouvenel.'

pour ma fille was not Ravel. On 14 April, Rouché wrote instead to Paul Dukas (1865–1935): 'Cher Maître et ami, Colette de Jouvenel has brought me a delightful libretto for a ballet-opera. Her wish is to read it to you so you can understand what she has in mind; you can also understand how happy I am to be the intermediary.'[7] Around the same time, Colette sent Rouché a manuscript draft (now lost), with a note attached: 'Cher Monsieur, here is the *Ballet pour ma fille* – have you found Dukas?'[8] Dukas, the composer of *L'Apprenti sorcier* (1897) and the masterly ballet *La Péri* (1912), would have been a natural choice for a *féerie-ballet*, not least because he was near at hand in Paris. Practical impresario that he was, Rouché may have been reluctant to offer a commission to a composer serving at Verdun. Dukas, however, refused the project by return post. Although full of praise for Colette's writing – 'I hugely admire Mme Colette de Jouvenel's talent, and I am certain that a Ballet authored by her could not do otherwise than refresh the genre' – he declared himself unwilling to participate in any sort of collaborative venture.[9] By the summer of 1916, therefore, Colette was writing once more to Rouché: 'Cher ami, Are you keeping the ballet, or will you send it back to me? If you're keeping it, have you got any thoughts about a composer with plenty of talent – and also haste?'[10]

We have no record of Rouché's initial approach to Ravel. It seems that a libretto was sent to Ravel during the latter part of 1916, but that it never reached him; in any case he was in no state to undertake a major project, hospitalized as he was with dysentery in the autumn and then distraught following the death of his mother in January 1917. It was probably not until April or May 1917 that Ravel agreed to take on the work (which figures in his correspondence only from June of that year). By then he had received a temporary discharge from the army on the grounds of ill health. Trying to restore the pattern of his life, he began to plan new musical projects and resuscitate long-abandoned ones. It appears that he was particularly interested in the fate of two works whose progress had stalled around the outbreak of war: the 'symphonic poem' *Wien* and the opera *La Cloche engloutie* (The Sunken Bell), based on Hauptmann's *Die versunkene Glocke*. Ravel had been working intermittently at both projects since about 1906, but had put them aside in the

---

[7] In Roger Nichols, *The Harlequin Years: Music in Paris, 1917–1929* (Berkeley and Los Angeles: University of California Press, 2002), 91.

[8] LAS Colette (3), Bm-O: 'Cher Monsieur, voici le *Ballet pour Ma Fille* – avez-vous trouvé Dukas?' This and the other five letters in this Bm-O catalogue reference (LAS Colette 1–6) are undated. Their sequence and tentative dates have been deduced from their context and provenance.

[9] LAS Dukas (Paul) (10), Bm-O (14 April 1916): 'J'aime infiniment le talent de Mme Colette de Jouvenel et je suis certain qu'un Ballet signé d'elle ne peut être qu'un rafraîchissement du genre.'

[10] LAS Colette (2): 'Gardez-vous le ballet, ou me le rendez-vous? Avez-vous, si vous le gardez, des vues sur un compositeur plein de talent – et aussi de hâte?' This letter is addressed from the de Jouvenels' home in Corrèze, where Colette spent most of summer 1916.

summer of 1914 (together with the newly begun *Le Tombeau de Couperin*, to which he would also return in 1917).

In January 1917 Ravel wrote to Sergei Diaghilev, formally giving his commitment to a new work for the Ballets russes.[11] Although the specified project (based on a scenario by the Italian Futurist poet Francesco Cangiullo) was never even partially sketched, what Ravel did eventually present Diaghilev with was *La Valse* (1920) – his realization of *Wien*. When, in spring 1917, Ravel agreed to consider the libretto that Rouché offered to him, he may similarly have been thinking of the drafted chunks of his abandoned opera. Indeed, some of his *Cloche engloutie* material was to find its way into the completed *L'Enfant*.

Before he finally accepted the libretto, however, Ravel seems to have requested some adaptations, possibly to facilitate a recasting of this existing material (as Orenstein notes, 'it is indeed a brief distance from the forest and dancing elves of Hauptmann's play to the garden and dancing animals of Colette's libretto').[12] Colette's next letter to Rouché reveals that her 'fantasy-ballet' was changing shape. Here at last, perhaps, we may sense the spontaneous enthusiasm which the mention of Ravel's name inspired in Colette: 'You have put fairies into my head. It's much more fun than a play or a novel. I'd like both to talk with you and to offer you two or three ideas. Where? When?'[13] Interestingly, a subsequent letter of 20 June 1917 from Ravel to Lucien Garban, his editor at Durand, also hints that the composer may have had a hand in determining the work's final form: 'I have several things to ask of you: firstly, the address of Colette Willy, which you will be able to find easily. I charged Rouché with a task [*commission*][14] for her, and have not yet had any response.'[15]

In 1917, no composer had set Colette's writing to music, and none other of that era ever would, save Francis Poulenc (the song 'Le Portrait' of 1937). Ravel's early engagement with this libretto is telling, therefore: fastidious as he was in his choices of texts, if he gave his support in principle to composing

---

[11] Arbie Orenstein (ed.), *Maurice Ravel: lettres, écrits, entretiens* (Paris: Flammarion, 1989), 164.

[12] Arbie Orenstein, *Ravel: Man and Musician* (New York: Dover Publications, 1991), 210.

[13] LAS Colette (6): 'Vous m'avez mis féeries en tête. C'est beaucoup plus amusant qu'une pièce ou un roman. Je voudrais à la fois vous consulter et vous soumettre deux ou trois idées. Où? quand?' The letter carries the printed letterhead '69 Boulevard Suchet / Auteuil 06–27', an apartment that Colette purchased on a fleeting visit to Paris in November 1916. From late summer 1916 until early April 1917 she was otherwise in Italy;

this letter probably dates from shortly after her return to France.

[14] Whilst not an artistic 'commission' in the formal sense (i.e. 'commande'), the French term has the sense of a task to be undertaken, or a message concerning such a task.

[15] Arbie Orenstein (ed.), 'La Correspondance de Maurice Ravel à Lucien Roger Garban. Première partie (1901–1918)', *Cahiers Maurice Ravel*, 7 (2000), 19–68: 66. 'J'ai plusieurs choses à vous demander: d'abord, l'adresse de Colette Willy, que vous trouverez facilement. J'ai chargé Rouché d'une commission pour elle, et n'ai pas encore de réponse.'

an opera-ballet on a libretto still incomplete or in need of some reworking, he must have been fairly certain that Colette's words would inspire music from him. In the event, Ravel did not receive a complete draft of the libretto until spring 1918,[16] and then applied himself to it only intermittently during the next five years (which saw the completion of *La Valse* and the Sonata for Violin and Cello). Only the arrival of Raoul Gunsbourg, director of the Théâtre de Monte Carlo, compelled him at last to bring *L'Enfant* to completion:[17] Gunsbourg offered Ravel a contract for the premiere, to take place in Monte Carlo in April 1925.

There is little documentary evidence to show the progress of *L'Enfant* until Gunsbourg's arrival precipitated Ravel into a flurry of belated activity. One undated letter from Colette to Rouché seems to have been written in autumn 1917: 'What is happening with the *Divertissement pour ma fille*? And with Ravel? I would love to hear any news about it.'[18] Colette must have addressed the same question to Rouché again in early 1919 (probably in person), for Rouché duly passed a message to Ravel, who replied to him on 20 February 1919:

> You see how timely your letter was: for days I have wanted to write to Colette de Jouvenel – I've just lost my address book, it's a disaster – to ask her if she still wants to have me as a collaborator […]
>
> I hope to return [from Mégève] in April […] and the first thing I intend to work on is Colette's 'opéra dansé'.[19]

There followed the first known direct communication between the collaborators; firstly from Ravel to Colette on 27 February 1919:

> While you were expressing your regrets to Rouché about my silence, I was thinking, amid all the snow, of asking you if you still wanted such an unreliable collaborator […]
>
> In truth, I am already working on it [our opera]: I'm taking notes – without writing any – I'm even thinking of some modifications… Don't be afraid, they're not cuts – on the contrary. For example, couldn't the squirrel's tale be extended? Imagine everything that a squirrel could say of the forest, and how that could be interpreted in music!

---

[16]   Orenstein, *Ravel*, 78.
[17]   In summer 1923, according to Paul Druilhe, 'Les Grandes Créations de l'Opéra de Monte Carlo: *L'Enfant et les sortilèges* de Maurice Ravel', *Annales monégasques*, 9 (1985), 7–26: 9. In two interviews given just before the premiere, however, Ravel says 'last spring' (that is, 1924): see Orenstein (ed.), *Maurice Ravel: lettres*, 349, 589.
[18]   LAS Colette (4): 'Qu'advient-il du "Divertissement pour ma fille?" Et de Ravel? J'en entendrais parler avec un grand plaisir.' This letter goes on to say that Henri de Jouvenel has just been in hospital; Colette writes that this is better than having him

at the front and hopes that she will not see him sent back there. De Jouvenel was given a civilian posting in Paris in July 1917 but was sent back to the front in November, remaining there until July 1918.
[19]   Orenstein (ed.), *Maurice Ravel: lettres*, 171: 'Voyez comme tombe bien votre lettre: depuis quelques jours, je voulais écrire à Colette de Jouvenel – je viens de perdre mon livre d'adresse; c'est un désastre – pour lui demander si elle veut toujours de moi comme collaborateur […]
'J'espère rentrer en avril […] et la première chose à laquelle j'ai l'intention de travailler est "l'opéra dansé" de Colette.'

> Another thing: what would you think of the cup and the teapot, in old Wedgwood – black – singing a ragtime? I confess that the idea of having a ragtime sung by two Negroes at our National Academy of Music fills me with great joy [...] Perhaps you will object that you don't usually write Negro slang. I, who don't know a word of English, will do just like you – I'll work it out.[20]

And then Colette's response to Ravel of 5 March 1919:

> Why certainly a ragtime! Why of course Negroes in Wedgwood! What a terrific gust from the music hall to stir up the dust of the Opéra! Go to it! [...] Do you know that orchestras in cinema houses are playing your charming *Mother Goose* suite while they show American westerns? If I were a composer and Ravel, I believe that I would derive much pleasure from learning that.
>
> And the squirrel will say everything that you wish. Does the 'cat' duo, exclusively miaowed, please you? We'll get acrobats. Isn't the Arithmetic business a polka?
>
> I wish you good health, and shake your hand impatiently.[21]

There is much that we can draw from this exchange. Ravel's writing is notably relaxed and informal, as it was only with friends and colleagues (he was meticulous in such matters). He and Colette had, after all, known each other for twenty years, encountering each other regularly at plays, theatres, and concerts, in the salons and even music halls. If their acquaintance had never ripened into close friendship, it had certainly matured into respect. There is an ease of communication between them and a quickness of artistic understanding: Ravel would indeed have been delighted to learn that cinema Westerns were rolling to the strains of *Ma mère l'Oye*. The letters are written in a spirit of comradeship and collaborative enthusiasm, offering evidence of a thoroughgoing exchange of ideas. 'Believe, chère Madame, in the lively artistic sympathy of your devoted / Maurice Ravel', the composer concludes, an entreaty whose foundation is bolstered by a subsequent letter to Roland-Manuel (August 1920), where Ravel confides, 'I'm working at the opera in collaboration with Colette – the final title is not yet fixed [...] Some inside information – I can assure you that this work, in two parts, will be notable for its *mélange* of styles, which will be severely criticized; this leaves Colette indifferent and me not giving a d[amn].'[22]

These letters, together with later communications, also return continually to the word and concept of *collaboration*. 'To see if she still wants to have me as a collaborator', Ravel writes to Rouché; 'our opera' and 'an unreliable collaborator' to Colette; and to Roland-Manuel 'I'm working [...] in collaboration

[20] Arbie Orenstein (ed.), *A Ravel Reader: Correspondence, Articles, Interviews* (New York: Columbia University Press, 1990), 188.
[21] *Ibid.*, 189.
[22] Roland-Manuel, *A la gloire de... Ravel* (Paris: Editions de la Nouvelle revue critique, 1938), 146: 'Je travaille à l'opéra en collaboration avec Colette – le titre définitif n'en est toujours pas fixé [...] Cette œuvre, en deux parties, se distinguera par un mélange de styles qui sera sévèrement jugé, ce qui laissera Colette indifférente et dont je me f...' See also Orenstein (ed.), *Maurice Ravel: lettres*, 185 (the two sources reproduce the letter slightly differently).

with Colette'. Almost four years later, in an interview published in May 1924, Ravel said, 'Now I am working with Colette on a very original piece, a kind of lyric fantasy.'[23] Perhaps he was being diplomatic; certainly Colette's name would have done nothing to harm the advance publicity. Yet, precise as he was, Ravel might as easily have said, 'I am working on a kind of lyric fantasy *on a libretto by* Colette.'

The little direct correspondence that links composer and librettist during this period need not indicate that there was no ongoing communication between them. Ravel and Colette were both based in or near Paris, moved in similar artistic and literary circles, and had telephones in their houses (which Colette certainly used for exactly that sort of purpose, as seen above in her request to Rouché to telephone her). It would be surprising indeed if they had not encountered each other between 1916 and 1925. In Ravel's eyes, Colette clearly held an artistic stake in his project. Equally, Colette's persistence in asking for progress reports, from 1916 into the 1920s, demonstrates that she saw herself as actively involved in its development. She had not handed over the libretto and vanished from the scene; the progress and the destination of *L'Enfant* clearly mattered to her.

On 16 March 1925, five days before the long-awaited premiere, Ravel wrote once more to Colette:

> When are you getting here? Despite the disastrous state of the parts – it's my fault… tsk… tsk… – we have managed to sort out the score, thanks to an excellent orchestra and a really extraordinary conductor [Victor de Sabata] […]
>
> Come quickly: your suite awaits you at the Hôtel de Paris, where the food is carefully prepared and indigestible […]
>
> See you soon. All the friendship and gratitude of your
> Maurice Ravel.[24]

Beyond its comradely enthusiasm, perhaps the most important feature of this letter is its salutation: 'Chère amie', Ravel begins. Nothing could demonstrate more clearly that between 1919 and 1925 Ravel and Colette remained in some form of contact: no polite Frenchman – certainly not the punctilious and gallant Ravel – would write 'Chère Madame' in 1919 and then send all his 'friendship and gratitude' to his 'Chère amie' six years later had he remained sealed in 'hermetic silence' in the interim.[25]

23 Orenstein (ed.), *A Ravel Reader*, 433.

24 Orenstein (ed.), *Maurice Ravel: lettres*, 232–3: 'Quand arrivez-vous? Malgré l'état désastreux du matériel – c'est ma faute… tsk…tsk… –, on est arrivé à débrouiller la partition, grâce à un orchestre supérieur, et à un chef vraiment extraordinaire […]

'Venez vite: votre appartement vous attend à l'Hôtel de Paris où la nourriture est indigeste et soignée […]

'A bientôt. Toute l'amitié et la reconnaissance de votre / Maurice Ravel.'

25 Choosing the correct appellation was of great importance to Ravel. His pupil Manuel Rosenthal recalled him agonizing over the wording of a simple letter of introduction to a Belgian conductor: 'Firstly, how to begin? "Mon cher ami?" But no, he's not really a friend. That's not it… and not "Monsieur Defauw" either, nor "Cher Monsieur".'

We may trace something more of the collaborative process in the changes of titles and form through which *L'Enfant* passed. The project was first referred to as a *ballet* (*pour ma fille*) in Colette's early correspondence and a *ballet-opéra* (in Rouché's initial letter to Dukas), but from the middle of 1917 Colette calls the work not *Ballet*, but *Divertissement pour ma fille*. This change occurs at exactly the time that Ravel became interested in the project, a telling indication of the clarifying focus which came with his involvement. A *divertissement* would necessarily make some sort of homage to opera-ballet of the eighteenth century, a period that was a lifelong source of inspiration to Ravel and would have been much on his mind in the second half of 1917, as he resumed work on *Le Tombeau de Couperin* (the completed manuscript of which is dated July 1914 and June–November 1917). The concept of a *divertissement* also carried clear structural implications, establishing the narrative around a series of dramatically and musically varied episodes. In addition, the changing title is also suggestive of a shifting balance between dance and song, perhaps tilting towards the latter in the shadow of *La Cloche engloutie*.

The idea of a *divertissement* may thus have been established early in Ravel's involvement, but the official title was to remain fluid for some time. Ravel's 1919 letter to Rouché calls the work an *opéra-dansé*; his subsequent letter to Colette refers simply to *notre opéra*. '[T]he final title is not yet fixed', Ravel wrote to Roland-Manuel in August 1920; two other letters written that summer refer to 'X… la machine pour l'Opéra' and 'la machine lyrique sans nom'.[26] Ravel, at least, had abandoned *Divertissement pour ma fille* by this stage,[27] although the title was still to provide Colette with a pun. In a later note, possibly sent in summer 1923, she writes to Ravel, 'Oh! cher ami, when, oh when, the *Divertissement pour ma… petite-fille*? Is it true, that it is going to be finished? With hope and friendship, Colette de Jouvenel.'[28] This was not, as

('D'abord, comment commencer? "Mon cher ami?" Mais non, il n'est pas vraiment un ami. Ce n'est pas, non plus, "Monsieur Defauw", ni "Cher Monsieur".') Marcel Marnat (ed.), *Ravel: souvenirs de Manuel Rosenthal* (Paris: Hazan, 1995), 121.

[26] Letters of 14 June and 24 August 1920, in Arbie Orenstein (ed.), 'La Correspondance de Maurice Ravel à Lucien Roger Garban. Deuxième partie (1919–1934)', *Cahiers Maurice Ravel*, 8 (2004), 9–89: 29, 34.

[27] In Colette, *En pays connu* (Paris: Ferenczi, 1950), 25, Ravel is quoted as pointing out, 'But I have no daughter' – an exchange already revealing more communication than 'Un salon en 1900' admits.

[28] Arbie Orenstein, '*L'Enfant et les sortilèges*: correspondance inédite de Ravel

et Colette', *Revue de musicologie* 52/2 (1966), 215–20: 216. 'Oh! cher ami, quand, quand, le "Divertissement pour ma… petite fille"? C'est vrai, qu'il va être fini? Avec espoir et amitié, Colette de Jouvenel'. Orenstein dates the note, written from Colette's house in Brittany, to January 1919. There is no record of Colette being in Brittany at this time, however, and the appellation 'cher ami' seems to suggest a later dating (since it would otherwise read oddly immediately before the more formal 'Cher Monsieur' and 'Chère Madame' of the February 1919 letters). The suggested alternative of summer 1923 is drawn from another rather frustrated message sent by Colette to Rouché (LAS Colette (5)), again from Brittany. Also undated, it was probably written around the same time: 'Alas, there is often assumed, an alternative title but a good-natured prod (the ellipsis gives it away): Colette's little daughter ('petite fille'), born in 1913, is growing up rapidly and if Ravel does not hurry up, Colette suggests, she will find herself with a granddaughter ('petite-fille') as well.

The final title seems not to have been decided upon until as late as Gunsbourg's arrival; no record survives of the exchanges that would necessarily have preceded its adoption. Not until autumn 1924 does *L'Enfant et les sortilèges* appear as such in Ravel's correspondence. Only in 1924, too, does Ravel refer to it as 'ma fantaisie lyrique'.[29] One final echo of the original title remained, for another undated letter from Colette to Ravel, probably sent shortly before the premiere, suggests that Ravel considered dedicating the work to the younger Colette: 'Cher ami, her first name is Colette, and, in full, Colette de Jouvenel. There she is, dedicatee, entering into glory through your labours! She will thank you… '[30] In the event, however, the work was published without a dedication.

The multiplicity of genre descriptions that followed *L'Enfant* from conception to premiere – ballet, opera, opera-ballet, ballet-opera, *opéra-dansé*, divertissement – reflects the intrinsic suppleness of its conception. The final appellation *fantaisie lyrique* overrides all distinctions and emphases (operaballet, ballet-opera) and reaches beyond formal description to musical, visual and dramatic realization.

Musical and poetic interplay

The one surviving draft page for the libretto of *L'Enfant* is the original version of the Cup and Teapot scene (later given by Colette to Hélène Jourdan-Morhange). In it the Cup, as the Teapot explains, can exclaim only

no sign of the *Divertissement pour ma fille* in the programme of *Ballets français*! My dear director and friend, I am most disheartened, I assure you!' ('Hélas, on n'annonce pas le "Divertissement pour ma fille" dans la série des *Ballets français*!… Mon cher directeur et ami, je suis bien découragée. Je vous assure!'). A series of *Ballets français* was announced at the Opéra in July 1923, following a first series announced in July 1922. If we accept Druilhe's assertion that Gunsbourg offered Ravel a contract for the Monte Carlo premiere in summer 1923, Colette's note to Ravel could suggest that she had had word of this – perhaps in a return letter from Rouché. The contractual negotiations that secured the Monte Carlo premiere are untraced.

29 Orenstein (ed.), *Maurice Ravel: lettres*, 230.

30 Orenstein, '*L'Enfant et les sortilèges*: correspondance inédite', 219: 'Elle s'appelle Colette, de son prénom, et Colette de Jouvenel en toutes lettres. La voilà, dédicataire, qui entre dans la gloire, par vos soins! Elle vous remerciera…' Orenstein interprets this letter to mean that Ravel was considering dedicating the work to Colette herself. Colette, however, never referred to herself in the third person and would probably have received any dedication under her professional name (especially since her marriage to Henri de Jouvenel broke down in 1924); it is much more likely that the dedication was intended for her daughter.

'Fouchtra!', 'because she is made of Limoges porcelain. It means "Shame!"'[31] Nor is this Teapot the African-American boxer-figure that would eventually emerge: 'vous avez khasié [cassée] la english théière de votre gram'ma!' he exclaims, his French scattered not with pugilistic 'franglais' but with phrases like 'cup of tea'. The recasting of this scene probably owed much to Ravel's 1919 suggestion of a ragtime Teapot in 'Wedgwood noir'. It seems to have taken Colette some time to come up with the definitive version, however: 'Always in the midst of work… I am at the "Wedgwood tea-pot and Chinese cup" on lines that Colette has just sent me', wrote Ravel to Ida Godebska on 13 October 1924.[32] Several more of the composer's suggestions may have found their way into the final text: Manuel Rosenthal cites the touches of soldiers' slang in the Cup's lines, for example, 'Kek t'as [qu'est ce que tu as] foutu d'mon kaoua?' ('What the hell have you done with my kava?'; see Fig. 37⁻¹), as typical of Ravel, who delighted in expressive argot.[33] If the Cup's and Teapot's Sitwellian nonsense is vintage Colette, the sentiments hidden within are entirely Ravelian: 'since we don't understand, it will always sound Chinese!'[34] (For more on the music at Fig. 28ff., see Chapter 6, under 'Ragtime rhythm and form'.)

Passages such as this have given rise to conjecture about the actual authorship of particular words, phrases, even scenes. Yet if the composer did rework parts of the libretto (we can now only guess), it was with an extraordinary alertness to established continuities of poetic and linguistic design, for there are no 'seams', no sense of piecemeal assemblage. A remarkable textual coherence runs beneath the contrasting episodes: from the first scene to the last, the same poetic gestures are used to generate the same distinctive affects. Much of this underlying consistency derives from subtle onomatopoeia: as Marie-Pierre Lassus observes, the characters of the individual 'enchantments' ('sortilèges') are all shaped by the sounds of their words as much as by their meanings.[35] The words of the inanimate creatures are distinguished by incisive vowels and cutting consonants (Lassus aptly

[31]   Draft page reproduced in Hélène Jourdan-Morhange, *Ravel et nous: l'homme, l'ami, le musicien* (Geneva: Editions du milieu du monde, 1945), plate IX: 'parce qu'elle est en porcelaine française de Limoges. Elle ne savait dire que Fouchtra! Ça voulait dire: "Shame!"' *Fouchtra* is an Auvergnat exclamation equivalent to the French colloquial *fichtre* (both derived from the coarse *foutre*).

[32]   Orenstein, 'L'Enfant et les sortilèges: correspondance inédite', 218: 'Toujours en plein boulot… J'en suis au "Wedgwood tea-pot and Chinese cup" sur mesures que Colette vient de m'envoyer.' Clearly, there had been another exchange of (now untraced) correspondence between Ravel and Colette.

[33]   Marnat (ed.), *Ravel: souvenirs*, 135.

[34]   'Puis'kongkongpranpa, Çaohrâ […] toujours l'air chinoâ' – i.e. 'Puisqu'on [ne] comprend pas, ça aura […] toujours l'air chinois' (Figs. 31–3).

[35]   Marie-Pierre Lassus, 'Ravel l'enchanteur: structure poétique et structure musicale dans *L'Enfant et les sortilèges*', *Analyse musicale*, 26 (1992), 40–7: 43–4; see also Emily Kilpatrick, '"Jangling in Symmetrical Sounds": Maurice Ravel as Storyteller and Poet', *Journal of Music Research Online*, 1 (April 2009), 1–19: 10–12; http://journal.mca.org.au (accessed 20 September 2009).

Example 2.1   Ravel, *L'Enfant et les sortilèges* (Fig. 40^{+1}): timbral emphasis in the Fire's aria

terms this affect 'la parole agressive'), while the animals and the Princess make more use of soft consonants and lighter vowels ('la parole tendre'). Typical of this are the sharp nasal vowels and menacingly rolled *r*s of the Fire ('Je réchauffe les bons, / mais je brûle les méchants. / Petit barbare, barbare imprudent, / tu as insulté à tous les Dieux bienveillants [...] Gare! Gare! Ah! Gare à toi!' [Figs. 40–6]), and the soft, drawn-out syllables of the Dragonfly ('Où-est tu? / Je te cherche... / Le filet... / Il t'a prise... / O toi, chère, / Longue et frèle' [Figs. 107–8]).

When Balliman observed that the text and music of *L'Enfant* were so intertwined that 'it is impossible to separate the collaborators', he was per-haps responding to how completely these linguistic affects are embedded in the score: Examples 2.1 and 2.2 demonstrate the rhythmic and timbral col-ourations with which Ravel emphasized the Fire's and Dragonfly's distinctive word-sounds. In Example 2.1, 'hard' vowels fall on the downbeats, with the attack of consonants reinforced by the staccato string accompaniment and the woodwind doublings. By contrast, in Example 2.2 the sustained string chords draw out 'soft' vowel sounds; gentle sibilants are emphasized by rhyth-mic placement, articulation, and orchestral colouring.

Changes of affect within scenes are conveyed with similar clarity. The first words of Maman to the Child stress the hard [e] and [a] vowels ('Bébé a été sage? Il a fini sa page?' [Fig. 3]), and are accompanied by incisive woodwind

Example 2.2 Ravel, *L'Enfant et les sortilèges* (Fig. 107): timbral emphasis in the Dragonfly's aria

chords. When she exhorts the Child to repentance ('Regrettes-tu ta paresse?' [Fig. 4]), the softer schwas and drawn-out double consonants are emphasized by the work's first string chords; see Example 2.3.

In all Ravel's vocal music, the closest approach to this sort of onomatopoeic characterization occurs in the choral settings of his own poetry, *Trois chansons pour chœur mixte sans accompagnement* (1914–15). In the first song, 'Nicolette', the sounds of the words define the characters of big bad wolf, beautiful page, and smelly, hunchbacked lord: the first rhymes on the deep nasal [ã] vowel ('Rencontra vieux loup grog*nant*' [Fig. 1]), the second on the light [i] ('Rencontra page jo*li*' [Fig. 2]), and the last on the sharp [y] ('Recontra seigneur che*nu*' [Fig. 3]). In the *Trois chansons*, as in *L'Enfant*, word-sounds are repeated and combined to create onomatopoeic soundscapes. The menacing percussive effect of the repeated *s* in the Animals' overlapping 'Unissons-nous!' in *L'Enfant* (Figs. 138–9) is the same as in 'Ronde', the last of the *Trois chansons*: 'Des satyresses, des ogresses, / Et des babaïagas, / Des centauresses et des diablesses, / Goules sortant du sabbat' (Fig. 2^{+8}). More threatening hisses emerge from the Numbers' chant of 'cinq et sept, cinq et sept' in the Arithmetic scene of *L'Enfant* (see Fig. 91), an allusion highlighted by the scene's culminating indication: 'Ronde folle' (Fig. 87). An even closer affinity links the Numbers to 'Nicolette': Ravel's clog-wearing heroine flees the wolf to an amusingly onomatopoeic 'ta-ka-ta-ka-ta-ka-ta-ka' in the altos and tenors (Fig. 1^{+8}); the vowel and consonant sounds are precisely those of the Numbers' repeated 'Quatre et quat'?' (around Fig. 88). In both works we sense the same almost tactile enjoyment of the sounds and rhythms of the language: 'Millimètre, Centimètre, Décimètre, Décamètre, Hectomètre, Kilomètre, Myriamètre, / Faut t'y mettre, / Quelle fêtre! / Des millions, Des billions, Des trillions, / Et des frac-cillions!' chants Mr Arithmetic (Figs. 83–4), echoing the dancing assonances of the 'Hamadryades, dryades, naïades, ménades, thyades, folettes, lémures' of the earlier 'Ronde' (Fig. 2^{+18}). Or consider the satisfyingly onomatopoeic gurgle Ravel found in one of Mr Arithmetic's puzzles: 'Deux robinets coulent (*coulent, coulent, coulent*) dans un réservoir!' (Fig. 84; the repetition – in the reprise [Fig. 86] – is that of the composer).

The authorship of the Arithmetic scene is not in question here: as Gregory Harwood has observed, its origins may lie in the bewildering mathematics class depicted in Colette's *Claudine à l'école*.[36] Rather, the commonalities between songs and *fantaisie lyrique* suggest that in Colette's text Ravel recognized vocal assonances that he had already used to expressive musical effect. 'The vocal line must dominate,' he said of *L'Enfant* in 'An Autobiographical

---

[36] Gregory Harwood, 'Musical and Literary Satire in Ravel's *L'Enfant et les sortilèges*', *Opera Journal*, 29/1 (1996), 2–16: 10.

Example 2.3 Ravel, *L'Enfant et les sortilèges* (Fig. 3⁺²): timbral emphasis of contrasting linguistic affects in the Mother's scene

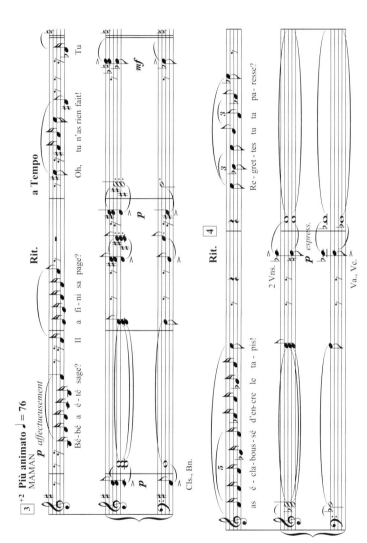

Sketch' of 1928, perhaps suggesting the extent to which his score was shaped by the sounds and rhythms of the libretto.[37]

This shared affinity for the interplay of music and language should not surprise us. Ravel was a friend of poets and writers, and recognized by those friends as a poet and writer of some distinction himself (Tristan Klingsor praised the *Trois chansons* highly).[38] André Mirambel wrote that Ravel's melodic lines often have the sense of written or spoken phrases: 'one could say that [he] elevated musical language to the heights of musical prose'.[39] Colette in turn was a capable pianist and worked for some years as a professional music critic;[40] music and musicians wend their way through all her published writings (particularly the autobiographical works). This musical engagement undoubtedly helped to shape a writing style notable for something akin to a composer's feel for resonance, metre, and cadence. The libretto she delivered was thus defined in large part by vocal affect and aural effect. Its evocative play of rhythm and assonance and its overall textual coherence, coupled with the striking affinities with Ravel's own poetry, suggest that composer and librettist shared a truly interdisciplinary sense of what an operatic libretto might be, were words to be shaped by musical sense and music by textual sonorities.

Structural interplay

So carefully crafted are the words of this libretto that they impact upon the architectural span and formal design of *L'Enfant*. The word 'sage', for example, imparts a large-scale reciprocity to the first and last scenes: the first words of Maman are 'Bébé a été sage?' and in the closing bars the Animals sing – and Ravel has them repeat in overlapping chorus – 'Il est bon, l'Enfant, il est sage, bien sage' (Figs. 150–4). The reiteration alerts us to the word's double meaning: when applied to children *sage* means 'well-behaved' – Maman uses it thus – but in its broader sense the word means 'wise'. We have come full circle, closing with the words of the opening; yet we are not quite back where

[37]   Roland-Manuel, 'Une esquisse autobiographique de Maurice Ravel' [1928], *La Revue musicale*, 19 (December 1938 [special issue]), 17–23: 23. 'C'est le chant qui domine ici.'
[38]   Tristan Klingsor, 'Maurice Ravel et le vers libre', *La Revue musicale*, 19 (December 1938 [special issue]), 121–3: 122–3.
[39]   André Mirambel, 'L'Inspiration grecque dans l'œuvre de Ravel', *La Revue musicale*, 19 (December 1938 [special issue]), 112–18: 116: 'on peut dire que Ravel a élevé la langue musicale à la hauteur de la prose musicale'.

[40]   See Margaret Crosland, 'Colette and Ravel: The Enchantress and the Illusionist', in Erica Mendelson Eisinger and Mari Ward McCarty (eds.), *Colette: The Woman, The Writer* (University Park, PA: Pennsylvania State University Press, 1981), 116–19; and Richard Langham Smith, 'Colette as Critic', *Music and Musicians*, 25 (1977), 26–8, and 'Ravel's Operatic Spectacles: *L'Heure* and *L'Enfant*', in Deborah Mawer (ed.), *The Cambridge Companion to Ravel* (Cambridge University Press, 2000), 188–210: 202.

we started, for the very sense of the words has grown – just like the Child himself. The allusion is heightened when the meandering oboe figurations of the opening scene are set in motion once more, now doubled by two violins (Fig. 153). Where once they were set against each other (as in Example 2.3), incisive and softer timbres are at last harmoniously intertwined.

Equally significant structural implications emerge from the words 'libre' and 'méchant'. Emphasized by the Child in the climactic phrases that frame his destructive rampage (Fig. 15), the words return at the climax of the work itself: 'libre' is heard three times in the Squirrel's aria (Fig. 132ff.), and in the Animals' uprising the incisive triplets of the repeated 'C'est le méchant' (Fig. 137^{-2}) propel the word to the forefront of the texture.[41] Although the Child initially declares himself free, as events unfold he comes to realize that he is spiritually as well as physically constrained by the consequences of his naughtiness: he cannot escape the Animals' wrath, though he can, at last, make reparation. In this slowly dawning recognition of his confinement we see, paradoxically, the Child's emotional horizons expanding: the callous little being of the opening scene learns how to feel fear, tenderness, sorrow, and remorse. Beyond the words 'libre' and 'méchant', the *ideas* of freedom and naughtiness (and its consequence, imprisonment) thus underpin the progression of the narrative.

This conceptual interplay is evoked with equal clarity in the gradual expansion of musical architecture across *L'Enfant*. The early scenes are compact and tightly focused, all based on ternary forms (except for the Child's opening monologue, which is even more self-contained, repeating its eleven-bar oboe figuration three times; on the second iteration the double-bass countermelody enters [Fig. 1]; on the third the Child begins to sing [Fig. 2]). The emotionally crucial episode of the Princess signals the slow unfolding of these tripartite structures, opening into – but still contained within – a meticulously balanced arch form (Figs. 62–73). After her disappearance, the questioning dominant pitches, B♭ and D, of the Child's little aria (Figs. 73–5) draw us away from the reflexive patterns of the early scenes: the Arithmetic Scene (Figs. 75–95) and Cats' Duet (Figs. 95–100) that follow are open-ended, one repeating and the other developing material *ad infinitum*.

With the move from interior scenes to the open Garden, we find the Child seeing himself no longer as a separate entity but as part of a wider world: 'Ah! what joy to find you again, Garden!' ('Ah! quelle joie de te retrouver, Jardin!'), he sings, arms outstretched in welcome (Fig. 102^{+3}). In response, the Animals do not appear and disappear in turn (as did the inanimate creatures) but

---

[41] Steven Huebner has also noted this: see 'Ravel's Child: Magic and Moral Development', in Susan Boynton and Roe-Min Kok (eds.), *Musical Childhoods* *and the Cultures of Youth* (Middletown, CT: Wesleyan University Press, 2006), 69–88: 86.

mingle on stage. Similarly interwoven are two alternating and overlapping groups of musical material, the open-fifth string chords and 'natural' sounds that depict the nocturnal Garden, and the waltz rhythms and melodic motives shared by the Dragonfly, Bat, Frogs, and Squirrel (Fig. 105ff.). These increasingly expansive and integrated structures derive directly from the dramatic shape of the libretto: as the Child's understanding deepens, so the musical forms open outwards.

An interesting coda to this may be observed in the set designs created by Alphonse Visconti for the 1925 premiere of *L'Enfant*; see Plates 2.1 and 2.2.[42] The interior opening set (Plate 2.1) is cluttered and constricting, the diagonal lines of the wood panelling heightening the sense of enclosure. Yet glimpses of tree and garden are visible through the windows, just as in the exterior second set (Plate 2.2) a spacious and enticing vista can be seen beyond the Garden itself. These images of a broader world serve to focus the scene and draw in the viewer. More subtly, they symbolize the Child's own expanding horizons. Almost certainly conceived without input from the work's musico-literary creators, the sets of the premiere are a perceptive visual response to the interplays of enclosure and liberation that underpin the libretto and score.

'The enchantress and the illusionist'

When Roland-Manuel coined the memorable phrase 'L'enchanteresse et l'illusioniste',[43] he was recognizing qualities and principles that, although differently inflected, were common to both the librettist and the composer of *L'Enfant*. Both Ravel and Colette were storytellers: besides creating compelling musical narratives, Ravel was renowned amongst the children of his friends as a teller of stories.[44] Both were keen observers, particularly of the animal world, which they regarded with amusement, wonder, and tender affection.[45] Like Ravel, Colette could make her point with exquisite elegance combined with simplicity and straightforwardness; like his, her work blends insight and tenderness with a satirical eye and a sparkling wit.

The presence of these shared traits has been observed by numerous commentators: Richard Langham Smith writes that 'the work may be regarded as a meeting of like minds', Judith Thurman that 'Ravel and Colette [...] shared a private wavelength'.[46] Yet in such reflections there is usually a lurking

---

[42] I am grateful to Charlotte Lubert (Société des bains de mer, Monte Carlo) for her generous assistance in obtaining these reproductions.

[43] Roland-Manuel, *A la gloire… de Ravel*, 158–9.

[44] See, for example, the recollections of Mimi Godebska Blacque-Belair, 'Quelques souvenirs intimes de Ravel', *La Revue musicale*, 19 (December 1938 [special issue]), 189–91.

[45] See, for example, Jourdan-Morhange, *Ravel et nous*, 31–3.

[46] Langham Smith, 'Ravel's Operatic Spectacles', 204; Judith Thurman, *Secrets of the Flesh: A Life of Colette* (New York: Knopf, 1999), 340.

Plate 2.1 Alphonse Visconti's set design for *L'Enfant et les sortilèges*: interior scenes (Monte Carlo premiere, 1925). Reproduced by kind permission of the Archives Monte-Carlo SBM

Plate 2.2 Alphonse Visconti's set design for *L'Enfant et les sortilèges*: garden scene (Monte Carlo premiere, 1925). Reproduced by kind permission of the Archives Monte-Carlo SBM

'but…': how do we reconcile these affinities with such dissimilar public personas, and in particular with the distant and mysterious Ravel whom Colette portrayed in 'Un salon en 1900'? One answer lies in the words of Hélène Jourdan-Morhange, an intimate friend of both artists:

> this seeming disparity [of personality] has never seemed so complete to me as has often been asserted: did they not share the same artisan's care for perfecting their work? And also, in the depths of their hearts, the same small vein that welled from the same source: reticence of soul? […] Ravel, candid as he was, left it easily discernible; Colette, woman amongst women, overdoes her colourful spontaneity the better to conceal her truth.[47]

Jourdan-Morhange identifies two crucial points: the notion of artisanship – to which we will return – and that of a shared personal 'reticence', or *pudeur*. The *pudique* Ravel insistently maintained the barriers between his personal life and his 'boulot' (work), a distinction that the often autobiographical Colette may seem to have blurred. Yet by publicly defining and declaring a personal narrative, autobiography itself can become a protective shield: as Jourdan-Morhange observes, behind Colette's mask of seeming self-revelation was a close-guarded private being. 'Can I say I really knew him, my illustrious collaborator, the composer of *L'Enfant et les sortilèges*?', 'Un salon en 1900' begins.[48] In the essay's mixture of candour and evasion, we see Colette drawing these boundaries between public and private space. Implicit in her reticence is a recognition of and respect for her colleague's *pudeur*, a reluctance to intrude – even after his death – upon the privacy of so intensely private a man.

In retreating from the personal in 'Un salon en 1900', however, Colette tacitly passed the task of writing more intimately about her collaborator to one better fitted for it, both from closer acquaintance and from being untrammelled by notoriety. Without Colette, Jourdan-Morhange's memoir *Ravel et nous* (1945) would probably not have been written. It was Colette 'who initiated her [Jourdan-Morhange] into the craft [métier] of the writer', drawing her out of the depression that had overtaken her when arthritis arrested her performing career,[49] Colette who supported and encouraged her friend through the writing of *Ravel et nous*, providing letters and the page of manuscript draft of *L'Enfant*, Colette who almost certainly facilitated the

---

[47] Jourdan-Morhange, *Ravel et nous*, 127–8: 'cette dissemblance ne m'apparaît plus aussi totale qu'on veut bien l'affirmer: n'ont-ils pas tous deux ce même scrupule d'artisan à parfaire leur ouvrage? Et aussi tout au fond de leur cœur, la même petite veine sourdant d'une même source: la pudeur d'âme? […] Ravel, candide, la laissait deviner; Colette, femme entre les femmes, outre sa spontanéité colorée pour mieux cacher *sa* vérité.'

[48] Colette, 'Un salon en 1900', 164: 'Puis-je dire que je l'ai vraiment connu, mon collaborateur illustre, l'auteur de *L'Enfant et les sortilèges*?'

[49] Bernard Villaret, 'Préface' to Colette, *Lettres à Moune et au Toutounet, 1929–1954*, ed. Bernard Villaret (Paris: Des femmes, 1985), 8: 'qui l'initia au métier d'écrivain'.

contract with Editions du milieu du monde,[50] and Colette who wrote the volume's graceful preface. And from the beginning to the end of their long published correspondence (spanning the years 1929–54), Colette addresses Jourdan-Morhange as 'Moune' – a nickname given to her by Ravel. In *Ravel et nous*, then, we may sense a second tribute, less explicit but perhaps more telling, from one *âme pudique* to another.

Perhaps most important, Ravel's direct and Colette's implicit separation of self and *métier* compels us to consider their collaboration in terms of what, for them, always came first: the practices and principles of their respective professions. Composer and librettist were linked by a shared sense of craft and a profoundly practical and unpretentious approach to their respective artistic callings. Both saw themselves less as 'artists' – with the associated implications of otherworldliness and 'temperament' – than as artisans (a word that crops up frequently in reflections on Ravel).[51] Their artistic – or artisanal – integrity led them to work in collaboration as the professionals they were, subsuming differences of personality in the interests of the work in hand. (For a broader discussion of relations between the artist and the artisan, perfection and *métier*, see Chapter 1.)

'[O]ne gives birth away from the flame, and with calculation,'[52] wrote Colette, echoing Ravel's assertion that he composed with the intellectual detachment that Edgar Allan Poe expounded in 'The Philosophy of Composition'.[53] Another of Ravel's rare reflections on the act of composition is equally revealing: 'A note at random, then a second one and, sometimes, a third. I then see what results I get by contrasting, combining and separating them.'[54] How many of Colette's essays and articles begin in precisely similar fashion, with an idea, image or even a word, that is repeated, worked over and gradually unfolded?

Ravel and Colette had a shared need 'to be precise, to be ready, to be in order' (as Colette put it),[55] in their physical environments – both lived and

---

[50] Editions du milieu du monde (Geneva) also published Colette's *Paris de ma fenêtre* (1944) and *L'Etoile vesper* (1947). *Ravel et nous* may have been drafted as early as 1941 (its publication perhaps delayed because of the Occupation); in a letter to Jourdan-Morhange (16 August 1941) Colette quotes a journalist colleague saying that 'Morhange has already written the finest book that could be written on him [Ravel]' ('Morhange a écrit sur Ravel le plus beau livre qu'on puisse écrire sur lui'): Colette, *Lettres à Moune*, 214. Four years later (2 August 1945), Colette wrote to Jourdan-Morhange again: 'I'm delighted that Rosset [of Editions du milieu du monde] is getting a move on with your book!' ('Je

suis ravie que Rosset se grouille pour ton livre': *ibid.*, 254.

[51] In addition to Jourdan-Morhange's reflection above, see Appendix to Chapter 1: excerpts from Roland-Manuel (*15*) and Léon-Paul Fargue (*19*).

[52] Colette, *L'Etoile vesper*, *Œuvres*, vol. 4, 853: 'on enfante à l'écarte de la flamme, et dans la mesure'.

[53] Orenstein (ed.), *A Ravel Reader*, 394, 433, 454.

[54] Quoted in Roger Nichols (ed.), *Ravel Remembered* (London: Faber and Faber, 1987), 55.

[55] Colette, *L'Etoile vesper*, 855: 'Être exacte, être prête, être en règle'.

worked in small spaces, in which the diverse tastes and accumulations of a lifetime were meticulously arranged – and in their creative life. Both composer and librettist, too, viewed their work against the sweeping background of centuries of cultural inheritance. Literary reminiscences and homages, direct and implicit, fill Colette's *œuvre*, just as Ravel's music and published writings are underlain with tributes to his musical and literary heroes. In both, a reverence for artistic heritage was coupled with an unselfconscious awareness of the quality of their own work (which both lived to see publicly recognized). Both made it clear that their *métier* demanded everything that they had to give, entailing a lifelong process of learning and striving. As Roland-Manuel recalled:

> He [Ravel] simply could not understand that an artist might tap other resources than those of his *métier*. One day I told him I was convinced I had to *start* by knowing my *métier* and he enquired with heavy irony what I intended to do the rest of the time, adding that one had to start by learning the *métier* of others and that a lifetime was not enough to perfect one's own.[56]

'French is quite a difficult language. After forty-five years of writing one just begins to appreciate this,' Colette wrote in *Journal à rebours*;[57] Ravel made the same point even more directly in his famous articulation of an aim he knew was impossible to achieve: 'My objective, therefore, is technical perfection […].'[58] This long, shared quest for precision and perfection is reflected in a mutual care for every element of their work, even those that an audience will never perceive directly. The poetic epigraphs with which Ravel headed *Jeux d'eau*, *Valses nobles et sentimentales*, and *Ma mère l'Oye*, for example, are similar in purpose to Colette's detailed and poetic stage directions in *L'Enfant*. Both form a kind of private dialogue between creator and performer and, if the words themselves are not communicated to the audience, their spirit should inform the performance.

'Un salon en 1900' is itself a kind of epigraph, offering an 'impression' of Colette's collaboration with Ravel that almost certainly captures more of its spirit than its substance. In her essay Colette elided and reduced, as a writer will, drawing from disjointed and miscellaneous happenings a coherent and graceful account. The narrative arches from the salon to the theatre, beginning with one set of curious characters – the habitués of Marguerite de Saint-Marceaux's Friday soirées – and effectively ending with the equally odd *sortilèges* dancing on another stage (her depiction of Ravel's declining years constitutes a poignant coda). Within this broad reciprocity are

---

[56] Roland-Manuel, quoted in Nichols (ed.), *Ravel Remembered*, 141–4: 143.

[57] Colette, 'La Chaufferette', *Journal à rebours*, 176: 'C'est une langue bien difficile que le français. A peine écrit-on depuis quarante-cinq ans qu'on commence à s'en apercevoir.'

[58] Orenstein (ed.), *A Ravel Reader*, 38. For the context of this remark, see Appendix to Chapter 1: excerpt (*1*).

held equivalent smaller moments of finely mirrored poetic logic: 'cela peut être long [...] Ça fut long' – echoes, perhaps, of the large- and small-scale arches, textual and musical, of *L'Enfant* itself; and are not colourfully reflexive phrases such as 'la lente frénésie'[59] themselves typically Ravelian?

In 'Un salon en 1900', Colette reshaped and disguised events, characters, and emotions in the service of narrative continuity and dramatic and poetic form ('I can allow myself this small indulgence: to be veracious from time to time,'[60] she wrote in the later and franker *L'Etoile vesper*, drawing attention retrospectively to the more opaque nature of her earlier memoirs). So the libretto was first offered not to Ravel but to Dukas; so the composer did not disappear entirely for eight or nine years; so the replacement of 'mouaô' with 'mouain' (or whatever) may signify that Ravel made several changes to the text. Ravel, of all composers, would have understood this skilful juggling of expression and form, since he was equally expert at manipulating the two. Writing to Roland-Manuel of his setting of Stéphane Mallarmé's 'Placet futile' (October 1913), he stressed the importance of 'the profound and exquisite tenderness which suffuses all of this' – having first noted that 'It was necessary to maintain the elegant deportment of the poem.'[61]

The existing documentation shows that the composer and the librettist of *L'Enfant* saw themselves as collaborators and considered their work a shared achievement. Yet they worked essentially in isolation, respect for professional and artistic integrity and shared *pudeur* keeping them at a distance. 'Ravel did not grant me any special privileges, neither explaining anything nor granting me an early hearing,' Colette confided in ruefully respectful acknowledgement of the demands of her collaborator's *métier*. (Late in life, she commented that most of her own work was done between ten at night and three in the morning – 'the indulgence of a writer relieved of telephone calls, friendly visits, or anyone's concern').[62] It was typical of Ravel to ensure that Colette would hear the work for the first time only on the stage of the Théâtre de Monte Carlo: he loved to offer gifts and surprise his friends, and he knew better than to spoil by premature revelation this of all gifts, all surprises. 'I had never imagined that this orchestral wave, spangled with nightingales and fireflies, could lift my modest work to such heights,' Colette wrote.[63]

Ravel and Colette were thus bound together by a shared sense of *métier*, a similar approach to the processes of creation, and a sympathetic conception

---

[59] Colette, 'Un salon en 1900', 166 (see n5).
[60] Colette, *L'Etoile vesper*, 868–9: 'Je peux bien me permettre cette petite douceur: être véridique de temps en temps.'
[61] Orenstein (ed.), *Maurice Ravel: lettres*, 133: 'Il fallait [...] la tenue élégante de ce poème. Il fallait, surtout, la profonde, l'adorable tendresse qui baigne tout cela.'

[62] Colette, *L'Etoile vesper*, 785–6: 'ébats d'écrivain dégagé du coup de téléphone, de la visite amicale et de la sollicitude quelle qu'elle soit'.
[63] Colette, 'Un salon en 1900', 167: 'Je n'avais pas prévu qu'une vague orchestrale, constellée de rossignols et de lucioles, soulèverait si haut mon œuvre modeste.'

of structural and expressive design, focused particularly in an enjoyment of the sounds and rhythms of the French language. 'Was not Ravel the musician whose heart could best understand Colette's heart?' wondered Carol-Bérard, reviewing the Opéra production of *L'Enfant* in 1939, 'Was it not he who could follow her most gracefully into the kingdom of dreams?'[64]

The success of this collaboration needs no defending in terms of its result: few other theatrical ventures have fused so successfully music and text, dance and drama, musical-poetic structure and visual design. Beyond this, however, *L'Enfant* is the result of a collaborative process whose richness may easily be underestimated. Ravel often worked closely with musicians in the preparation of his works for performance, and with designers and directors in their staging. None of his other scores, however (with the possible exception of *Daphnis et Chloé*), owes its very existence and form to creative interaction in the way that this one does. There is in Ravel's letters to Colette an eagerness that is rare in his correspondence: he enjoyed and was inspired by his engagement with an artist whose precepts and practices were so close to his own. In the final assessment, it is perhaps in that eagerness that true collaboration lies.

---

[64] Carol-Bérard, '*L'Enfant et les sortilèges*' [review], *L'Epoque* (19 May 1939): 'Ravel n'était-il pas le musicien dont le cœur pouvait le mieux comprendre le cœur de Colette? N'était-il pas celui qui pouvait la suivre avec plus de grâce dans le domaine du rêve?'

3 Memory, pastiche, and aestheticism in Ravel and Proust

Michael J. Puri

The lives of Marcel Proust (1871–1922) and Maurice Ravel naturally invite comparison with one another, and not only because they created bodies of work that place them at the pinnacle of their respective arts. Born four years apart, these two inveterate Parisians were both mummy's boys, dandies, queer (arguably), salon denizens, night owls, and insomniacs that showed admiration for each other's work in two gestures: Proust wanted Ravel's *Pavane pour une infante défunte* played at his funeral, while Ravel had Proust's complete, multi-volume novel *A la recherche du temps perdu* bound in hardcover and incorporated into his compact but select library at Montfort-l'Amaury.[1]

Subsequent efforts to sketch out a shared life are soon confounded, however, as there appears to be no record of their interaction. In fact, the only mention of one in the correspondence of the other appears in a letter Proust wrote to Mme Jean Cruppi in 1914. Apparently responding to her request that he introduce her to the editors of the *Nouvelle Revue française*, Proust refers her instead to Ravel, the composer of 'remarkable' music whom he understands to be both friendly with her – she was, after all, the dedicatee of *Noël des jouets* and *L'Heure espagnole* – and well respected at the *Nouvelle Revue*.[2] If this polite and expedient reference to Ravel betrays little of Proust's estimation of Ravel, hope for further revelation surges momentarily upon learning that the artists' paths crossed posthumously in the figure of Céleste Albaret. Albaret, Proust's maid and confidante during the last decade of his life, gave tours of Ravel's home in Montfort-l'Amaury and tended to its upkeep when Ravel's brother, Edouard, could no longer do so. Unfortunately, her tour commentary did not reveal any relationship or artistic affinity between the two, but rather was said to have focused on Proust almost to the exclusion of Ravel![3]

---

[1] Proust's semi-autobiographical novel seemingly formed part of Ravel's collection of memoirs by French authors, which also included those by Bourrienne, Madame de Caylus, Madame d'Epinay, Chateaubriand, and Saint-Simon.

[2] Marcel Proust, *Correspondance*, established, presented, and annotated by

Philip Kolb, 21 vols. (Paris: Plon, 1970–93), vol. XIV [1915], 351–2.

[3] Albaret mentions this episode briefly in her autobiographical reminiscences: 'For several years I was occupied with the Musée Ravel at Montfort-l'Amaury, near Paris. People came to see me there; I confess to having spoken more about Mr Proust than Ravel to

Rumours persist to this day that Proust disliked Ravel, in which case Albaret's unusual conduct as a volunteer guide for what is now the Musée Maurice Ravel might have demonstrated partisanship more than ignorance or lack of interest in the composer's life. However, instead of giving undue credence to these rumours – which may derive as much from Proust's close friendship with Reynaldo Hahn (1875–1947), a rival composer and the author of some trenchant reviews of Ravel's music, as from any deep-seated feelings on his part – it is better to devote our attention to the sole passage in *A la recherche* in which Proust refers to Ravel.

Ravel's cameo in Proust

The passage in *Time Regained* in which Proust refers to Ravel begins with a young man listening to a recital who rises to find another seat after no longer being able to tolerate the distraction caused by the narrator chatting nearby with the Duchess of Guermantes. Having lost his place in the programme, he mistakenly believes that Beethoven's 'Kreutzer' Sonata is a composition by Ravel, 'which he had been told was as beautiful as Palestrina but difficult to understand'.[4] As he moves around in the darkened room in search of a different seat, he accidentally bumps into a writing desk. Rather than being troubled by the noise, the other audience members are actually happy to be relieved from the 'torture' of having to listen 'religiously' to the Beethoven. After witnessing the 'unfortunate little incident' that they helped to cause, the narrator and the Duchess leave the room, which brings the scene to an end.[5]

Clustering together several ironies, this quintessentially Proustian comic vignette illustrates how certain social rituals and circumstances can transform music from a source of pleasure into a source of obligation. The first irony arises from the discrepancy between the serious young man's imposition of these obligations upon himself and his basic inability to fulfil them, since he apparently cannot distinguish Beethoven from Ravel, much less evaluate the complex claim that the latter is 'as beautiful as Palestrina'. The second results from his inadvertent collision into the desk, which ends up

the museum's visitors' ('Pendant quelques années, je me suis occupée du musée Ravel, à Montfort-l'Amaury, près de Paris. On venait m'y voir; je m'accuse d'avoir beaucoup plus parlé de M Proust que de Ravel aux visiteurs du musée'): Céleste Albaret, *Monsieur Proust: souvenirs recueillis par Georges Belmont* (Paris: Editions Robert Lafont, 1973), 436. André van Praag, 'De Maurice Ravel à Marcel Proust', *Synthèses*, 24 (1969), 91–104, also contains an interview with

Albaret about Proust and Ravel conducted during her time at the Musée Maurice Ravel.
[4]   Marcel Proust, *Time Regained*, in *Remembrance of Things Past*, trans. C. K. Scott Moncrieff, Terence Kilmartin, and Andreas Mayor, 3 vols. (New York: Vintage Books, 1981), vol. III, 1080. (See too the further revision by D. J. Enright: *In Search of Lost Time* (London: Chatto and Windus; New York: Modern Library, 1992).)
[5]   Proust, *Time Regained*, 1080.

disrupting the reverential silence he was trying so hard to honour and preserve. The third stems from the audience's surprising reaction to this distraction, in responding with relief rather than the exasperation that the young
man had felt toward his chatting neighbours. With these three ironies, Proust
exposes the tyranny which such rituals exert over salon audiences that want –
and can cope with – little more from music than mere diversion.

   While this passage may appear in a work of fiction, it nevertheless shows a
reasonably good understanding of Ravel's music. The fact that Proust chose
to contrast Ravel's music with Beethoven's – represented here by the middle-
period 'Kreutzer' Sonata, an especially non-Ravelian piece for its earnestness,
ferocious physicality, and symphonic proportions – demonstrates a clear
awareness of its aesthetic profile.[6] Next, the notion that Ravel's music is 'as
beautiful as Palestrina but difficult to understand' is not simply a red her-
ring introduced to tax further the young man's musical understanding for
the reader's amusement, but rather seems to have held a particular meaning
for Proust, a clue to which appears in his 'Fragments of Commedia dell'arte'.
Here, Proust explicitly associates Palestrina with an 'artificial return to
nature' – a renunciation of modern music (including Wagner, Franck, and
d'Indy) for Renaissance and Baroque music, represented by Handel, Haydn,
and Palestrina.[7] Thus, the comparison between Palestrina and Ravel in *A la
recherche* seems to imply a rejection of Wagnerian influence and an 'artificial return' to more traditional tonal materials and forms, both indisputable
aspects of Ravel's work. The additional qualification that Ravel's music is
more 'difficult' than Palestrina's places this commentary squarely within the
contemporary discourse surrounding Ravel's music, which often cracked its
teeth on the novel harmonies of such works as *Miroirs* and the *Valses nobles et
sentimentales*.[8]

Imagination and transposition

In comparison to the slim pickings offered by biography and commentary,
aesthetics and poetics provide more opportunities to interrelate Ravel and
Proust. Nourished in their youth on trends alternately dubbed Symbolism,

[6] In case we might think that Proust was
implicitly contrasting the 'Kreutzer' with
Ravel's Sonata for Violin and Piano, we
should recall that the latter had not yet been
composed when Proust died in 1922.
[7] Marcel Proust, 'Fragments of Commedia
dell'arte', in *The Complete Short Stories of
Marcel Proust*, compiled and translated by
Joachim Neugroschel (New York: Cooper
Square Press, 2001), 53.

[8] Philip Kolb, the editor of Proust's collected
correspondence, has identified this episode
as an example of Proust 'satirizing a type of
snobbery of the musical avant-garde', and
has grouped it with similar scenes from *The
Guermantes Way* and *Cities of the Plain*.
My brief explication tries to show that its
citation of music is not merely satirical, but
in fact demonstrates substantial musical
understanding. See Proust, *Correspondance*,
vol. IX [1909], 239.

Decadence, or Aestheticism, both prized the imagination as the artistic faculty and prerogative *par excellence*. A direct declaration of this principle appears in 'Contre Sainte-Beuve', where Proust asserts that 'when the art that claims to be realistic suppresses that inestimable truth, the witness of the imagination, it suppresses the only thing of value; and on the other hand, if it records it, it enriches the meanest material'.[9] In Ravel's work, the same principle manifests itself in an unabashed love for travelling back in time (the antique), across great distances (the exotic), and into fantastical spaces (the oneiric, or 'dream-like'); the opening song of the cycle *Shéhérazade*, which invokes 'Asie' three times before launching forth into a litany of literary and musical orientalisms, is an exemplary instance of the Proustian 'place-name', which typically evokes vivid associations and arouses pungent desire despite – or, rather, because of – its dissociation from real, first-hand experience. The great value that both artists ascribed to the imagination led them, on the one hand, to devalue the utilitarian for its contact with vulgar reality and, on the other, to entertain the idea of translating aesthetic experience from one medium into another, especially the audible. Near the beginning of *The Captive*, the narrator echoes in the following passage earlier sentiments made by Swann about sound being able to reflect 'like water, like a mirror':[10]

> There were days when the sound of a bell striking the hour bore upon the sphere of its sonority a plaque so spread with moisture or with light that it was like a transcription for the blind or, if you like, a musical interpretation of the charm of rain or the charm of sunlight. So much so that, at the moment, as I lay in bed with my eyes shut, I said to myself that everything is capable of transposition and that a universe that was exclusively audible might be as full of variety as the other.[11]

Inherent in the neologistic title of Ravel's *Sites auriculaires* – an early work for two pianos which contains its own bell music in the movement entitled 'Entre cloches' – Ravel's ambitions for transposing the nonmusical into music became explicit in his comments on two related works: the opera *L'Heure espagnole* and his setting of five prose poems from Jules Renard's *Histoires naturelles*, which served as preliminary studies for the opera. On 12 January 1907, the day the composer's *Histoires* were to be premiered, Ravel visited Renard to invite him to the concert, allegedly remarking that he had tried 'to say in music what you say in words when you're gazing at a tree'.[12] Ravel's comments in an interview that appeared a few days prior to the May 1911

[9] Marcel Proust, 'Against Sainte-Beuve', in *Marcel Proust on Art and Literature, 1896–1919*, trans. Sylvia Townsend, second edition (New York: Carroll & Graf, 1997), 54.
[10] This remark is made by Swann in *Within a Budding Grove* as he notes how the personal meaning for him of Vinteuil's sonata – and particularly its synecdochical *petite*

phrase – has changed over time. See Proust, *Remembrance*, vol. I, 575.
[11] *Ibid.*, vol. III, 78.
[12] Jules Renard, *Journal*, eds. Léon Guichard and Gilbert Sigaux (Paris: Gallimard, 1960), 1100–1, trans. and cited in Roger Nichols (ed.), *Ravel Remembered* (London: Faber and Faber, 1987), 78.

premiere of *L'Heure* acknowledge more strongly the mediating presence of language in the opera's gestures towards transposition. There, Ravel says that he intended the harmonic setting of the libretto 'to seem funny, like puns in language', a notion he then elaborates by claiming that he even 'heard funny' while composing it – a deliberate wordplay that captures the strangeness of intermedial transposition by not only describing it, but also emulating it.[13]

A penchant for pastiche

Proust and Ravel were two artists so heavily invested in the power of the imagination to transform experience, hybridize media, and transport the self, that it makes full sense that they shared an interest in pastiche, which allows an artist to adopt a historical style and genre in order to inhabit virtually another time and place – and even to slip into the skin of another artist. Although Proust had long dabbled in literary pastiche, his 'Lemoine' series, based on a real diamond-fabrication hoax that had taken him and several others for dupes, appeared in *Le Figaro* in early 1908 when he was in his late thirties. Including short pastiches of Honoré de Balzac, Edmond and Jules de Goncourt, and Gustave Flaubert, among others, this series followed on the heels of another collection entitled *A la manière de...* (In the Style of...) by Paul Reboux and Charles Müller, which was quite influential in its day; the 1913 edition can be found in Ravel's library at Montfort-l'Amaury.[14] For his series, Proust chose writers for whom he felt a special affinity, explaining that his pastiches allowed him not only to come to grips with that influence, but also to purge himself of it. In addition, literary pastiche gave him the opportunity to exercise a peculiar talent, which he liked to describe in musical terms:

> When I began to read an author I very soon caught the tune of the song beneath the words, which in each author is distinct from that of every other; and while I was reading, and without knowing what I was doing, I hummed it over, hurrying the words, or slowing them down, or suspending them, in order to keep time with the rhythm of the notes, as one does in singing [...] My ear for this sort of thing was sharper and truer than is common, which was what had enabled me to produce literary imitations; since when one picks up the tune the words soon follow.[15]

13   Maurice Ravel, cited in René Bizet, 'L'Heure espagnole', in Arbie Orenstein (ed.), *A Ravel Reader: Correspondence, Articles, Interviews* (New York: Columbia University Press, 1990), 411–13: 411.

14   The edition that appears in Ravel's library is: Paul Reboux and Charles Müller, *A la manière de... Troisième série* [Third series] (Paris: Bernard Grasset, 1913).

15   Proust, 'Against Sainte-Beuve', 265. Jean Milly has noted that 'it is almost always with the aid of musical metaphors that [Proust] expresses the originality and unity of a writer's work': Proust, *Les Pastiches de Proust, édition critique et commentée par Jean Milly* (Paris: A. Colin, 1970), 38.

While most accounts of this work focus on Proust's pastiche of Flaubert, we can get a sense of Proust's skill in this domain – which he might have called his 'musicality' – by reading an excerpt from one of his lesser-known pastiches. Written about 1911 but unpublished in his lifetime, this pastiche transposes the quotidian scenario of the loss of a hat into the language of the libretto for Debussy's *Pelléas et Mélisande*:

MARKEL: You were wrong to leave this hat! You will never find it again!

PELLÉAS: Why won't I ever find it?

MARKEL: We never find anything again… here… It's lost forever.

PELLÉAS: As we're leaving, we'll just take one – that looks like it!

MARKEL: There is none that looks like it!

PELLÉAS: So what did it look like?

MARKEL: *very softly*:

It was a poor little hat

Like everyone wears!

No one could have said whose home it came from… it seemed to come from the end of the world…!

[…]

PELLÉAS: What is that noise?

MARKEL: It's the cars leaving.

PELLÉAS: Why are they leaving?

MARKEL: We will have scared them off. They knew that we would go very far away from here and they left. They will never return.[16]

While the pastiche is a distinct and relatively isolated phenomenon in Proust, it is widespread in Ravel, and can be applied to many pieces he composed during the thirty years that separate the archaizing *Ballade pour la reine morte d'aimer* (*c*.1893) from the 'Blues' movement of the Sonata for Violin and Piano (1923–7). Although it is not possible here to survey pastiche in Ravel comprehensively, we can nevertheless gain insight into it by examining his subtle but masterful *A la manière de… Borodine*, which was composed in 1913, together with the somewhat slighter *A la manière de… Emmanuel Chabrier*.

---

[16] Excerpted from Proust, 'Pastiche de Pelléas et Mélisande', in *Contre Sainte-Beuve, précédé de Pastiches et mélanges et suivi de Essais et articles*, ed. Pierre Clarac with the collaboration of Yves Sandre (Paris: Gallimard, 1971), 206–7:

MARKEL: Vous avez eu tort de laisser ce chapeau! Vous ne le retrouverez jamais!

PELLÉAS: Pourquoi ne le retrouverai-je pas?

MARKEL: On ne le retrouve jamais rien… ici… Il est perdu pour toujours.

PELLÉAS: En nous en allant, nous en prendrons un, – qui lui ressemble!

MARKEL: Il n'y en a pas qui lui ressemble!

PELLÉAS: Comment était-il donc?

MARKEL: *très doucement*:

C'était un pauvre petit chapeau

Comme on porte tout le monde!

Personne n'aurait pu dire de chez qui il venait… il avait l'air de venir du bout du monde…!

[…]

PELLÉAS: Quel est ce bruit?

MARKEL: Ce sont les voitures qui partent.

PELLÉAS: Pourquoi partent-elles?

MARKEL: Nous les aurons effrayées. Elles savaient que nous nous en allions très loin d'ici et elles sont parties. Elles ne reviendront jamais.

The impulse to write a pair of pastiches appears to have come not from Ravel but from his friend and fellow composer-pianist Alfredo Casella (1883–1947). Two years earlier, Casella had performed and published a set of musical pastiches of six contemporary German (Wagner, Brahms, and Richard Strauss) and French composers (Fauré, Debussy, and Franck); the title of this collection, *A la manière de...*, indicates that it drew inspiration from the same literary anthology by Reboux and Müller that had helped to motivate Proust to write his Lemoine sketches.

'Every pastiche,' as Richard Dyer has noted, 'has its particular group that gets it.'[17] In the case of Casella's *A la manière de...*, the intended audience was not simply the broadly literate listener of the time – as Proust's pastiches for *Le Figaro*, for example, targeted the broadly literate reader of the time – but more specifically those in attendance at the concerts of the newly founded Société musicale indépendante (SMI).[18] In tune with the mandate of the SMI to provide provocative alternatives to the more earnest, tradition-bound programmes of the Société nationale de musique (SN), Casella's first series flagrantly violates the latter's tenets of seriousness and originality to offer, instead, spot-on imitations of six major composers that land just on the gentler side of parody – with the possible exception of the brutal Strauss pastiche, entitled tellingly 'Symphonia molestica'.

By alternating pastiches by Casella with those by Ravel, the second series of *A la manière de...* gives an even stronger sense of the project's embeddedness within the SMI community by including contributions from its unofficial ringleader, Ravel. At the same time, the juxtaposition of pastiches highlights their individual differences in tone. While Casella's pastiches of d'Indy ('Prélude à l'après-midi d'un Ascète') and Ravel ('Almanzor ou le mariage d'Adélaïde') continue unapologetically the parodic practice of the first series, Ravel's pastiches of Chabrier and Borodin are better described as homages. For one reason, they unfold and develop just as smoothly and sweetly as they taper off, as if they issued from nostalgic reverie upon their models. For another, they bear witness to the artistic genealogy both of Ravel and of the generational subset of composers to which he belonged, a group well represented within the founding committee of the SMI.

Painting a portrait of Chabrier improvising a 'paraphrase' on an aria by Gounod, *A la manière de... Emmanuel Chabrier* might seem, at first glance, to be more significant than the Borodin pastiche for its double gesture of homage, with the one nested within the other; certainly it was the more

[17] Richard Dyer, *Pastiche* (London and New York: Routledge, 2007), 3.
[18] Premiering these pieces himself at the SMI concert of 6 March 1911, Casella also used the cover page of their publication to dedicate the first series to Fauré and the other members of the SMI's committee, including A. Z. Mathot, the committee's secretary who published both series and whose longstanding musical coterie had formed the basis for the society's founding membership.

Example 3.1   Ravel, *A la manière de… Borodine* (bars 1–16)

popular of the two pastiches at the premiere performance, where the audience called for its encore.[19] Upon closer inspection, however, we cannot so easily dismiss *A la manière de… Borodine* as the 'purely superficial' rendering of the Russian composer that one of the concert's reviewers would have us understand it to be.[20] Granted, the opening phrase of this ABA', as reproduced in Example 3.1, does cluster together elements typically associated with Borodin: pedal points, a gently undulating melody, and a streak of chromaticism towards the end. These elements belong to the Russian musico-literary topic that Richard Taruskin has identified as *nega*: 'sweet bliss', connoting a blend of the erotic and the exotic. As Taruskin as shown, while this topic dates back at least to Glinka's *Ruslan and Lyudmila*, it reaches 'maximum strength' in Borodin, especially in the orientalist Polovtsian music from *Prince Igor*, which Diaghilev and his Ballets russes had helped to popularize in Paris several years before Ravel composed his pastiche.[21]

[19]   The encore is mentioned in Jean Poueigh's review of the SMI concert of 10 December 1913, in *La Revue musicale de la SIM*, 9 (supplement of 15 December 1913), 9.
[20]   *Ibid.*, 9: 'M Ravel a dessiné, sur un rythme de Scherzo-valse, un Borodine d'un pittoresque saisissant; un Borodine

purement extérieur il est vrai' (Mr Ravel has drafted, in the rhythm of a Scherzo-Valse, a strikingly picturesque Borodin, but one that is, admittedly, purely superficial').
[21]   Richard Taruskin, 'Entoiling the Falconet', in his *Defining Russia Musically: Historical and Hermeneutical Essays* (Princeton

Example 3.2 Borodin, *Prince Igor* (Act II, No. 17, bars 1–4)

Example 3.3 Borodin, *Prince Igor* (Act II, No. 7, bars 25–8)

A la manière de… Borodine does not rest content with creating a pastiche of Borodin through general citations of *nega*, however, but strives beyond them in three respects. First, Ravel renders the sound of Borodin even more closely by penetrating its harmonic and melodic details. A good potential model for Example 3.1 is the closing chorus of the Polovtsian maidens from Act II of *Prince Igor* (No. 17 in the Belaieff vocal score of 1889), whose first phrase is reproduced in Example 3.2. The debt of one to the other should be clear upon comparing the two: they both begin off-tonic and swerve into a cadence on the submediant harmony that coincides with a distinctive, descending three-note formula in the melody. The initial chorus of the Polovtsian maidens from Act II (No. 7), one of whose internal phrases (bars 25–8) is reproduced in Example 3.3, supplies a good model for the second half of Example 3.1: both open with a move to the dominant of the subdominant, followed by a series of diminished seventh chords in the upper voices which add pangs of longing to the slow chromatic fall

University Press, 1997), 170. As Taruskin points out, *nega* signified the sensual and seductive Eastern Other for Russian audiences, whereas French audiences would have understood it as representing the Russians in their Eastern otherness.

Example 3.4 Ravel, *A la manière de… Borodine* (bars 57–61)

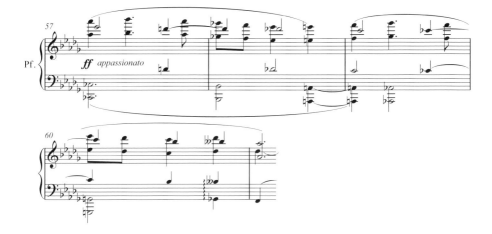

of the inner voice. While these features may participate equally with the pedal points and the melodic undulation in the projection of *nega*, they add a further level of detail that may be even more effective if it remains subliminal.

The second testament to the ambition of *A la manière de… Borodine* also involves modelling on a *nega*-drenched Polovtsian number from *Prince Igor*, but is located instead in the B section of the pastiche. The climax of the piece, which occurs at bar 57 and is reproduced in Example 3.4, seems to be based on the love duet between the daughter of the Polovtsian Khan and Igor's son (No. 12), whose pertinent bars – the declaration of their passion for each other at bars 4–9 after rehearsal letter D – appear in Example 3.5. As can be seen in the music scores, both moments are marked 'appassionato' (a direction so unusual in Ravel's music as to suggest external influence or allusion). Both moments feature a chromaticized series of first-inversion chords that descend stepwise from the dominant to the tonic.[22] The B Section, therefore, is not just an internal episode incorporated for the sake of contrast with the surrounding A sections, but rather offers a complementary perspective on Borodin's Polovtsian music that exchanges the mass choral sentiments of *nega* for more intimate declarations of desire. Whether wittingly or not, the climax in Ravel's pastiche ends up occupying the same relative position as the love duet in Borodin's opera: both are the hearts that beat at the centre of their respective works.

The careful design of the B section, which cycles through the same phrase four times until the high, delicate tinklings of the initial statement have metamorphosed into the robust outpourings of the climax, is an instance of the

---

[22] Taruskin remarks of this passage that the bass line 'gives out one of those complete chromatic descents that signal *nega* at full sensual strength': *ibid.*, 176.

Example 3.5 Borodin, *Prince Igor* (Act II, No. 12, letter D^{+4})

third respect in which *A la manière de… Borodine* commands attention as a pastiche: its seamless commixture of the styles of the two composers. In this case, the initial and final presentations of the B theme are clearly indebted to Borodin, while the theme's gradual intensification and registral behaviour (in particular, a slow registral descent across its length, coupled with a quick ascent at its end, as in Waltz IV of the *Valses nobles et sentimentales*) are Ravelian hallmarks. Moreover, the waltz that is *A la manière de… Borodine* could pass for a member of either the *Valses nobles* or Borodin's *Petite suite*,[23] whereas the abundant use of hemiola in the A sections, as well as the metronomic discipline required by the marking 'Allegro giusto', pulls the pastiche slightly closer to Ravel. The coda, which wedges out texturally while attentuating dynamically, is a Mendelssohnian vanishing act that is as characteristic of one composer as the other. In short, Ravel has fulfilled magically in this piece one of the earliest definitions of pastiche: that it be neither an original, nor a copy, but a fascinating *tertium quid*.[24]

---

[23] Ravel may, in fact, have taken the opening motive of *A la manière de… Borodine* almost note by note from the beginning of the coda in the Mazurka from the *Petite suite*, which is also in D♭ major.

[24] Dyer cites the following definition of pastiche by Roger de Piles from 1677: 'Tableaux, qui ne sont ni des Originaux, ni des Copies': Dyer, *Pastiche*, 22.

The resurrections of memory

Memory, the third and final topic of this chapter, might very well be the least obvious way to interrelate Proust and Ravel since it would seem to mean different things in the separate contexts of their work. In Proust's novel, it is primarily a phenomenon that takes place in the mind of the narrator, while in Ravel's music it manifests itself mainly as an abiding dependence on the distant historical past, most noticeable in his avid use of antique forms: the minuet, the waltz, the pavane, the passacaglia, and the tombeau (with its individual movements). As we will see, however, some moments in Ravel make use of the same trope of memory favoured in Proust: the miracle of resurrection and reanimation, which brings the dead to life and pulls the past into the present. In Proust, the key context for the use of this trope is the *moment bienheureux*, or 'felicitous moment'.

The *moment bienheureux* results from a chance encounter with a sensation that seems to refer the present to a special moment in the narrator's past, thereby triggering a 'search for lost time';[25] instances of such precipitating sensations in *A la recherche* include a stumble across uneven paving stones, the clattering of spoons in a dining room, the glimpse of a book from childhood in another person's library – and the classic example of the taste of a cake dipped in tea. In the scene involving the latter, the narrator is overcome by vague feelings of nostalgia upon tasting a madeleine soaked in some lime-blossom tea. After two unsuccessful attempts to conjure up the source of this sensation by sheer will, a recollection begins to stir of its own accord. When it finally emerges to reveal a moment from his childhood in Combray, the narrator experiences the past as resurrected in his mind, rather than merely as recollected:

> As in the game wherein the Japanese amuse themselves by filling a porcelain bowl with water and steeping in it little pieces of paper which until then are without character or form, but, the moment they become wet, stretch and twist and take on colour and distinctive shape, become flowers or houses or people, solid and recognisable, so in that moment all the flowers in our garden and in M. Swann's park, and the water lilies on the Vivonne and the good folk of the village and their little dwellings and the parish church and the whole of Combray and its surroundings, taking shape and solidity, sprang into being, town and gardens alike, from my cup of tea.[26]

---

25   Roger Shattuck defines the *moment bienheureux* as 'a moment of pleasure and communion caused by involuntary memory,' whereby one 'recognizes the past inhabiting the present': Shattuck, *Proust's Binoculars* (New York: Random House, 1963), 27. The catalogue of these moments that he offers in *Proust's Binoculars* (69–79) reappears, in slightly varied form, in an appendix to his *Proust's Way* (New York and London: W. W. Norton, 2000).
26   Proust, *Remembrance*, vol. I, 51.

In addition to associating memory with resurrection, the madeleine scene introduces three further paradigmatic aspects of the *moment bienheureux* that will prove useful to us when considering similar moments in Ravel. First and foremost, as already suggested in the brief description of the scene above, it provides the moment with a detailed phenomenology. The moment usually catches the subject of memory in the midst of an ongoing process, whose repetition often breeds disenchantment; just before the narrator raises the madeleine 'mechanically' to his lips, he describes himself as feeling 'dispirited after a dreary day with the prospect of a depressing morrow'.[27] Against this backdrop, the momentary encounter with a past sensation is all the more extraordinary, taking the narrator by surprise and compelling him to devote full attention to it by suspending physical movement, turning his mind inwards and clearing it of distracting thoughts and sensations. As he does so, he sharpens his sensitivity to the feeling of a mystical *correspondance* between him and the object that caused the precipitating sensation, imagining that it is a soul 'calling' out for him to recall it, and thereby deliver it from a state of limbo.[28] Access to any such recollection is possible only through 'involuntary memory', which allows the reminiscing individual during the *moment bienheureux* to re-experience the past in its full, sensual presence, in contrast to 'voluntary memory', which, as the author himself described in an interview, 'belongs above all to the intelligence and the eyes [and] offers us only untruthful aspects of the past'.[29] Although these efforts to remember might very well come to nothing (as in the episode with the three trees near Balbec), in the madeleine scene they eventually succeed after several failures; as the memory gradually nears consciousness, the narrator seems to feel 'the resistance' of the long-forgotten memory and hear 'the echo of great spaces traversed' as it rises from the murky depths of his psyche.[30] When the memory is finally revealed, the density and richness of the experience that it bears trigger feelings of elation that overwhelm the narrator.

The remaining two aspects of the madeleine scene that make it the paradigmatic *moment bienheureux* supplement its phenomenology. Firstly, its haphazard occurrence in the life of the narrator does not mean that it occupies a random position within the rhetorical design of the narrative; on the contrary, the madeleine scene is a pivotal event that creates the climax of the introduction to *A la recherche* while launching simultaneously the main account of his childhood. Secondly, the narrator leaves open the possibility

---

[27]   *Ibid.*, 48.
[28]   On the 'souls' that 'call out' from material objects, see Proust, *Remembrance*, vol. I: 47–8, 622, 733.
[29]   This interview, conducted by a reporter from *Le Temps* in the autumn of 1913, has

been translated into English and included in the Appendix to Roger Shattuck, *Marcel Proust* (Princeton University Press, 1974), 166–72.
[30]   Proust, *Remembrance*, vol. I, 49.

for the operations of memory to involve acts of imagination – in other words, for memory to be creative, rather than merely reproductive. His acknowledgement, during the madeleine scene, that the remembering mind is 'face to face with something which does not yet exist, to which it alone can give reality and substance'[31] expands into more ambitious thoughts towards the end of the novel. There, he suggests that mnemonic activity offers a general, heuristic model for poetics, which compels us to make 'efforts of the same kind as those that we make to recall something that we have forgotten, as if our finest ideas were like tunes which, as it were, come back to us although we have never heard them before and which we have to make an effort to hear and to transcribe'.[32]

The most obvious candidates for a Proustian *moment bienheureux* in Ravel's music appear in his score for the Russian ballet *Daphnis et Chloé*. Beginning work on this piece in 1909 – the same year in which Proust began to write *A la recherche* – Ravel would later describe this 'choreographic symphony' as an attempt to 'compose a vast musical fresco, less concerned with archaism than with faithfulness to the Greece of my dreams'.[33] On the one hand, the disavowal of 'archaism' expresses the divergence of opinion between Ravel and his librettist and choreographer Mikhail (Michel) Fokin(e) (1880–1942), who originally wanted *Daphnis* to be as historically accurate as possible, reproducing not only the text of the third-century-CE Greek novel by Longus, but also authentic rhythms and melodies from Ancient Greece.[34] On the other hand, the allusion to 'the Greece of my dreams' implies the intermingling of memory and imagination in *Daphnis*, even the prioritizing of imagination over memory. As in Proust, the faculty that gives shape to Ravel's fantasies about the past is a *mnemonic imagination*.[35]

The Introduction (opening–Fig. 4) of *Daphnis* corresponds to the madeleine scene in Proust's novel insofar as both are not only the first but also the paradigmatic *moments bienheureux* within their respective works. The Introduction falls into two halves (opening–Fig. 2 and Figs. 3–4), each of which describes registrally an arc. The first half begins as a *creatio ex nihilo* with an almost inaudible rumble on a low A in the timpani and double basses. After an indeterminate length of time (with a pause marking), the music begins to ascend slowly from the A via a series of perfect fifths in the muted *pianississimo* strings and harp; the resulting sound evokes playfully

---

31 *Ibid.*

32 *Ibid.*, vol. III, 912.

33 Roland-Manuel, 'An Autobiographical Sketch by Maurice Ravel' [1928], in Orenstein (ed.), *A Ravel Reader*, 29–37: 31.

34 Fokin relates his original intentions for *Daphnis* in Michel Fokine, *Fokine: Memoirs of a Ballet Master*, ed. Anatole Chujoy, trans. Vitale Fokine (Boston: Little, Brown,

1961), 196. (On Fokin, see too the opening of Chapter 8.)

35 Ravel's alleged description of *Tzigane* as an attempt to 'bring the Hungary of my dreams to life' (['la difficulté diabolique] fera revivre la Hongrie de mes rêves') is even more explicit about the power of the imagination to resurrect the (imagined) past; cited in Marcel Marnat, *Maurice Ravel* (Paris: Fayard, 1986), 550.

Example 3.6   Ravel, *Daphnis et Chloé*: thematic material in Introduction

(a) 'Appel' (Fig. 1^{-1})
(b) 'Nymphes' (Fig. 1)
(c) 'Daphnis/Chloé' (Fig. 2^{-3})

the tuning of a cosmic lyre, whether that of Orpheus or Apollo. At the raising of the curtain midway through the series of fifths, we see an unpopu-
lated Grecian meadow and sacred grove at the same time that we hear the
first statement in the muted horns of the primary motive, labelled 'Appel'
(Call) in Example 3.6a. This undulating motive, which in the first half of the
Introduction passes several times between the orchestra and the invisible
chorus, introduces into the landscape a mysterious animism that we may
relate to Proust's souls, who call out to be recalled ('rappelé') to life. Indeed,
the participation of music in the (re-)enchantment of the world is an integral part not only of *Daphnis*, but also of Ravel's aesthetic in general, for, as
Emile Vuillermoz once mused, 'The orchestra for Ravel is, in effect, a forest of
Brocéliande whose every tree imprisons a fairy.'[36]

The D♮ that marks the end of the series of ascending fifths is the same
note that begins the first statement of the 'Nymphes' (Nymphs) theme in
the solo flute. As is evident from Example 3.6b, the simple, sinuous line of
the Nymphes, unfurling within a static harmony and inevitably bringing to
mind the opening melody of Debussy's *Prélude à L'Après-midi d'un faune*,
evokes a shepherd's improvisatory piping *en plein air* on a lazy afternoon – a
quasi-diegetic music emitted seemingly by the antique, pastoral landscape
itself, since there is no actual shepherd in sight. Counteracting the leisurely
affect of the Nymphes line is a palpable tension introduced by the first violins

[36] Emile Vuillermoz, 'Le Style orchestral de
Maurice Ravel', *La Revue musicale*, 6 (April
1925 [special issue]), 22–7: 26. 'L'orchestre est
en effet pour Ravel une forêt de Brocéliande
dont chaque arbre emprisonne une fée.'
Brocéliande is the name of an enchanted
forest within Arthurian legend.

(Fig. 1ff.): a high tremolo on A, at the octave in harmonics, presented *presque imperceptible* ('almost imperceptible') at *pianissississimo* dynamic; a piquant dissonance also arises from the tritone between the incipit D♯ of the theme and various occurrences of the tonic A in the accompaniment. As soon as the Nymphes material comes to a close, 'Daphnis/Chloé', the love theme of Daphnis and Chloé, appears in the solo horn (Example 3.6c). Migrating into different instruments and harmonic fields, like the peregrine 'Appel', this thematic pairing of the Nymphes and Daphnis/Chloé alternates one more time before the first half of the Introduction comes to an end.

Like the first half, the second begins with a gradual registral ascent (Fig. 3) that culminates in a statement of the Nymphes theme; unlike the static and quiet first half, however, the second is dynamic and climactic. A billowing texture of triplet quavers starts quietly low down in the cellos, but soon increases in volume and register to figure the gradual filling of the stage with young men and women, who carry votive offerings for the Nymph statues in the sacred grove. The arrival at Fig. 4, which features a return to the tonic harmony at the same time that the invisible chorus comes onstage, is superseded three bars later by a climactic harmonic shift that supports simultaneous, *fortissimo* statements of both the Appel motive in the full chorus and that for the Nymphes in the flutes and trumpets. Each facet of the musical texture seems to correlate to an onstage action: the Nymphes theme coincides with the crowd's reverence before the Nymphs' altar, the Appel figure sounds the crowd's praise of the deities, and the high, scintillating, heterophonic refraction of the Appel motive in the harps and violins swirls around the Nymphes material just as the flower garlands, placed by the young women, encircle the pedestals of the Nymphs. As the texture subsides, the Introduction gives way to the 'Danse religieuse' (Fig. 5ff.).

From this overview, we can see that the Introduction not only presents the main motivic-thematic material of the ballet, but also follows the basic phenomenology of the *moment bienheureux*. Interrupting an ongoing process (the series of ascending fifths), a fascinating event (the sound of the Nymphes theme with its spellbinding D♯, together with the sight of the landscape) engenders a state of enthralment (rhythmic and harmonic stasis in the accompaniment, made suspenseful by tremolos in the high strings and low timpani). Deserted except for a few grazing sheep, the pastoral setting nonetheless seems alive, calling out audibly for recognition and release from its state of limbo (created by the Appel motive and alternating Nymphes and Daphnis/Chloé themes). The stasis, distance, and disembodiment in the first half then yields to the dynamism, proximity, and embodiment of the second as the sound grows, the stage fills, the invisible chorus comes into view, and the texture and tempo are enlivened ('Animez progressivement' at Fig. 3). A 'musical time warp'[37] fusing the past with the present, the second half crowns this *moment bienheureux* with a climax that is overwhelming in its sublime, synaesthetic fullness.

Similar to its role in Proust's novel as a 'starting point' or 'foundation stone' for the narrator's life,[38] the phenomenon of the *moment bienheureux* is crucial to the large-scale structure of Ravel's most extensive score. The initial resurrection of an idyllic past plays the same role in Ravel as the madeleine scene did in Proust, bringing the Introduction to a head while also launching the main body of the work. The Introduction then recurs in altered form in both the Nocturne (Fig. 70) and the 'Lever du jour' (Daybreak; Fig.152), which begin, respectively, the second and third panels of this triptych. Like the Introduction, both feature scenes of reanimation: in the Nocturne – whose conspicuous evasion of a climax at the invocation of Pan makes it more of a 'failed' *moment* – the three Nymphs are brought back to life, descending from their pedestals to perform a 'slow and mysterious dance', while the 'Lever du jour' represents the dawn as the joyous restoration of the pastoral world, along with the even more ecstatic reunion of the couple. In fact, if Fokin's early draft scenario for *Daphnis* had become its definitive libretto, there would have been an additional scene of reanimation; in this version, Act II opens on a trampled garden which one of the Nymphs restores to life, suddenly and magically, with a simple wave of her hand.[39]

The reliance upon *moments bienheureux* in both Proust's novel and Ravel's ballet score may lend shape and coherence to the overall design of these extended works, but it also betrays a fundamental anxiety that the past – miraculously made present by the mnemonic imagination – will soon become past once again. Neither artist is oblivious to this threat. When the narrator's lover dies suddenly in *A la recherche*, he immediately makes a conscious effort to preserve her memory from imminent oblivion, searching in particular for a 'sweet' recollection, since he knows it will continue to resonate in his mind 'like a sort of vibration, prolonged by a pedal', long after he will have forgotten many other details about her and their life together.[40] In *Daphnis*, just as the concluding, frenetic Bacchanale is about to obliterate all traces of the idyllic romance, Ravel presents us with just such a 'sweet' scene to vibrate in our memories: 'Daphnis and Chloé embrace tenderly' ('s'enlacent tendrement') to a fragment of their love theme (Fig. 195). Valedictions in both Proust and

---

[37] The concept of the 'musical time warp' derives from commentary on Debussy's *Chansons de Bilitis* in Julie McQuinn, 'Exploring the Erotic in Debussy's Music', in Simon Trezise (ed.), *The Cambridge Companion to Debussy* (Cambridge University Press, 2003), 117–36: 130. For a complementary reading of this passage from

Daphnis, see Deborah Mawer, *The Ballets of Maurice Ravel: Creation and Interpretation* (Aldershot: Ashgate, 2006), 94–6.
[38] Proust, *Remembrance*, vol. III, 262.
[39] Cited in Simon Morrison, 'The Origins of *Daphnis et Chloé* (1912)', *19th-Century Music*, 28/1 (2004), 50–76: 55.
[40] Proust, *Remembrance*, vol. III, 400–1.

Ravel do not forbid mourning, but foster it; after all, if we felt no sadness over the loss of experience, we could not feel the joy of its involuntary recollection in the *moment bienheureux*. As Proust wrote so famously – a bittersweet truth which applies just as well to the Greece of Ravel's dreams in *Daphnis* – 'the true paradises are the paradises that we have lost'.[41]

[41] *Ibid.*, 903.

4   Erotic ambiguity in Ravel's music

Lloyd Whitesell

Scant evidence remains from which to form a picture of Ravel's erotic-affectional life. There are conflicting accounts of a marriage proposal made when he was in his forties; but he remained a lifelong bachelor.[1] To our knowledge he was never linked romantically with anyone, unless we are to make something of his early attachment to the poet Léon-Paul Fargue: according to Hélène Jourdan-Morhange, Fargue was 'united to Ravel by a tender friendship of youth'.[2] As for sexual encounters, several friends mention casual visits to female prostitutes.[3] This is an equivocal piece of information, however, since by Ravel's time the Parisian *demimonde* had developed a repertoire of ruses to disguise same-sex contacts.[4] All in all, the facts are too inconclusive to establish a clear hetero- or homosexual identity.

People who knew Ravel, both straight and queer, remarked on the inscrutable character of his intimate emotional life. His insistence on utter privacy has baffled those seeking to place him as a sexual subject. In a homage after the composer's death, Emile Vuillermoz spoke of the 'sexual enigma' of Ravel and likened him to the 'indifférent' from his song cycle *Shéhérazade*.[5] Many

---

[1] Marguerite Long related the story of the marriage proposal as told to her by 'a very dear [male] friend': Long, *Au piano avec Maurice Ravel* (Paris: Julliard, 1971), 184–5. In 1985, Manuel Rosenthal claimed that Hélène Jourdan-Morhange had confided to him the circumstances of Ravel's proposal to her; see Rosenthal, 'Entretiens avec Rémy Stricker', *France Culture* (1985), quoted in Marcel Marnat, *Maurice Ravel* (Paris: Fayard, 1986), 463. There is, however, no mention of any such proposal in Jourdan-Morhange's memoir: Hélène Jourdan-Morhange, *Ravel et nous: l'homme, l'ami, le musicien* (Geneva: Editions du milieu du monde, 1945). According to Orenstein: 'friends of Ravel have told me that he wanted to marry [Jourdan-Morhange] but she refused, and others have claimed that she wanted to marry Ravel but he refused'; see Arbie Orenstein (ed.), *A Ravel Reader: Correspondence, Articles, Interviews*

(New York: Columbia University Press, 1990), 17.
[2] Jourdan-Morhange, *Ravel et nous*, 48. See too comments on Fargue in Gerald Larner, *Maurice Ravel* (London: Phaidon Press, 1996), 220.
[3] Long, *Au piano avec Ravel*, 184; Rosenthal, in Marnat, *Maurice Ravel*, 464; Désiré-Emile Inghelbrecht, in Hans Heinz Stuckenschmidt, *Maurice Ravel: Variationen über Person und Werk* (Frankfurt am Main: Suhrkamp Verlag, 1966), 138. See also Larner, *Maurice Ravel*, 221.
[4] Lloyd Whitesell, 'Ravel's Way', in Sophie Fuller and Lloyd Whitesell (eds.), *Queer Episodes in Music and Modern Identity* (Urbana and Chicago: University of Illinois Press, 2002), 49–78: 60–1.
[5] Emile Vuillermoz, 'L'Œuvre de Maurice Ravel', in Colette et al., *Maurice Ravel par quelques-uns de ses familiers* (Paris: Editions du tambourinaire, 1939), 1–95: 65.

have since sought to enlist him under one known category or another, and there is indeed a tenacious underground tradition of claiming Ravel as gay.[6] Roger Nichols cites a psychological study from 1963 whose author classifies the composer as belonging to a type whose characteristics include 'a virtual absence of sexual appetite'.[7] Others have surmised a highly reticent heterosexual orientation.

Comparison between Ravel and Flaubert

Ravel himself preferred a type of self-presentation wherein the self is understood as an aesthetic project free from sexual entanglements – the dandy in the avant-garde of fashion and disdainful of bourgeois conventions; the solitary bachelor wedded to his art. In this stance he is akin to other sexual enigmas within his social orbit, such as Ricardo Viñes, Erik Satie, and Manuel de Falla. In personal statements made to friends, Ravel averred that his vocation as an artist rendered him unsuitable for marriage: 'Morality… this is what I practice, and what I am determined to continue. We artists are not made for marrying. We are seldom normal, and our lives even less so.'[8] These lines echo mildly Gustave Flaubert's repudiation of marriage and family in the service of art; Fargue even compares Ravel with Flaubert in his creative isolation: 'He reminded me of Flaubert, who would withdraw, sensitive and bitter, to compose his masterpieces.'[9] However, roles such as dandy and bachelor-artist are inherently ambiguous in signification, since the selfsame aestheticist poses were common evasive accommodations adopted by homosexual people in the face of social stigma. Marcel Proust drew attention to the 'solitary' figure who shuns temptation as one distinct type among the varieties of 'inverts' observable in French society.[10] (For detailed discussion of Proust, see Chapter 3.) Both André Gide and Jean Cocteau went through dandyist periods in their youth before adopting more overtly queer personas.[11] Across

6   Whitesell, 'Ravel's Way', 51–2.

7   Roger Nichols, *Ravel* (London: J. M. Dent, 1977), 152. The author, Dr S. D. M. Pallaud, also claims that Ravel was arrested at the 'anal-sadistic' stage.

8   Ravel to Hélène Casella (19 January 1919), in Arbie Orenstein (ed.), *Maurice Ravel: lettres, écrits, entretiens* (Paris: Flammarion, 1989), 169: 'La morale… c'est celle que je pratique et que je suis décidé à continuer. Nous ne sommes pas faits pour nous marier, nous autres artistes. Nous sommes rarement normaux, et notre vie l'est encore moins.' See too Jacques de Zogheb, 'Souvenirs Ravéliens', in Colette et al., *Maurice Ravel par quelques-uns de ses familiers*,

171–5: 172: 'Au fond, ma seule maîtresse, c'est la musique', and Rosenthal cited in Marnat, *Maurice Ravel*, 463.

9   Léon-Paul Fargue, 'Autour de Ravel', in Colette et al., *Maurice Ravel par quelques-uns de ses familiers*, 153–61: 156: 'Il me faisait songer à Flaubert, qui se retirait, sensible et amer, pour composer des chefs-d'œuvre.'

10   Marcel Proust, *In Search of Lost Time*, trans. C. K. Scott Moncrieff and Terence Kilmartin, revised by D. J. Enright, 6 vols. (London: Chatto & Windus, 1992), vol. IV, 22–3, 27–31.

11   Arthur King Peters, *Jean Cocteau and His World: An Illustrated Biography* (New York: Vendome, 1986), 30–7.

Europe, the pose of the aesthete provided cover for homoerotic pursuits, as is well documented in the cases of Walter Pater and Oscar Wilde.[12] Thus the identity types which Ravel embraced may or may not have served a protective function. Nevertheless, while in themselves empty of sexual content, they are still queer insofar as they resist conformity to heterosexual scripts.[13]

Such determined resistance is palpable in Flaubert's correspondence: 'When will I get married, you ask me? [...] Never, I hope [...] As for my moral disposition, I will keep the same one until the new order [...] I've found my footing, my centre of gravity [...] Marriage for me would be a terrifying breach of faith'; and 'A curse upon the family, which softens the heart of the brave, which encourages every kind of cowardice, which extracts every conceivable concession, and which marinates you in an ocean of milk and tears.'[14] The vehemence of his language can be traced to an experience fundamentally at odds with social norms. As Jean Borie has shown, the bachelor in the later nineteenth century faced strong currents of suspicion, as a figure whose refusal to participate in the social order classified him not only as sterile, but as antipatriotic and a corrupting influence. Public health officials recommended the imposition of a tax on the unmarried, while pathologists branded bachelorhood as tantamount to sexual deviance.[15] The attempts of certain individuals to create 'original ways of life, oppositional (*contestataires*) alternatives to the cloying tide' of the family should be viewed in relation to the inhospitable environment.[16]

---

[12] Richard Dellamora, *Masculine Desire: The Sexual Politics of Victorian Aestheticism* (Chapel Hill: University of North Carolina Press, 1990); Ellis Hanson, *Decadence and Catholicism* (Cambridge, MA: Harvard University Press, 1997); Richard A. Kaye, 'Gay Studies/Queer Theory and Oscar Wilde', in Frederick S. Roden (ed.), *Palgrave Advances in Oscar Wilde Studies* (London: Palgrave Macmillan, 2004), 189–223.

[13] Michael J. Puri has argued similarly for the queer import of dandyism, 'In this essay, we [...] will allow the dandy to maintain his fullness as a *queer* figure whose embodied opposition to bourgeois norms extends to his sexuality': Puri, 'Dandy, Interrupted: Sublimation, Repression, and Self-Portraiture in Maurice Ravel's *Daphnis et Chloé* (1909–12)', *Journal of the American Musicological Society*, 60/2 (2007), 317–72: 320.

[14] Flaubert, letter to his mother (15 December 1850), quoted in Jean Borie, *Le Célibataire français* (Paris: Le Sagittaire, 1976), 25–6: 'A quand la noce? me demandes-tu [...] A

jamais je l'espère [...] Pour ce qui est de mes dispositions morales, je garde les mêmes jusqu'à nouvel ordre [...] J'ai trouvé mon assiette, mon centre de gravité [...] Le mariage pour moi serait une apostasie qui m'épouvante'; letter to Louis Bouilhet (5 October 1855), quoted in Michelle Perrot, 'En marge: célibataires et solitaires', in Perrot (ed.), *Histoire de la vie privée*, vol. IV: *De la Révolution à la Grande Guerre* (Paris: Seuil, 1987), 287: 'Malédiction sur la famille qui amollit le cœur des braves, qui pousse à toutes les lâchetés, à toutes les concessions, et qui vous détrempe dans un océan de laitage et de larmes.' Compare with Gide's youthful cry of resistance of forty years later (from *Les Nourritures terrestres*, 1897): 'Families, I hate you! closed circles round the hearth; fast shut doors; jealous possession of happiness', in André Gide, *Fruits of the Earth*, trans. Dorothy Bussy (London: Secker & Warburg, 1949), 67.

[15] The writings of Auguste Ambroise Tardieu and Dr P. Garnier are cited in Borie, *Le Célibataire français*, 90–7.

[16] Perrot, 'En marge: célibataires et solitaires', 287.

Queer incongruity and its responses

The question remains as to whether social alienation due to a committed non-conformist stance has any bearing on one's artistic expression – in Ravel's case, whether his particular brand of aestheticism might be related to an underlying awareness of being 'at odds with his surroundings' (as a young Viñes described his friend).[17] A theoretical framework offering insight into this question is elaborated in the work of the Danish sociologist Henning Bech. In his book *When Men Meet: Homosexuality and Modernity*, Bech takes a phenomenological approach to 'the conditions and possibilities of life in contemporary modern societies', as exemplified by the social predicament of the male homosexual. He argues that, due to his erotic preference, experience of oppression, and exposure to prevailing cultural discourses, the homosexual has an especially close affinity to the problematic conditions of modern life.[18] Bech's analyses draw on Heideggerian concepts of experiential life-worlds and existential 'moods' or 'tunings' (German *Stimmungen*).[19] While we need not debate the terms of his wider argument here, his investigation into specific tunings stimulates thought about the question at hand. Bech introduces a tongue-in-cheek fable designed to capture the experiential key of 'wrongness'. Slyly, he circumvents mention of sexuality *per se*, sketching instead the picture of a temporary renter in a beach house community who falls foul of the neighbours through his non-observance of established social customs: 'Once the massive majority in one's surroundings takes a disapproving view, one begins to feel wrong oneself and sets to work trying to detect shortcomings in oneself.' Bech goes on to suggest the possible range of personal responses to an awareness of feeling odd or wrong. He describes twelve such responses, including: 'I adapt', 'I avoid people', 'I pretend to ignore', 'I defy', 'I sneer', 'I rage', 'I flee', and so on.[20]

Immediately, we can see a number of these reactions at play in the vicinity of bachelorhood. Flaubert's declarations of self-sufficiency, as cited above, combine rage, mockery, and defiance. Ravel's own moral stance sounds very similar to Bech's third type of response:

> 3. I *rationalize*; I am a bit of a character, but for *highly respectable* reasons; the fact that I have neither a dog nor a wife is because it would disrupt my work, which is very important and to which I am utterly devoted.[21]

[17] Ricardo Viñes, journal entry for 1 November 1896, trans. Nina Gubisch [-Viñes], 'Le Journal inédit de Ricardo Viñes', *Revue internationale de musique française*, 1 (1980), 154–248: 190.

[18] Henning Bech, *When Men Meet: Homosexuality and Modernity*, trans. Teresa Mesquit and Tim Davies (University of Chicago Press, 1997), 2; furthermore,

the homosexual is 'a particularly open or exposed defile' for these modern conditions – 'the city, the collapse of norms, the absence of safe and secure communities and identities […] the external surveillance of the police and the internal analysing of science', 154.

[19] Bech, *When Men Meet*, 5–6, 221.

[20] *Ibid.*, 92–4.

[21] *Ibid.*, 93.

A most intriguing feature of Bech's list, however, is its implicit suggestion that psychologically defensive strategies contain the seeds of aesthetic/expressive strategies as well:

> 7. I *persevere*, exaggerate, put on extra-provocative clothes, flash in front of the windows.
>
> […]
>
> 9. I *lord it over them*, I have breeding, I do not listen to music with the windows open, and when I do, it is classical […]
>
> 10. I *rage,* or I *cry*, at their stiff-necked norms or my own stiff-necked deviancy […] and fantasize about things being different.[22]

Item 10 of the list conflates three different emotional responses – indignation, lament, and escapism – each of which has clear associations with a distinct artistic genre or mode: namely, protest, melodrama, and fantasy. The provocative stance of item 7 hints at aesthetic stratagems designed to *épater les bourgeois*. Item 9 (together with items 5, 'I pretend to ignore', and 8, 'I sneer') conjures up a pose of aristocratic aloofness or ironic detachment, as embodied in the figure of the dandy. Thus, without being reductively direct or monolithic, Bech's analysis allows us to see how queer forms of cultural expression may have their roots in social phenomena as experienced by a queer subject.

Aesthetic strategies in Ravel's *Shéhérazade* (1903)

To test this hypothesis I turn now to Ravel's music. While I believe that queer subjectivity can have far-reaching consequences for one's cognitive and creative orientation, for the scope of this chapter it makes sense to concentrate on the musical treatment of erotic desire. In life, the composer carried himself as if aloof from desire, establishing such distance through aesthetic perfection or irony.[23] As Vuillermoz recalled, Ravel 'handled paradox and deadpan irony with a formidable facility'.[24] We might even supplement Bech's list of responses in order to capture nuances important to Ravel, as follows: 'I am dismissive of my sense of difference or of desire altogether; I evade the issue'. The evasive turn is evident in his music as well as in his life.

Consider, for instance, the early orchestral song cycle *Shéhérazade*,[25] with its setting of texts by Tristan Klingsor that are overtly erotic. In the second song, 'La Flûte enchantée', a concubine is roused from her bed by a nocturnal melody brushing against her cheek like a kiss, while in the third,

[22] *Ibid.*, 93–4.
[23] For detailed treatment of aesthetic perfection, see Chapter 1.
[24] Vuillermoz, 'L'Œuvre de Maurice Ravel', 3.

[25] The reader is referred here to the full orchestral score of Maurice Ravel, *Shéhérazade* (Paris: Durand, 1914).

'L'Indifférent', the narrator is seduced by the charms of a graceful youth pass-ing by. The first song, 'Asie', mentions dark amorous eyes, bright teeth, and sumptuous clothing in its catalogue of exotic sights. Ravel responds to the poems with music of dazzling colour and sensuality. In 'Asie', even the initial statement of yearning to travel is conveyed through powerfully eroticized gestures. As the singer imagines the boat in the harbour ready to embark, the orchestra gathers itself into a magically rocking, pulsing texture, simul-taneously oceanic and corporeal. Woodwind dyads bob on lapping waves of muted strings (Fig. 2ff.); at the same time, the orchestral mass, in its warmth, density, and swell, evokes a breathing body passionately aroused. The irony is that such an intense erotic sensation should be invoked to glamorize an image of solitude – the lone vessel, 'mystérieuse et solitaire' (Fig. 3^{+4}), surro-gate for the subject immersed in fantasy.

In fact, desire is conceived ironically throughout the cycle. In choosing his texts, Ravel avoided those poems from Klingsor's collection that featured explicit nudity or sexual encounters.[26] Instead, though the primary images in the poems that he chose seem to imply a free circulation of sensual desire, they are embedded within scenarios of disappointment. Thus in the poem for 'La Flûte enchantée', music takes on properties of physical touch. The identi-cal rhyme of 'joue/joue' ('my beloved *plays* / from the flute to my *cheek*' [Fig. 4^{-1}; Fig. 5^{-1}]) captures in a single word the transformation from floating mel-ody to bodily caress. Yet this 'mysterious kiss' is only an imaginary compen-sation in the aesthetic realm for thwarted sexual desire. In the real world, the lovers are separated by a lattice (symbol of female seclusion) through which only sound can penetrate. The flute melody meandering through the song is thus ambivalent in its symbolism, countering frustration with languorous display and sublimating the forbidden passion into decorative patterns like the organic curves of Islamic architecture.

The poem for 'L'Indifférent' begins with a visual caress, as the narrator drinks in the young stranger's beauty and traces the curve of his face. At the mention of his lips the youth begins to sing 'in an unknown tongue', as if the erotic gaze were translating directly into musical response – or as if the lips and tongue of the poet were achieving an imagined union with those of the boy. (Here there is a significant echo of the close of 'Asie', where the poet calls attention to his/her own lips in the act of narration: 'raising my cup to my lips from time to time to interrupt my tale artfully'.) The youth appears to pause at the doorstep, on the brink of physical intimacy, while the narrator essays

---

[26] See Tristan Klingsor, *Schéhérazade* (Amiens: Edgar Malfère, 1926), 126; from poem 76, 'L'Etranger': 'Dans un bain parfumé de jasmin / Tu n'auras qu'à te plonger / Et mon esclave rasé / Massera d'une savante main / Ton corps fin, ton derrière puissant / Et ton sexe lourd / Qui pend entre tes jambes d'adolescent / Comme un sachet précieux de velours'.

a discreet sexual advance ('Come in! Let my wine cheer you'). But the youth moves on with a wave of the hand. Once again, Ravel has selected a scene of thwarted desire. New to this poem, however, is the element of teasing. The narrator is teased with the promise of sensual pleasure, and with the hope that his/her invitation will be recognized for what it is. The poem also teases us as to the youth's sexual awareness: is he truly 'heedless' of the onlooker's desire, or, in his bearing, gestures, and music making, is he coquettishly playing on his own attractiveness?

Ravel's Asia is a land whose erotic delights remain paradoxically just out of reach. Or rather, the text withholds them while the music realizes them, bathing the listener in sensuous pleasure. Returning to 'Asie', the opening ten bars (up to Fig. 2) pose musical gestures of powerful yearning – in the terraced vocal melody, the prolonged deadlock between the triadic elements of E♭ minor and D major, and the chain of dissonances delaying resolution. Yet traditional (V–i) cadential fulfilment does arrive at the close of this section. The elapsed bars now sound preparatory to the launching of the oceanic texture described above, as the initial harmonic ambiguity dissolves into an E♭ modal sonority (Fig. 2), almost undisturbed for fifteen bars. This sonorous field engulfs the solitary traveller of the poem in erotic plenitude. The same textural-motivic complex recurs at the song's climax (Fig. 15), once again approached via the V–i cadence, now heightened in intensity to suggest crashing waves and spasmodic physical release. The remainder of the song acts as an envoi ('And then I would return to tell my adventure'; Fig. 17), returning to the initial E♭/D opposition and chain of dissonances, before dissolving at last (this time chromatically and thus irrationally) into a decaying reminiscence of the voluptuous tonic field. The climax and its after-echo, textless passages embodying long-range fulfilment, are thus interrupted by a span of harmonic irresolution, just at the point where the text re-establishes an arch narrative distance and alludes to a storytelling tactic of withholding fulfilment, in the manner of the fictional Sheherazade.

'L'Indifférent' begins immediately with its own enveloping texture in lush extended harmonies. Gently rocking figures in the muted strings evoke buoyancy as well as the stirrings of a warm pulse (Michael Puri characterizes this opening as a 'barcarolle in compound duple meter that exudes luxury, repose, and pleasure').[27] The introductory gesture crests at bar 7 with a sigh of yearning, where the woodwind melody reaches a dissonant ninth (against F♯ minor) and falls down by a fifth. Soon after the voice enters, this gesture is answered by a different sighing figure in the strings: this time an exhalation of pleasure (cresting on a C♯^{9} chord; Fig. 1). The yearning motive returns in distilled form at the moment of invitation (the Bm^9 chord at 'Entre!'; Fig. 4^{-3}),

---

[27] Puri, 'Dandy, Interrupted', 331.

only to have the texture and tonality break down entirely as the youth rejects the invitation. In conclusion, however, following the singer's last drooping phrase, the flutes, now supported by violas, resume the yearning motive (again on $F_{\sharp}m^9$; Fig. 5^{-1}), leading directly to a secure tonal resolution and restoring the sensory fullness of the opening. Thus, regardless of the scenario of unrequited desire, the music presents a lasting, though interrupted, span of languid fulfilment. It is as if the composer has translated the poet's state of one-sided longing into a sonorous envelope of aesthetic pleasure.

With such an aestheticizing move Ravel accomplishes a number of things. He establishes an incongruous relation between musical and textual perspectives. He removes the object of desire from the frustrating world of social dynamics, substituting the perfection of the musical object, and evades wholehearted investment in the scene of desire through distance and paradox. This evasive turn can be interpreted in terms of a defensive response to stigma – but it is not merely defensive. It also has the potential to pique or provoke the listener. The authorial pose of ironic detachment is especially evident in the teasing attitude towards the listener, conveyed through calculated but temporary disruptions.

Let me take a moment to clarify the focus of my analysis. One could certainly insist on the presence of semantic markers of queerness in this cycle, latent as they often are in the vocabulary of exoticism. In the descriptions of 'un *mystérieux* baiser' ('La Flûte enchantée', Fig. 5^{-1}), '[un] jeune *étranger*' ('L'Indifférent', Fig. 1), 'une langue *inconnue*', and 'une musique *fausse*' ('L'Indifférent', Fig. 3), there is a suggestion of desire moving along unfamiliar paths, under the spell of enigmatic objects. But I am making a different point here. I am arguing for the recognition of an aesthetic posture of irony, teasing, and evasion, traceable to the phenomenal experience ('tuning') of queer incongruity.[28] My examples centre on the representation of erotic desire in order to make the queer connections more cogent, but the posture I describe has more comprehensive implications: the *Shéhérazade* persona's tactic of artful interruption, for instance, implies a fundamental aesthetic of teasing, whether or not sex is directly involved. Jonathan Dollimore has approached the work of Oscar Wilde from a similar angle. In an extremely helpful formulation, he identifies a queer aestheticist posture in terms that highlight its dissident force: 'In Wilde's transgressive aesthetic […] the survival strategies of subordination – subterfuge, lying, evasion – are aesthetically transvalued

---

[28] In her comprehensive study of the concept of irony, Linda Hutcheon plots a diagram of irony's various functions. A number of the aesthetic strategies I am concerned with here (ambiguity, teasing, indifference, distancing, self-protection, evasion, and subversion) are situated on her diagram. Her schema recognizes a multiplicity of strategies (with differing 'affective charges') while bringing them together within a single rhetorical family. See Linda Hutcheon, *Irony's Edge: The Theory and Politics of Irony* (London: Routledge, 1994), 44–56.

into weapons of attack, but ever working through irony, ambiguity, mimicry, and impersonation.'[29] In Ravel's case, any 'attack' on bourgeois conformity is generally not spelled out in terms as flamboyantly confrontational as in Wilde. It can be sensed rather in attitudes of indifference or subtle sardonic gestures – 'the mocking smile' that 'must sometimes stifle lyrical ardour'.[30]

Evasion in *Gaspard de la nuit* (1908)

For a further illustration I turn to Ravel's piano cycle *Gaspard de la nuit*,[31] where the prose poems by Aloysius Bertrand inspiring these pieces prefigure a decadent sensibility in their evocation of bizarre, dreamlike tableaux and morbid, neurotic emotions. The first piece, 'Ondine', is the only one with an overtly erotic scenario. A water spirit appears in the moonlight outside the window, singing of a magical realm beneath the lake. She addresses the narrator, pleading with him to marry her and descend to her underwater palace. When the man refuses, she cries a few tears, then bursts out laughing and vanishes in showers that trickle down the windowpanes. Once again we have a scene of thwarted desire, but this time the desire is directed at the narrator from outside himself, troubling his solitude. He chooses to resist Ondine's enticements, guarding his privacy, and keeping the windows closed.

In Ravel's pianistic setting, Ondine is personified as a voice – an importunate lyrical melody swathed in shimmering sonorities. Desire is figured through the sinuous arches of her melody as well as through the volatility of her watery medium. A caressing touch and an extremely supple technique are required to coax the piano to breathe and shiver, spout and cascade. Ravel's melding of vocal and water figuration results in a textural ambiguity whereby the central tune intermittently loses its status as a stable melodic entity amid the mercurial arpeggiation. The opening passage of the melody is like a human voice in its single line, lying mostly below the tremolo accompaniment. But suddenly, at bar 10, the voice-leading is broken (the implied E$\sharp$ does not appear); the melody is displaced above the accompaniment, then expanding into a pianistic 'voice' doubled at the octave (bar 14). The melodic phrase at bar 10 initiates a new registral strand, giving the impression (at least momentarily) of a new voice entering from a different direction. From now on the melody appears generally in octave doubling, dwindling to the original

[29] Jonathan Dollimore, *Sexual Dissidence: Augustine to Wilde, Freud to Foucault* (New York: Oxford University Press, 1991), 310.

[30] Vlado Perlemuter and Hélène Jourdan-Morhange, *Ravel d'après Ravel*, fifth edition (Lausanne: du Cervin, 1970), 8: 'Ravel expliqu[ait] à Vlado pourquoi le sourire narquois devait quelquefois juguler l'ardeur lyrique'.

[31] See Maurice Ravel, *Gaspard de la nuit*, Urtext edition ed. Roger Nichols (London: Edition Peters, 1991). Bar numbers in the text follow this edition, which does not count the opening half-bar.

song-plus-tremolo texture only at important structural moments (bars 32, 42, and 80). Several cadential phrases dissolve into spume with no stable melodic arrival (e.g., bars 29–31, 40–1, and the final bars). The developmental middle section (bars 42–61) expands upon the broken voice-leading of the opening, alternating between the primary soprano persona and a shadow voice erupting from the depths. In the piece's final moments, the voice and water elements dramatically dissociate. A mournful unaccompanied tune (voice alone; bar 84) gives way to biting dissonant arpeggios, causing the melody to disperse and vanish in the swirling texture. (Note the overlapping patterns of interruption in this crucial passage across bars 83–7: the temporary suspension of watery figuration; the D minor of the solo passage as an irrational disruption of the black-key harmonic field; the single enigmatic $G_\sharp$ inflection *within* the D minor solo.)

In sum, the Ondine voice is deceptive in its very substance. It is also ambiguous in its expression. This is brought home most palpably in the Janus-faced *dénouement*, where the weeping of the rejected supplicant turns instantly into the laughter of the haughty queen. But the seeds of this ambivalence can be found much earlier. For most of the piece (bar 16 through to the 'solo' at bar 84), the poetic scenario of unsuccessful seduction and unrequited love is well reflected in the abortive tonal progressions. Almost none of the numerous chords implying a dominant function resolve tonally. (The few that do resolve do so in passing; see, for example, bars 27–8.) Tonal expectations are mostly evaded by oblique moves to newly asserted key areas. (Thus across bars 16–22, $F_\sharp^7$ moves to $G_\sharp$ major; in bars 29–30, B^7 moves to $G_\sharp$ minor/major; in bars 55–6, A^7 moves to a G chord, followed by $C_\sharp$ octatonic; and so on.) A compounded feeling of frustration climaxes at bar 66, where the rhetorical arrival (a build to *fortissimo*) corresponds to a peak in harmonic tension. The copious release of kinetic energy at this point is unsupported by any tonal arrival. (A strongly implied $F_\sharp$ arrival is withheld until bar 74, its status as goal undermined by the C major interruption.) The prevailing gestures described so far are not ambivalent in representation; they clearly express thwarted desire. But the opening passage (bars 1–15) is a different matter. Here the underlying progression ($C_\sharp$–$A_\sharp^7$–$D_\sharp m$–$F_\sharp m$–$D_\sharp^{\varnothing 7}$–$C_\sharp$) follows a lucid tonal logic, moving into subdominant sonorities before returning to the Mixolydian-inflected tonic. The twinge of longing evoked by the half-diminished seventh chord (bars 11–12) is immediately folded back into $C_\sharp$ and the identical arching figures with which the melody began.[32] Thus the opening passage displays successful, even cyclical formal closure, as if the vocal persona is self-reliant

32 Contrast this treatment of the half-diminished seventh chord with its appearance during the first climactic passage (bar 70), where the prolonged $G_\sharp^{\varnothing 7}$, together with the registral highpoint, serves to intensify the sense of deferred, frustrated desire for resolution.

and has no need to search elsewhere for fulfilment. Expressive ambivalence then arises between the sovereign composure established during the opening and the naked desire revealed as the piece unfolds. When the Ondine voice eventually surrenders to a seeming resignation (with the D minor solo), the effect is somehow stagy and the ensuing laughter casts doubt on the sincerity of the previous emotions. Indeed, the laughing cadenza (bar 88) represents a second climax of physical release, as if Ondine takes the greatest pleasure in dismissing cruelly her mortal plaything.[33] As the turbulence subsides, it resolves tonally by way of the cadential progression (D$\sharp^{o7}$–C$\sharp$) from the opening, thus restoring the original aura of indifference.

Marguerite Long interprets the mournful solo as the expressive core of the piece, a moment of especially intimate revelation:

> The waves quieten for a moment, but only to enable the ever-loving Ondine to show her exquisite femininity for the last time in a profundity of solitude and silence. Then, in rustling dissonances, Ondine vanishes into the depths which hold her palace, to hide her vexation and her tears. The sudden and calm indifference of the waters conceals from sight and memory the so recent past as nothing else could.[34]

I hear it in exactly opposite terms, as a *pose* of naked vulnerability, theatricalized rather than sincere and immediately exposed as a ruse. In the mocking disappearance of the luscious Ondine voice, might we not detect a cynical authorial comment on the Romantic tendency toward personification, and the gullibility of the listener? The point about listening perspective raises another intriguing question regarding Ravel's rhetorical handling of the scene – namely, what has become of the poem's male persona? Bertrand's poem is grounded by the perspective of the narrator who resists seduction, but Ravel's piano offers no counterpart. Given the indeterminacy of textless music, there are several ways to understand this. One interpretation sees the narrator in his sheltering room as the true expressive subject of the poem, occupying the position of interiority which Ravel chooses to leave blank, or tuck out of sight. Another interpretation situates the *listener* as the one at the mercy of the troubling voice – only with no power to express resistance. But of course the music is open to more ambiguous paths of identification, with the listener (like the composer) free to imagine himself now as the vulnerable solitary, now the mocking siren, thus creating a satisfying 'closed circuit' between personas.

Siglind Bruhn has pointed out how Bertrand's poem deviates from previous tellings of the story (such as that by La Motte-Fouqué) in that there is 'no mention of Ondine's longing for a soul, and her need for [a man's] love to

---

[33] Compare with the imagery of ejaculation ('giboulées qui ruisselèrent blanches') at the poem's conclusion.

[34] Marguerite Long, *At the Piano with Ravel*, ed. Pierre Laumonier, trans. Olive Senior-Ellis (London: J. M. Dent, 1973), 90.

obtain it'.[35] This important alteration allows Ravel to refashion the archetypically Romantic Ondine into a modernist persona, indifferent to principles of inwardness. He creates a portrait of 'lyrical ardor' within a paradoxical framework by which the expressive intent is thoroughly ironized. Here the specific thematics of desire and the general aesthetics of musical expression are closely intertwined. We can see how a sceptical treatment of erotic subjectivity overlaps with a mistrust of expressive subjectivity in broader terms – that is, how modernist detachment may be motivated by queer evasiveness.

In 'Scarbo', the third piece from *Gaspard*, the scenario once again concerns a narrator whose solitude is threatened, this time by an imp who defies locked doors. Scarbo is a nastier creature from the spirit world, intruding into the inner sanctum, scratching at the narrator's bed curtains, tormenting him during the hours of sleep. Ravel's piano setting elaborates upon the imp's unpredictable, tricky nature, his ability to vanish and reappear at will. At times he erupts from hiding with a fanfare (bars 32, 110, and 386), causing violent startlement; at other times he lurks ominously, his victim waiting with jangling nerves (bars 1, 121, and 395). He spends much of the while dancing about, shifting craftily between waltz (bars 32, 65, and 314) and flamenco figurations (bars 52, 73, and 318).[36] The piece is not about eroticism, but rather about anxiety and suspense; nevertheless, the element of teasing is very much to the fore. In a sense, Ravel has taken the idea of the mocking gesture from the conclusion of 'Ondine' and given it an extended treatment.[37] Overall, the piece proceeds by way of many feints and reversals towards two climaxes of Mephistophelean frenzy (bars 366 and 563). A curious thing happens soon after the first climax. The tumult settles down to a recapitulation of the jangled-nerve gesture (bar 395ff.). Instead of recommencing with frenetic activity, however, the figuration gradually calms and liquefies until the entrance of the repeated-note theme from the flamenco, now in a slow dreamy haze. For the next eighteen bars (bars 430–47) an entirely different sound world is evoked – strongly recalling 'Ondine' in its tempo, melodic doublings, and

[35] Siglind Bruhn, *Images and Ideas in Modern French Piano Music: The Extra-Musical Subtext in Piano Works by Ravel, Debussy, and Messiaen* (Stuyvesant, NY: Pendragon Press, 1997), 141, 181; quotation from 185.

[36] Roy Howat, 'Ravel and the Piano', in Deborah Mawer (ed.), *The Cambridge Companion to Ravel* (Cambridge University Press, 2000), 71–96: 87.

[37] A subtle but specific connection between all three pieces centres on the harmonic colour of the half-diminished seventh chord. In 'Ondine', a $G\sharp^{\o7}$ sonority (bar 70) appears as a crowning symbol of thwarted desire. In 'Le Gibet', an $F^{\o7}$ chord (bar 12) – the referential 'Tristan chord' at its original pitch (later transposed in bars 17 and 35) – epitomizes the decadent, perverse sensory fixations of the poem. In 'Scarbo', both of these sonorities materialize in the midst of the opening flamenco: $G\sharp^{\o7}$ at bar 65, the Tristan chord (spelled as $E\sharp^{\o7}$) at bar 92. Here the Tristan chord appears as a sharp dramatic accent at the peak of a crescendo, but its tensions are immediately and playfully resolved, as if to say that the emotional ordeals it symbolizes will have no place in this antic context.

shimmering sonorities – as if the vexatious Scarbo has assumed the form of the seductive Ondine. On the surface, this comes across as another prank. But introducing eroticism (however ironically) into the piece brings an added psychological layer to its paranoid, insomniac fantasy. Furthermore, this shape-shifting passage calls attention to an ambiguity of interlocution underlying the entire piece. That is to say, the Scarbo persona's attitude towards the listener/narrator is difficult to pin down: harassment shades into horseplay shades into flirting and teasing. The elusive nature of the persona extends to the tone and manner of its address.

Comparison with *Jeux d'eau* (1901)

The evasive strategies I have been describing can be readily identified in works without appended poems – even in works not concerned directly with erotic desire. The earlier piano piece *Jeux d'eau*,[38] also composed of water imagery, makes for an intriguing comparison with 'Ondine'. As with the later piece, Ravel provides a modernist update of a Romantic model (specifically, the Lisztian travel sketch *Les Jeux d'eau à la Villa d'Este*). In *Jeux d'eau* the convention of programmatic water music provides a pretext for an essay in aesthetic objectification. Ravel avoids any melody modelled on the voice, opting for complex textures of interlocking figuration. The undulating arpeggios of the first theme are far from unpredictable; instead they swell and scintillate with the precision of a mechanism. A second theme (bar 19), gently percussive rather than lyrical, is set amid a ringing cloud of bell-like sonorities, while the third theme (bar 29; 'a Tempo'), still percussive, assembles rocking figures into a layered texture. The build-up to the climax (across bars 38–49) proceeds in stylized increments of mounting tension. At its recapitulation (bar 62; 'Ier Mouvt'), however, the first theme undergoes a crisis: motivated by harmonic conflict, the musical texture dissolves into random spray, then erupts skyward into harsh cascades (bars 67–72, prefiguring the cadenza from 'Ondine'). Nevertheless the 'randomness' is stylized into sequential progressions and highly regular rhythmic motion. The effect is paradoxical – a picture of disruption in which the placement of every note is carefully arranged. Even through the crisis, the reigning tone is one of impeccable composure.[39]

---

[38] See Maurice Ravel, *Jeux d'eau* (Paris: E. Demets/Editions Max Eschig, 1902).

[39] Compare with Vladimir Jankélévitch's discussion of apparent randomness or disorder as an ironic façade in Ravel: 'Lack of precision here is only one more type of precision, a refinement of finesse, just as studied negligence is only a form of supreme elegance [...] Someone who [...] appears to despise details when they have been arranged with precision [...] these are traits revealing a clever man, a teasing, mischievous man [*l'espiègle, le malicieux*] who is as cunning as Ulysses': Jankélévitch, *Ravel*, trans. Margaret

The pulsing jets eventually coalesce into a statement of the third theme (bars 73–7; 'Un peu plus lent qu'au début'). These five bars stand out as anomalous in respect to the surrounding high gloss. Initially, the theme slows to a caesura as if the fountain mechanism is winding down. Then it resumes (bar 75; 'Lent') – but for the first time in the piece, Ravel marks the passage *très expressif*, as if belatedly acknowledging a subjective origin for the musical gesture (as if 'longing for a soul'). The contrast between the prevailing impassive tone and this very expressive utterance casts the Romantic rhetoric into exaggerated relief. Yet the moment is brief, curtailed by the intrusion of a single wry dissonance ($C\natural/B\sharp$ prolonged over $F\sharp^9$, at bars 76–7). The salient tritone is motivically cogent, deriving from the cadential element of the third theme (see bars 32–4), and embodying the C/F$\sharp$ clash from the cadenza just heard. Nevertheless Ravel contrives to emphasize and isolate the C [B$\sharp$] as a note out of place (bar 77), a 'mocking smile' that ironizes the foregoing lyrical passage. As the dissonance moves to resolution, the expressive persona is swept away like a phantom by the entry of the second theme (bar 78), restoring composure in an exquisite, shimmering, crystalline expanse. We may note the remarkable analogy to the *dénouement* of 'Ondine': a hyper-expressive phrase, flawed by a single enigmatic pitch, gives a shrug and returns to indifference. While the proportions of sentiment versus detachment are different in *Jeux d'eau*, there is the same travesty of expressive ardour and the same symbolically charged evacuation of a subjective persona.[40]

Desire in *Valses nobles et sentimentales* (1911)

With my final example, I return more specifically to the thematics of desire, as dramatized in a dance suite. In his piano cycle *Valses nobles et sentimentales*, modelled on the waltz collections of Schubert, Ravel invokes the erotic connotations of this dance, with its closed position and gliding rotation, as well as the imagined context of fashionable ballroom society. Yet Ravel's waltzes are notorious for their acerbic tone; one might even say that the whole collection is governed by the metaphor of the mocking smile. The comments of Vladimir Jankélévitch are pertinent to the issues at hand:

> The waltz, which is the most passionate and expressive of all dance forms, composes in this instance valuable [*précieuses*] figures for divertissement; with Liszt and Chopin the waltz was laden with all the ardours of the soul, but with Ravel the tender waltz reveals sharp harmonies, all prickly with stalactites and fine needles.[41]

Crosland (Westport, CT: Greenwood Press, 1976), 131.

[40] Compare with Puri's suggestive reference to the Baudelairean concept of the 'vaporization of the self': Puri, 'Dandy, Interrupted', 347.

[41] Jankélévitch, *Ravel*, 42.

By choosing such a dissonant harmonic idiom, the composer introduces a subliminal element of aggression into the dynamic of partnership; thus the stinging offbeat clusters at the opening of the piece have the feel of love bites.

In his own, well-known analysis of the middle section of the seventh waltz, Ravel illustrates how his spiked harmonic language can be understood in terms of 'unresolved appoggiaturas'.[42] What may strike us as irrational imported dissonance, or conflict between harmonic planes, actually has a logical basis in the underlying voice-leading. Ravel makes liberal use of chromatic neighbour notes while displacing the syntax to emphasize or prolong their dissonant, active-tone function and to withhold their resolution. The basic technique yields a dazzling array of different effects. In the opening bars of the first waltz, multiple dissonances bunch into accents, which are given sharp relief by vaulting into an exposed register. In bars 25–32, harsh cross-relations (B/A♯ and A/G♯ between the hands, D/D♯ in the left hand) are prolonged gratuitously for eight bars before resolving at the last minute. (This is an effect similar to the passage analysed by Ravel, where the right hand suggests E major for ten bars over F major in the left.) In the cadential passage leading to the recapitulation (bars 57–60), the contrary-motion passing notes are handled perversely so as to include as many cross-relations as possible. Later, the lumbering sequential appoggiaturas of the sixth waltz suggest a clumsy physicality. Often the syntactic displacements seem to toy with the listener's expectation of resolution, as in the main theme of the seventh waltz (bars 19ff. after the introduction), whose piquant chords hang enigmatically in the air. Sometimes they never do resolve properly: for example, the A♭ minor chord, over D, in the first waltz (bar 24); and the rogue A♯ (the 11th) added to the E^{13} chord at the main cadence of the seventh waltz (see bars 64 and 156). Ravel's mischievous, negligent handling of voice-leading syntax imbues the very musical fabric with ironic desire.

On a larger structural level, there is an alternation of 'noble' and 'sentimental' statements. The dissonant idiom features in both, but takes on a distinct emotional rhetoric depending on the context. In the languid passages, irresolution tends to suggest an expressive intensity or sincerity of some kind: the fifth waltz ('dans un sentiment intime') is a good example of this. Meanwhile, the second waltz ('avec une expression intense') alternates calmer modal phrases with outbursts of anguished dissonant chords. On the other hand, in the brilliant passages, displaced resolution suggests the capricious or derisive manipulation of emotions. In its rhythmic fluctuation between the two attitudes, *Valses nobles* creates a structure of teasing ambivalence, inviting the listener repeatedly to engage in sentiment, and then airily dismissing it. Such a game of invitation and rejection underscores the theme

---

[42] Orenstein (ed.), *A Ravel Reader*, 519–20.

of romantic courtship. But it also plays a signifying role in relation to the social aspect of the dance. That is, the sentimental passages evoke a context of intimacy or interiority, while the brilliant passages evoke public display. In this sense the large-scale alternation enacts a dramatic movement between an exterior and interior *mise-en-scène*. In accordance with its bifocal rhetoric, the work has two endings: the extrovert seventh waltz, and the languid, impressionistic eighth (labelled 'Epilogue'). If the first ending presents a climax of brilliant display, the second – in its static processes, freely associative form, and indulgence in distorted reminiscence – presents a climax of interiority. In this final passage, the active or emotive attitudes of the previous waltzes are succeeded by a retreat into pleasant reverie. I see this epilogue as another glamorization of solitude, in which the dance is completely removed from the social sphere and the fulfilment of aesthetic-erotic desire is achieved in a reflective circuit of self-communion.

In its aimless replaying of musical flourishes and its slackening of waltz gestures into a stylized, undanceable slow motion, the Epilogue epitomizes the dandyist sentiments expressed in the work's epigraph: '… the delightful and always novel pleasure of a useless occupation'.[43] This throwaway manifesto passes over bourgeois ideals of productiveness for a more blithe doctrine: dance and art as opportunities for mere diversion, stylish *divertissement* rather than formal belabouring, pleasure for its own sake. Here too aesthetic and erotic discourses meet. The elevation of style-consciousness and non-productive pleasure may also be read as a statement of sexual nonconformity on the part of the bachelor wishing to turn imputations of uselessness, sterility, and narcissism on their heads.

The pose of indifference

Much of what I have been exploring in this chapter relates to Ravel's particular brand of aestheticism, and what happens to the representation of desire in such a context. Aestheticism involves a displaced relationship to the object of desire. Arguably the most influential articulation of aestheticism's principles as a theory of art and life is found in Walter Pater's collection of essays *The Renaissance* (1873). The disinterestedness of aesthetics, as described by Immanuel Kant, means that appreciation demands the experience of sensual pleasure while disregarding the actual object that causes such pleasure.[44]

---

[43] '…le plaisir délicieux et toujours nouveau d'une occupation inutile', quoted from Henri de Régnier's novel *Les Rencontres de Monsieur de Bréot* (Paris: Mercure de France, 1904).

[44] Dennis Denisoff, 'Aestheticism', in George E. Haggerty (ed.), *Gay Histories and Cultures* (New York: Garland Publishing, 2000), 15.

An aestheticist appreciation removes the beautiful object from the world of social interaction. It embraces sensual pleasure for its own sake while adopting an evasive, ambiguous attitude toward the origin of pleasure. From one perspective it can serve as a protective manoeuvre (a 'survival strategy of subordination', in Dollimore's words),[45] allowing one to indulge in questionable forms of desire while disavowing desire itself. From another perspective it represents an oppositional pose, by refusing to be caught in prevailing systems of moral value. According to Ross Chambers, irony becomes a tactic of resistance when it 'produces the subject as elusive [and] indefinable'; thus it may be argued that a queer pose of evasion 'derives its power as opposition from [its] refusal to be pinned down' by any schemes of sexual determination.[46] A queer pose of indifference has the potential to cast doubt upon the universal validity of dominant narratives of desire.

In a portrayal of the lonely 'invert' who resorts to subterfuge in the hopes of meeting someone like-minded, Marcel Proust describes the pose of indifference in its protective aspect:

> Then the solitary [...] loiters upon the beach, a sterile jellyfish that must perish upon the sand, or else he stands idly on the platform until his train leaves, casting over the crowd of passengers a look that will seem indifferent, disdainful or abstracted to those of another race, but [that] would not deceive the connoisseur [...] of a pleasure too singular, too hard to place, which is offered him, the confrère with whom our specialist could converse in the strange tongue.[47]

In the pose as characterized by Proust, the language of glance and gesture is deliberately ambiguous, broadcasting an apparent disregard for desire while signifying desire to the trained eye. Richard Dellamora identifies the same rhetoric of 'doubled discourse' (that is, a merging of general and specialized meanings) in the works of Pater: he reads the late story entitled 'Apollo in Picardy' (1893) as a coded cautionary tale of a medieval prior 'who self-consciously quells his sexual and emotional attraction to other males'.[48] A disturbing erotic influence is exerted by Apollyon, a herdsman and harpist, who at one point plays music for the labourers as they construct a monastic building. For my purposes, the significance of this story lies in the manner in which Pater himself calls attention to diverging paths of artistic interpretation. The muse-figure Apollyon is memorialized in a sculpture at the top of the building, a portrait of 'an idle singer' with a harp – 'King David, or an angel? guesses the careless tourist'.[49] As Dellamora argues, '"the careless tourist" who misidentifies the sculpture also misses its erotic expressiveness.

---

[45] Dollimore, *Sexual Dissidence*, 310.
[46] Ross Chambers, *Room for Maneuver: Reading (the) Oppositional (in) Narrative* (University of Chicago Press,

1991), 55. His argument at this point is not specifically queer-inflected.
[47] Proust, *In Search of Lost Time*, vol. IV, 30–1.
[48] Dellamora, *Masculine Desire*, 219, 186.
[49] Pater, quoted in *ibid.*, 221.

He (or she) is a figure of the uncomprehending bourgeois in his/her approach to culture.'[50] In contrast, Pater refers to another kind of onlooker, 'the expert', whose knowledge is ostensibly art-historical, but whose aesthetic expertise also stands for an awareness of the homoerotic impulses animating classical antiquity.[51]

In Ravel's case too, the 'careless tourist' might miss the productive significance of queer subjectivity for his musical representation. But for listeners attuned to its significance, Ravel's exploration of ambiguous desire is oppositional in its dramatization of problematic personas which refuse to be pinned down. His exploration of a posture of indifference offers a sardonic commentary upon the cultural importance invested in well-worn scenarios of seduction, partnership, and transcendent desire.

---

[50]   *Ibid.*, 221.
[51]   Pater, quoted in *ibid.*, 220–1.

5 Crossing borders I: the historical context for Ravel's North American tour

Nicholas Gebhardt

'Take America as it is: the country to make money and nothing else.'

Bernard Ullman[1]

'Maurice Ravel is in America', declared the *Musical Courier* in January 1928. 'That is a fact of importance so great that for the moment it seems to overshadow other things. To have with us a musician who for the past generation has been recognised as one of the greatest composers in the world is a rare privilege that no music lover is likely to underrate.'[2] And nor did they. From 4 January, the day he stepped off the ship in New York, until his departure four months later on 21 April, Ravel appeared in over thirty concerts, attended countless social engagements, and was the subject of a sustained critical debate about the merits of his music and his capacities as a performer.[3] He received standing ovations, parties were organized in his honour, and the music press constantly sought his views on everything from the future of modern music to American orchestras. Daily performances were punctuated by rehearsals, overnight train journeys, and after-hours entertainment in clubs and theatres, often to the point of exhaustion. 'If I return to Europe alive,' he wrote to his brother, Edouard, after the first few days in New York, 'it will prove that I am long-lived!'[4]

Although Ravel was surprised at the attention lavished on him, his experiences were not unusual. In a review of Ravel's New York debut, the critic Leonard Liebling reported: 'These are exciting days in our musical circles, what with the comings and goings of the famous European conductors and the naively disinterested visits of the distinguished composers from across the seas.'[5] Musicians were lured by the large sums of money on offer, the

[1] Letter from Bernard Ullman to Hans von Bülow (18 April 1876), quoted in R. Allen Lott, '"A Continuous Trance": Hans von Bülow's Tour of America', *Journal of Musicology*, 12/4 (1994), 529–49: 542.

[2] [Uncredited], 'Ravel Predicts a Return to Melody', *Musical Courier* (26 January 1928), 14.

[3] For details, see the 'Appendix: Itinerary for Ravel's tour' at the end of this chapter.

[4] Letter from Ravel to his brother Edouard Ravel, Boston (13 January 1928), quoted in Arbie Orenstein, *Ravel: Man and Musician* (New York: Dover Publications, 1991), 95.

[5] Leonard Liebling, 'Ravel is Hailed at Concert', *New York American* (16 January 1928), quoted in Norman Vance Dunfee, 'Maurice Ravel in America – 1928' (DMA dissertation, University of Missouri – Kansas City, 1980), 115.

celebrity status they often enjoyed, the high standards of musicianship they encountered, and the enthusiastic response of both critics and audiences, so that extended tours of North America by European artists were not only commonplace but hugely significant events, part of a much larger cultural revolution that had been under way since the nineteenth century. This revolution involved two related transformations: firstly, the emergence of the corporate music industry or show business and, secondly, the reconstruction of artistic value and practice in terms of mass forms of entertainment. The purpose of this chapter is to examine Ravel's tour in terms of these transformations and to consider its significance in clarifying the meaning(s) of musical modernism.

American audiences had been familiar with Ravel's music for at least a decade and, in the year before he toured, two major profiles were published in anticipation of his arrival. In the *Musical Quarterly*, Edward Burlingame Hill set out to place Ravel's development as a composer within the wider context of French and, more broadly, European music; in the *New York Times* Olin Downes discussed the composer's recent works.[6] Both authors highlighted the composer's distinctive Gallic qualities, focusing on his elegance and poise, as well as his compulsive attention to detail. They also agreed that in every aspect of his existence, from his hillside 'retreat' in Montfort-l'Amaury to his compositional technique, Ravel embodied the tension between an aristocratic past and a democratic present that had become the preoccupation of European artists following the upheavals of World War I. For these critics, at least, Ravel's 'genius' was in his capacity to reconcile this tension, to 'bring about a fusion of quasi-archaic sentiment and contemporary means'.[7]

The issue was put even more forcefully by Downes in an article published during the course of Ravel's tour: 'Is this art [of Ravel's] the fruition, or the last vestige, or the mere mirage of a defeated and vanishing culture?'[8] His answer involved trying to clarify the composer's historical position in terms that were consistent with the ways in which American audiences were coming to understand the claims of modernism.[9] 'A characteristic product of ideas refined and re-refined by centuries of an aristocratic culture,' he wrote, '[Ravel] has been watching with coolness and curiosity the formation of a new and cruder society and its gropings in the field of expressive culture. He

[6] Edward Burlingame Hill, 'Maurice Ravel', *Musical Quarterly*, 13/1 (1927), 130–46: 135; and Olin Downes, 'Maurice Ravel, Man and Musician', *New York Times* (7 August 1927), X6.

[7] Hill, 'Maurice Ravel', 136.

[8] Olin Downes, 'Mr Ravel Returns', *New York Times* (26 February 1928), section 8, 8.

[9] Joseph Horowitz points out that 'Downes's ideal critic was one who so identified with an audience as to disappear into it.' See Joseph Horowitz, *Understanding Toscanini: A Social History of American Concert Life* (Berkeley: University of California Press, 1987), 10.

has surely felt the pressures, the potencies and the swirling forces of a young, impulsive people.'[10]

An awareness of how these pressures, potencies, and 'swirling forces' were affecting music can certainly help to explain Ravel's initial reticence about performing in North America. His friend the pianist and promoter E. Robert Schmitz (1889–1949), had first approached the composer about a tour in 1922 and continued to do so regularly, but Ravel always turned him down: 'I am not a pianist,' he would say. 'I do not care to be exhibited like a circus.'[11] Yet in spite of his reluctance, Ravel was also conscious that musical developments taking place in the United States (and the Americas more broadly) had become increasingly influential amongst European artists. For Ravel this centred above all on the problem of identifying new compositional materials adequate to and expressive of what he called 'a world brotherhood of art'.[12] In 1926, Schmitz tried again, offering a guarantee of $10,000 for three months, and Ravel was finally persuaded to sign a contract.

Schmitz's organization, Pro Musica, was just one of many new music societies that were formed during the 1920s to support tours of North America by the leading European modernists. Above all else, these societies aimed to provide a sympathetic context within which the music of modern or avant-garde composers such as Stravinsky, Schoenberg, Debussy, Varèse, Milhaud, Bartók, Ives, Copland, and many others could be heard and, more important, understood. While the International Composers' Guild (founded by Varèse and Carlos Salzedo) and the League of Composers remain the best known and documented of these societies, Pro Musica was arguably more significant, as much for the scale of its operation as for what Ronald Wiecki terms its 'alternative vision of musical possibilities'.[13]

Schmitz conceived of Pro Musica as a means by which people throughout the United States (and not just in the major artistic centres, such as New York or Boston) would have the 'opportunity of contact with the leading musicians of all the countries including America'.[14] By 1928, the organization had a national membership of over 3,500, divided into fifteen chapters, and had already sponsored tours by Alfredo Casella (1925), Prokofiev (1926), the Pro Arte Quartet (1926), Milhaud (1926–7), Alexandre Tansman (1927), and Bartók (1927–8).[15] Ravel's tour, however, proved to be Pro Musica's greatest achievement. Not only did the concert series raise the profile of the organization through extensive press coverage, but many of its chapters reported

---

[10] Downes, 'Mr Ravel Returns'.
[11] Ravel in Madeleine Goss, *Bolero: A Life of Maurice Ravel* (New York: Tudor Publishing Company, 1940), 217.
[12] Downes, 'Mr Ravel Returns'.
[13] Ronald V. Wiecki, 'A Chronicle of Pro Musica in the United States (1920–1944): With a Biographical Sketch of Its Founder, E. Robert Schmitz' (PhD dissertation, University of Wisconsin – Madison, 1992), 15.
[14] Letter from E. Robert Schmitz to Geneve Lichtenwalter (15 September 1923), quoted in Wiecki, 'A Chronicle of Pro Musica', 21.
[15] *Ibid.*, 231–343.

record box office receipts and substantial increases in membership. Such was Ravel's international reputation by this time that many of those new members joined just to hear him perform, while in Detroit a Pro Musica chapter was set up specifically so that Ravel could appear in that city.[16]

Ravel's reception in the United States, therefore, was inseparable from the growing influence and success of Pro Musica and the ideas and principles it espoused. These had their origins in Schmitz's attempt to found a type of International of contemporary music that would counteract the commercial exploitation of artists and reconstitute the relationship between composer, performer, and audience on more egalitarian and authentic terms. This was by no means a simple task. As Joseph Horowitz argues, the development of classical music in nineteenth-century America was by and large a history of the emergence of a 'culture of performance' centred upon a canon of 'masterworks' and celebrity interpreters.[17] Schmitz's determination to assert the 'truth' of the music against an ethos of 'performativity' – the art historian Michael Fried calls it 'theatricality' – set Pro Musica at odds with this development.[18] 'There is a general tendency,' Schmitz told a journalist in 1921, 'of elevating the soloist at the expense of the music, and considering him in the light of the autocrat of the music world.' Ravel's tour was thus an integral part of Schmitz's plans to reverse this tendency and restore to art a 'common purpose, a democracy of spiritual freedom and equality'.[19]

Orpheus in the New World

I will return to critical debate about Ravel's music and performances below. Before doing so, however, I want to examine the sources of Schmitz's dissatisfaction with the new and difficult conditions faced by modern artists. This necessarily involves a rather lengthy discussion of the American tours undertaken by a number of key figures in European music during the nineteenth century. In the final section of this chapter, I intend to demonstrate that through their mutual association Schmitz and Ravel both confronted and, in different ways, tried to resolve the problem of artistic independence (Ravel calls it 'individuality') that had preoccupied their predecessors as much as it was of concern to their contemporaries. This problem took on heightened significance in the United States for several reasons. Firstly, there was no legacy

---

[16] *Ibid.*, 205, 547. Pro Musica Detroit is the only chapter of the organization that still exists.
[17] Joseph Horowitz, *Classical Music in America* (New York: W.W. Norton & Co., 2005), xiii–xv.

[18] Michael Fried, *Theatricality and Absorption: Painting and Beholder in the Age of Diderot* (University of Chicago Press, 1988).
[19] Rosalie Housman, 'An Interview with E. Robert Schmitz', quoted in Wiecki, 'A Chronicle of Pro Musica', 111.

of aristocratic or court control of artistic life from which musicians sought their independence; secondly, it was a principle that the state should not interfere in the lives of its citizens by providing subsidies for artistic activity; and, thirdly, the primary contexts for music were commercial, which meant that the constraints on artists and the possibilities for success were of an entirely different order to the ones they were used to in European societies.

The assimilation of the 'American Dream' into European culture has a long history which extends to well before the first settlements were established in the New World. It reached its greatest intensity in 1776 with the American Revolution, which became the primary example of and a focal point for the Enlightenment belief in the regeneration of humanity, only to be overtaken in 1789 by the revolutionary dream of the French. Because the French Revolution was above all a confrontation with Europe's past, the newly formed United States was quickly pushed to the periphery once again, its prosperity idealized as a fortuitous combination of geography and industry. It did not take long, however, before the succession of revolutions and counter-revolutions that swept European societies in the wake of the French experiment with democracy created renewed interest in the idea of America as a promised land in which humanity was to be reborn and the individual remade (and, thus, self-made).

This was certainly a view common to the millions of Europeans who made the long journey across the Atlantic throughout the nineteenth century, whether by desire or necessity, in search of a better life or, at the very least, the new opportunities which seemed to exist there. Professional musicians were no more exempt from this dream than anyone else, and by the 1860s it had become common to refer to the United States as the 'El Dorado of the musical world'.[20] The well-publicized tours made by virtuosos such as Henri Vieuxtemps (1820–81), Jenny Lind (1820–87), and Sigismond Thalberg (1812–71), as well as the regular visits by composers, bandleaders, conductors, and travelling opera troupes, served merely to confirm for European artists just how great the possibilities were.

While success in Paris, London or Vienna made the names and consolidated the reputations of the great virtuosos throughout Europe, it was the American tour that made them their fortune.[21] As Paderewski wrote of his first trip to the United States in 1891, 'America, then as now, was a "promised

[20] Katherine K. Preston, *Opera on the Road: Traveling Opera Troupes in the United States, 1825–1860* (Urbana: University of Illinois Press, 1993), 142.
[21] In the 1840s, Heinrich Heine wrote that, 'The piano virtuosos come to Paris every winter like swarms of locusts, less to gain money than to make a name for themselves here, which will help them all the more to a rich pecuniary harvest in other countries. Paris serves them as a kind of billboard on which their fame may be read in enormous letters.' Heinrich Heine quoted by Arthur Loesser, *Men, Women and Pianos: A Social History* (New York: Dover Publications, 1954, reprinted 1990), 376.

land" to all European artists, a land of fantastic and fabulous legend, with money and appreciation flowing out to meet the artist from the great and lively and generous American public.'[22] Even Eduard Hanslick was moved to comment that 'America was truly the promised land, if not of music, at least of the musician.'[23]

Because many of the touring virtuosos were composers as well or claimed close contact with the leading composers of the European concert hall and operatic traditions, they provided American artists and audiences with a direct means of incorporating themselves into those traditions. The continuous appearance of virtuoso performers also convinced American musicians of the importance of developing artistic institutions that were sufficiently durable and audiences that were sufficiently knowledgeable about the classical tradition to meet the demands of these artists. Louis Moreau Gottschalk explained this process in the 1860s:

> I was the *first* American pianist, not by my artistic worth, but in chronological order. Before me, there were no piano concerts except in peculiar cases – that is to say, when a very great name arriving from Europe placed itself by its celebrity before the public, which, willing or unwilling, through curiosity and fashion rather than from taste, made it a duty to go and see the lion. Now piano concerts are chronic.[24]

The pianist Henri Henze's tour in 1846 did more than any other to establish the precedents for European musicians' participation in the emergence of a mass musical culture in the United States, in which the virtuoso recital increasingly became the most visible and important element. This was mostly due to the efforts of a young promoter, Bernard Ullman, who offered to take on the management of Henze's tour believing that 'to plan concerts well in America one must possess imagination, a sense of what is fitting, a knowledge of the human heart, and a grasp of strategy'.[25] What this meant above all was carefully organized travel plans, advance publicity, and wide coverage in the press, generally obtained by coming up with 'bizarre, impossible things' which would excite 'the interest of potential concert-goers'.[26] The result of Ullman's new conception of artistic management was that Henze gave over ninety-eight performances in forty-two cities in his first season, far more than any other comparable figure at the time. Already, then, we can see how Schmitz's Pro Musica aimed to modify the demands placed upon artists by entrepreneurs such as Ullman, yet without sacrificing the financial rewards

[22] Ignace Jan Paderewski and Mary Lawton, *The Paderewski Memoirs* (London: Collins, 1939), 197.

[23] Eduard Hanslick, quoted in John H. Mueller, *The American Symphony Orchestra* (London: John Calder, 1958), 22.

[24] Louis Moreau Gottschalk, *Notes of a Pianist* (New York: Da Capo, 1979), 239.

[25] Henri Henze, quoted in R. Allen Lott, 'Bernard Ullman: Nineteenth-century Impresario', in Richard Crawford, R. Allen Lott, and Carol J. Oja (eds.), *A Celebration of American Music*: *Words and Music in Honor of H. Wiley Hitchcock* (Ann Arbor: University of Michigan Press, 1990), 174–91: 176.

[26] Henze, quoted in Lott, 'Bernard Ullman', 176.

available to them. Compared with Henze's intensive schedule, the structure of Ravel's tour opened up a space for critical engagement between the artist, the audience, and performers that had all but disappeared in the final decades of the nineteenth century.

It was Thalberg's tour in 1856–7, however, which consolidated Ullman's ideas of artistic management along with his reputation, both in the United States and in Europe: so much so in fact that the journalist John Sullivan Dwight wrote in one of his editorials of 'Ullman the indefatigable, who flies back and forth over the Atlantic like a shuttle, weaving star after star of European theatre and concert notoriety into the great American web of Art and – speculation'.[27] Rather than wait for European performers to arrive in the United States, Ullman and several other managers began travelling to Europe to sign contracts with recognized celebrities and search for new ones. This was the context for the arranging of Thalberg's tour, in the course of which the famous pianist performed over 340 concerts in more than seventy-five North American cities. Indeed, so carefully planned were his appearances that the *New York Dispatch* duly noted

> It were folly to deny the management of [Thalberg's] business affairs, the arrangement of his concerts and matinees, the quickness of his movements, the combination of attraction, the selection of hours and places for performances, the economy of time, are all more perfect, more closely calculated, and more energetically carried out, than was ever any similar undertaking in this or any other country.[28]

What such an undertaking required was a detailed knowledge of rail timetables, concert venues, hotels, all of which Ullman combined into a relentless schedule that kept performers continuously on the move and on the stage, six days a week, and sometimes even twice a day. Perhaps his most important innovation, though, was his use of the press, of which he had intimate knowledge.[29] Early on he had decided that 'the newspaper was the key to artistic success', pursuing publicity of any kind so long as it attracted an audience, and thereby gained further publicity for the artists he managed as well as for the management of artists in this way.[30] To this end he regularly gave away free tickets on the principle that crowds attract crowds; he encouraged his performers to give free concerts for school children and got the press to report on them favourably; he devised unusual stage settings for his performers; and he was the first to make agreements with new American piano manufacturers

---

[27] Dwight, quoted in *ibid.*, 174.
[28] Quoted in *ibid.*, 177–8.
[29] As was the case with many of the performing arts entrepreneurs, Ullman had had experience in newspapers before becoming a manager. Cosima Wagner recalled Ullman giving a lecture in Europe

[30] on 'how to achieve an understanding with the press': quoted in *ibid.*, 185.
[30] Henze, quoted in *ibid.*, 183. Lott also mentions that the motto 'scandal is the system and secret of all management in the United States' was attributed to Ullman by his business associate Max Maretzek, 183.

such as the Chickering Piano Company of Boston in exchange for their support of his tours.

The American tours of Anton Rubinstein and Hans von Bülow

All of this meant that when the fiery Anton Rubinstein (1829–94) landed in New York in 1872 – because of the American Civil War he was the first major European performer to do so since Thalberg in 1858 – the ground was well prepared for him to turn the public recital into the foremost mass cultural event for visiting European artists and to redefine the meaning of virtuosity. Rubinstein fused an overtly passionate approach to the piano, a volatile or 'Romantic' temperament, and a conception of the piano which emphasized its orchestral rather than lyrical qualities (and thus positioned it as a rival to the symphony orchestras, which were then becoming popular) into a single vision of the artist as interpreter of, rather than merely a medium for, the composer's ideas. So successful was he in this and so large were the box office receipts for his concerts that he set a new standard for what touring artists might expect and what their audiences demanded from them. According to Robert Grau's account:

> [Rubinstein] opened at Steinway Hall in September, 1872, to an audience which represented at the box office $1,700, at that time regarded as something phenomenal [...] As an illustration of the public desire for classical music as interpreted by these artists, it is recorded that the largest results of the entire tour were at a Monday matinee recital, when $3,100 was taken in at the box office.[31]

Over the two years he was in the United States, Rubinstein performed 215 concerts (and frequently more than six concerts a week), and became renowned for his 'compelling power and sweep, a zeal for expression and communication, such as Americans had not yet experienced'.[32] His originality lay in featuring, to the exclusion of all else, a canon of piano works – those by Beethoven, Chopin, and Schumann above all else.

  Although critics were divided on Rubinstein's musical choices, everywhere he went he was accorded the cult status he felt a great *interpretative* artist deserved and which great music *interpreted* by such an artist required of its listeners. Aside from the lively critical debate that emerged regarding his controversial style and choice of repertoire, in which the great pianist himself was an active participant, the other significant legacy of the tour was a reflection on his experiences which he published in an autobiography a decade later.[33]

---

[31] Robert Grau, *The Business Man in the Amusement World* (New York: Broadway Publishing Company, 1910), 16.

[32] Loesser, *Men, Women and Pianos*, 515.
[33] Anton Rubinstein, *Autobiography*, trans. A. Delano (London: S. Low, 1890).

Many of the European artists who visited the United States left some record of their journey, in which they invariably reflected on what they felt was happening to music and to musicians once they arrived in the New World. The theme that dominates these accounts is their preoccupation with the problem of artistic autonomy. Reflecting on the demands of continuous performance, Rubinstein was quite explicit about its effects: 'Under these conditions there is no chance for art – one grows into an automaton, simply performing mechanical work […] It was so tedious that I began to despise myself and my art.'[34] Echoing longstanding concerns that musicians had rendered themselves subservient to mere entertainment, Rubinstein referred to the 'slavery' he endured and commented frequently on the fact that his schedule allowed no time for rehearsing new pieces.

This theme was to emerge even more strongly with Hans von Bülow (1830–94), Rubinstein's major rival for the title 'Greatest Pianist in Europe,' who arrived in the United States in 1876, a year after the Russian had departed. Managed by Ullman and contracted for an equally demanding performance schedule, Bülow toured for eight months, played 139 concerts in thirty-nine American cities and, like Rubinstein, frequently performed six nights a week (even though he was contracted for no more than five.)[35]

Whereas Rubinstein was preoccupied with perfecting and defending his conception of interpretation as it took shape through the idea of musical 'masterworks', and in proving that the pressures of continuous performance prevented the full realization of such a concept, for Bülow something more was at stake. Although during his initial negotiations with Ullman, the pianist admitted that he did not have 'the talent to grab, to stir up the masses' as had Rubinstein, he was far more open to the possibility of artistic self-transformation.[36] The idea appears most forcefully at the beginning of his tour, in a letter he wrote to his mother:

> Yes, truly, Europe is old and lame – there are only two young countries, Russia and America. If I were half as old as I am, it [this realization] would draw me to the former; with my almost 46 years (excuse this lack of gallantry as a son), I belong *here*, as every hour these last eight weeks has shown me […] I am an entirely new man, a new artist.[37]

For the first few months of the tour Bülow returned again and again to the same theme, the irresolvable differences he felt existed between the Old World and the New. In another letter to his mother he described how 'I am living it up here as I would not have thought I would ever be able to do again – housed and served like a prince […] I have never, nowhere, for so long, felt so well, I could say, happy […] with horror I think back on the old rotten European

---

34   *Ibid.*, 115.
35   Lott, '"A Continuous Trance": Hans von Bülow's Tour of America', 536.
36   *Ibid.*, 536.
37   *Ibid.*, 531.

world.'[38] He even felt that he had managed to achieve a degree of contractual autonomy where Thalberg and Rubinstein had not: 'As you know, I am a real artist, not a public entertainer […] If my colleagues, the great Thalberg and the, after all, more dignified Rubinstein, had done better, more systematic preparatory labor in my sense for the genuine and true, things would be in a much better condition.'[39] As a result of his preparation and the fact that he was able to pursue his singular artistic vision, which he called his mission to educate, Bülow felt America was 'the place where, for the first time, I can be entirely *myself*'. Such was his attachment to the United States in the first few months that he began the process of becoming a citizen, commenting, 'I consider myself henceforth dead and buried as far as Europe is concerned.'[40]

This feeling of rebirth was not to last, however. The frenetic pace of the tour, the demands, technical and aesthetic, he placed upon himself, and the fact that he was compelled to perform the same pieces over and over without any chance to practise or rework his repertoire began to wear him down. By April 1876, after 132 concerts (and with 33 still to go), Bülow asked Ullman to release him from his 'eight months of servitude', wishing as well that he had paid more attention to Rubinstein, who had warned him of the adverse effects the tour would have on his artistic integrity if he undertook it.[41] The paradox was that in seeking to secure his autonomy as an artist by means of the huge financial rewards made possible by American show business, Bülow found himself in the reverse situation: 'You have no idea how terribly depressing, nauseating, and exhausting this slavery is.'[42]

Nevertheless, prior to their arrival in New York, no performer such as Rubinstein or Bülow was entirely innocent of the demands of celebrity and mass music events. William Weber reminds us that the Promenades which began in London and other cities in the 1830s regularly attracted crowds of between 1,000 and 3,000 people, and notes the widespread decision amongst the music societies with big subscription bases to acquire the use of concert halls seating upwards of a thousand people to support their massed events. For Weber, a concert at the Palais de l'industrie in Paris in 1859 in which 6,000 singers from 204 choral societies performed to an audience of 40,000 was evidence of 'a desire to celebrate the emerging urban-industrial civilisation with a grand thronging together in public places'.[43] He also makes the critical point that we cannot separate the rise of mass culture and the elevation

---

[38] *Ibid.*

[39] *Ibid.*, 537.

[40] *Ibid.*, 541.

[41] Siegmund Levarie, 'Hans von Bülow in America', *Institute for the Study of American Music Newsletter*, 11/1 (1981), 8–10: 10; and Lott, '"A Continuous Trance": Hans von Bülow's Tour', 532n.

[42] Lott, '"A Continuous Trance": Hans von Bülow's Tour', 543–4.

[43] William Weber, 'Mass Culture and the Reshaping of European Musical Taste, 1770–1870', *International Review of the Aesthetics and Sociology of Music*, 25/1–2 (1994), 175–90: 184.

of the classical masters.[44] In this sense, until the later part of the century, the musical culture of United States was more an extension and amplification of this mass culture than a new form of it, with few if any permanent institutions available to sustain the immense post-Revolutionary artistic events as envisaged by Berlioz or Wagner.

It is also worth remembering that when Bülow undertook his North American tour, neither Carnegie Hall (which would come to be the setting for one of Ravel's triumphs), nor the Metropolitan Opera House, nor the Boston Symphony Orchestra (with which Ravel would later act as a guest conductor) existed. In the final decades of the nineteenth century, concert life in the United States underwent a dramatic change, with a speed and intensity that surprised even those performers who were best placed to benefit from the expansion in opportunities and the demands that accompanied them.

The turn-of-the-century experiences of Paderewski and Busoni

Prior to his first tour in 1891, Ignacy Jan Paderewski (1860–1941) recalled, he had expected that the tour would be a carefully balanced mixture of selected concerts interspersed by rehearsals and periods of rest. The reality was different:

> [...] it was concert after concert with only a day or two between: a continuous tour, and I had to begin in New York with *three orchestral* concerts, at which I had to play *six* piano concertos in one week and a group of solos. It was incredible! [...] Why, in Europe, I might not have an opportunity of playing six concertos in one season [...] But in New York, I was expected to play six concertos in one week![45]

From the moment he arrived in New York, Paderewski was overwhelmed by the 'lack of time', as he rushed from one concert to the next, often on the same day. Accustomed to the discipline of practice and rehearsal, he was completely unprepared for the 'sheer physical task' that lay ahead of him. 'When I was told that the rehearsal for my next concert was to take place directly after my first one', he wrote, 'it is not an exaggeration to say that I really was overcome.'[46] Things got no better once he left New York. Since he was contracted by the Steinway Company for so many concerts in quick succession, he was unable to reach Chicago in time to rehearse with the orchestra there, arriving in the morning in time for a 2.30p.m. concert: 'I had never seen the hall, never heard the orchestra, and never seen [Theodore] Thomas [the orchestra's conductor] himself, and it was my first appearance in Chicago.'[47]

44 *Ibid.*, 189.
45 Paderewski and Lawton, *The Paderewski Memoirs*, 201–2.
46 *Ibid.*, 204.
47 *Ibid.*, 223.

In his account, Paderewski continually returns to the immense strain the tour placed on him and the problems it raised for his conception of the artist as communicator. Yet he remained surprisingly positive about the opportunities for musicians in the United States, far more so than either Rubinstein or Bülow. He was impressed by the size of the country, its enormous resources, and, most important, its 'energetic, enterprising, and laborious population'. Like many of his fellow Europeans, the one thing he particularly noted was the national obsession with money. This manifested itself in the 'atmosphere of intense competition, of continuous effort, and of speed – speed, speed, even then. Nearly every one was thinking and speaking about money.'[48]

While Paderewski managed to shape his performances in response to the demands placed upon him and, in doing so, gained renewed public legitimacy as an artist from his willingness to adapt to the new conditions, his equally popular contemporary Ferruccio Busoni (1866–1924) remained far more ambivalent about the New World. Busoni undertook five tours of the United States between 1891 and 1915. His appearances thus cover an important period, during which the corporate form of show business was consolidated throughout North America.

As with Rubinstein and Bülow, Busoni's initial admiration and hope in the possibilities open to performing artists in the United States gradually turned into profound disenchantment and, at times, outright hostility. Echoing the themes of rebirth evident in Bülow's letters, in 1910 Busoni wrote to his wife Gerda, 'I am bound to admit that America is young; that it is not yet born […] It still has work to do for centuries to come.'[49] The following year, in an article published in the *Musical Courier*, he noted that America was 'rapidly coming into its own, particularly in its interest and appreciation of music', and that 'American audiences have come to know what they want and insist upon getting it. Mediocre compositions and mediocre performances have been tabooed by the men and women forming the audiences that attend the musical undertakings of this country.'[50] His early enthusiasm was repaid by his audiences: a reviewer at one of his concerts reported that the 'audience fairly hurled its applause at Busoni after each number and the *Don Juan* ended in a riot of cheers, hand clapping and foot stamping so clamorous that the hall appeared to shake with cyclopean tumult'.[51]

Busoni's own compositions proved much less successful. In a review of Karl Muck's performance of Busoni's *Geharnischte Suite* in Boston in 1906, Louis Elson said, 'While we emphatically do not like the school, we demand

48 *Ibid.*, 231.
49 Ferruccio Busoni, *Letters to His Wife*, trans. Rosamond Ley (London: Edward Arnold, 1938), 168.
50 'Busoni's Tribute to America', quoted in Marc-André Roberge, 'Ferruccio Busoni in the United States', *American Music*, 13/3 (1995), 295–332: 312.
51 Quoted in Roberge, 'Ferruccio Busoni in the United States', 303.

for Busoni the same respect that is accorded to other modern dissonancists [*sic*]. The more we get of this rambling, difficult, 'impressionist' school, the better, for the fever will have sooner run its course.'[52] Reconciling his considerable talents as a performer with his ambitions as a composer proved an increasingly difficult task, for him as much as for his audiences. Four years later, during his third tour, he complained to Gerda that the United States had become 'joyless', the land not of 'unlimited possibilities' but of 'impossible limitations'.[53]

By 1915, on what was to be his last tour, all pretence at admiration was abandoned. In a letter to his friend Harriet Lanier, he wrote: '[every one] of the five visits has proved a disappointment, and every time I have returned with renewed faith and with hopeful anticipations [...] All my achievements and hardest labours during a lifetime do not prove of any value to the American managers and to the public of this country.'[54] He felt that in order to make money he had been forced to 'prostitute' himself in front of a public who, with the exception of a 'handful of people', had remained indifferent to his efforts. His final comments, reportedly made to a friend on his deathbed, outdid even Bülow's disappointment. 'They [the Americans] make shit a religion [...] shit [...] this is America.'[55]

The growing dissatisfaction that Busoni felt with the United States and the position of the artist there was deeply bound up with his ideas about the future of music and the meaning he attached to modernism as a specific solution to the deteriorating relationship between the composer, performers, and the public. In his 'Sketch of a New Esthetic of Music', published in New York in 1911, he had referred to the modern musician as 'a pilgrim who has succeeded [...] in freeing himself from earthly shackles'.[56] The sense of rebirth he believed possible in America was inseparable from the rebirth he imagined for music; the failure to realize that rebirth was a failure to realize the promise of the New World, and only served to remind Europeans of how difficult it was to escape their past.

Ravel received: 1928

We are now in a position to understand why Ravel might initially have been reluctant to undertake a tour and, moreover, why eventually he accepted Schmitz's offer. During the first decades of the twentieth century, European

[52] Quoted in *ibid.*, 309.
[53] Busoni, *Letters*, 161.
[54] Quoted in Roberge, 'Ferruccio Busoni in the United States', 314.
[55] Quoted in *ibid.*, 315.

[56] Ferruccio Busoni, 'Sketch of a New Esthetic of Music', in Elliot Schwartz and Barney Childs (eds.), *Contemporary Composers on Contemporary Music* (New York: Da Capo, 1998), 16.

artists tended to view the United States with an equal measure of attraction and repulsion, often because of the published accounts by performers such as Rubinstein or Bülow. The vitality and power of its culture was irresistible to many performers, especially those who counted themselves as modernists; yet its crass commercialism seemed incomprehensible and destructive of those artistic values for which they ultimately stood. The positive aspects of this view were exaggerated by World War I, which had brought musical life in Europe to a virtual collapse and served only to highlight the artistic energy and immense creativity emerging from cities such as New York and Chicago. The jazz age thus intensified the already complex narratives of decline and renewal, of constraint and emancipation, of ancient and modern, that characterized the experiences of the artists I have described above.[57]

As far as Ravel was concerned, the prospect of a tour was framed by what he already knew of musical life in the United States, a knowledge derived in part from his contacts with American composers such as Gershwin and Copland, but also from his encounters with American performers in the café-concerts and music halls of Paris.[58] As Deborah Mawer confirms in Chapter 6, Ravel had for some time been interested in the possibilities of American vernacular forms such as ragtime, jazz, and blues and, along with many of his French contemporaries, he had already experimented with aspects of these forms. If nothing else, then, the tour was an opportunity to hear this music first-hand and to test his ideas in front of American audiences. Nonetheless, that the negotiations between Ravel and Schmitz took so long suggests that, even though the financial rewards were substantial, the composer remained ambivalent about what such a tour could achieve.[59]

While there are similarities between the experiences of Ravel on tour and those of the virtuosos such as Busoni and Paderewski, these similarities are mostly superficial. Elements of the tour were undoubtedly exhausting, and the schedule of concerts more or less followed those of the earlier artists in covering most major North American cities.[60] What made all the difference, however, as I argued above (page 95), was the growing influence and success of Pro Musica. The interest in Ravel's music and the extensive press coverage of the tour was the result of almost a decade during which Schmitz (along with many other leading performers and composers, many of whom

[57] The most comprehensive account of the influence of European modernism upon American composers and performers is found in Carol J. Oja, *Making Music Modern: New York in the 1920s* (New York: Oxford University Press, 2000).
[58] Jeffrey H. Jackson, 'Music-Halls and the Assimilation of Jazz in 1920s Paris',

Journal of Popular Culture, 34/2 (2000), 69–82.
[59] In his response to E. Robert Schmitz, Ravel wrote: 'vous ne pouvez me blâmer de comparer les avantages avant de vous donner une réponse définitive'. Ravel, quoted in Wiecki, 'A Chronicle of Pro Musica', 285.
[60] See again the Appendix to this chapter.

had emigrated to the United States before or during the war) actively sought to open up a social space for music that would counteract the commercial exploitation of artists and the reification of 'masterworks', bringing them a new dignity and creating a new field for the imagination. 'To understand modernism properly,' he stated in an interview in 1923, 'we must, first of all, accept the sincerity of the moderns, and believe they are genuinely striving towards emancipation.'[61] For Schmitz, the triumph of Ravel's tour was as much a triumph for his vision of a new relationship to music.

The critical response to Ravel's tour indicates the extent to which the efforts of Pro Musica and the other new music societies in supporting national tours by modernist composers, as well as leading performers, had made this acceptance possible. Although the tone and focus of coverage in the daily newspapers as well as the specialist music press varied immensely, most reviewers commented on Ravel's refusal to make any concessions to virtuosity, whether as a pianist or conductor, and on how finely formed (or even 'studied') his compositions were.[62]

In the *Chicago Evening Post*, for example, Karleton Hackett praised Ravel's intimate and reserved conducting style, noting that his lack of theatrical sense enabled him to bring clarity and force to the music.[63] Downes had noted the same qualities in his compositions, in a review published in the *New York Times*. 'The precision and taste of his [Ravel's] workmanship', he wrote, 'the complete technical mastery of his medium, the care with which each different musical idea was worked out complete, impeccable in form and style, were striking manifestations of the art of a composer whose works rebuke the pretense and dilettantism so fashionable in many quarters of Paris today.'[64] And in *Musical America*, following Ravel's concert in San Francisco on 3 March, Marjory Fisher described Ravel as 'an aristocrat', adding 'The things of the vulgar world do not interest him save as spectacles for the comment of his detached observation.'[65]

As we saw above (pages 93–4), the 'aristocratic' quality evident in Ravel's music (and in his life more generally) was one of the most important themes to emerge in the course of his tour, as critics tried to make sense of the role

[61] Schmitz, quoted in Wiecki, 'A Chronicle of Pro Musica', 59.

[62] In what was (and still is) a common view of Europeans' attempts to incorporate ideas from American vernacular music into their compositions, Roy Harris argued that, 'When Ravel attempted to incorporate our rhythmic sense into his violin sonata, it sounded studied.' See Roy Harris, 'Problems of American Composers', in Henry Cowell (ed.), *American Composers*

on American Music (Stanford University Press, 1933), 151.

[63] Karleton Hackett, 'Ravel Conducts Chicago Symphony', *Chicago Evening Post* (21 January 1928), 5, quoted in Dunfee, 'Maurice Ravel in America', 87.

[64] Olin Downes, 'Ravel in American Debut', *New York Times* (16 January 1928), 25.

[65] Marjory M. Fisher, 'San Francisco Events', *Musical America* (3 March 1928), 39, quoted in Dunfee, 'Maurice Ravel in America', 132–3.

of artists and the value of art for Americans. Aware of how important the issue was to his audiences, Ravel often asserted a concept of 'aristocracy' as an active principle in his practice. In an interview with the *San Francisco Examiner*, he suggested (provocatively) that 'music always was and always will be an aristocratic art. That is why musicians should be discouraged. Encourage them and you flood the world with mediocrities. You couldn't discourage a Beethoven. The more obstacles you put in his way, the more obstinate he becomes.'[66]

The use of the term 'aristocratic' in this context was synonymous with notions of refinement, control, distinction, restraint, taste, and tradition and, as such, prompted critics to compare Ravel with the emerging stars of the concert stage, from Horowitz to Heifetz. Of his debut in New York City, on 15 January, a writer in the *New York World* noted that Ravel was '[d]eeply absorbed in the problems of creative work and little concerned with self exploitation'.[67] At no point, however, were these qualities perceived to be at odds with his modernism. As the reviewer in the *St Paul Pioneer Press* put it: 'While he [Ravel] is one of the most erudite of contemporary composers, a man steeped in the tradition of the classics, and a music maker of meticulously careful workmanship, he is likewise one of those musicians who look steadily forward and register the influences of today as sensitively as those of yesterday.'[68]

This review underlines why Ravel's tour for Pro Musica was so successful. Amidst great social and political changes provoked by the rise of corporate capitalism in the United States and the collapse of European societies after the war, and the musical changes resulting from expressionism, atonalism, serialism, and neoclassicism, Ravel's music was not just a symbol of the 'crisis in culture'; it was not simply a reflection of the conflicts and contradictions that were transforming European and American societies in this period. His experiments involved discovering how musical conventions of the past were capable of securing music's independence (and the individuality of the artist along with it) at just that moment when those conventions were no longer able to provide such a guarantee. Rather than merely repeating old compositional formulas, however, he annulled the generic properties of a minuet, passacaglia, blues melody or fugue, subordinating their historical

---

[66] Redfern Mason, 'Ravel Here to Conduct Symphony', *San Francisco Examiner* (1 February 1928), 6, quoted in Dunfee, 'Maurice Ravel in America', 153.
[67] [Unsigned], 'Maurice Ravel Makes Debut Tonight in Program of His Own Works', *New York World* (15 January 1928), quoted in *ibid.*, 155.

[68] [Unsigned review], 'Ravel, Eminent Composer, to Play Own Music Here Friday Night', *St Paul Pioneer Press* (11 March 1928), quoted in Wiecki, 'A Chronicle of Pro Musica', 298.

or ethnic appeal to the *individuality* of the treatment. The meaning of each form or motive, along with its relationship to the specific tradition or culture from which it was taken or derived, was likewise transformed into a musical experience both self-contained and unrepeatable. Only the integrity of the artist could testify to its truth, its authenticity.[69]

In his pre-tour interview with Downes in 1927, Ravel commented that Igor Stravinsky's '[latest] work, *Oedipus Rex*, showed that while he plays with old forms, he is actually finding something new'.[70] This is an equally good description of Ravel's compositional practice, although he was arguably less concerned with inventing new musical structures than with the problem of sound textures. As Charles Rosen suggests in a perceptive article on Ravel's piano music, the prelude of *Le Tombeau de Couperin* achieves the *sonority* of eighteenth-century instruments, but in a manner derived mostly from the innovations of Schumann or Fauré. Likewise, Rosen argues that in the fugue from the same piece, any resemblance to the superficial 'polytonality' of the baroque form was suppressed by Ravel in order to amplify the rhythmic complexity of the syncopation.[71]

Thus it was that in the Piano Concerto in G (1929–31) Ravel indicated his debt to Gershwin on many levels; in the view of one scholar, it was the greatest compliment ever paid by a European to an American composer.[72] However, it was not Gershwin's stylistic innovations that proved attractive to Ravel, but the American's ability to produce seemingly endless melodic ideas from the combination of blues notes and syncopation. This melodic priority was incorporated into the larger schema of the Concerto in G in which Ravel sought to reconstruct the concerto's classical form, through a continual reworking of Basque, Spanish, and American folk melodies. In a movement from France to America and back again, therefore, Ravel had discovered the possibility of combining the most contrary of elements within a single work: conveying through the holistic *spirit* of classicism the individualized *sound* of the jazz age, and, in doing so, modifying the relationship between the two. (For a further perspective on this theme, see Chapter 6.)

[69] These ideas were developed in the lecture that Ravel gave as part of his recital in Houston on 7 April and which was later published by the Rice Institute: Maurice Ravel, *Contemporary Music*, Rice Institute Pamphlet 15/2 (1928), 131–45. This lecture was read before each Pro Musica event, usually by a committee member.

[70] Downes, 'Maurice Ravel, Man and Musician'.

[71] Charles Rosen, 'Where Ravel Ends and Debussy Begins', *High Fidelity*, 9/5 (1959), 42–4 and 117–21: 42–3.

[72] David Schiff, *Gershwin: Rhapsody in Blue* (Cambridge University Press, 1997), 75. The significance of Ravel's tour is manifested in terms of the form that the concerto took and the sonorities it achieved, though the tour also delayed the actual composition of the work until 1929. In answer to a query from Schmitz about performing the concerto in the United States during his tour, Ravel replied simply 'Concerto abandonné.' Telegram from Ravel to Schmitz (13 January 1927), quoted in Wiecki, 'A Chronicle of Pro Musica', 286.

In a summary of the final years of Ravel's life, which includes a brief discussion of the North American tour, Arbie Orenstein argues that the success of Ravel's tour 'brought his international reputation to its zenith'.[73] Although Orenstein remains surprisingly circumspect on this point, I take him to mean that only after Ravel's trip did his significance as a composer become fully apparent to those American musicians whose art he influenced. Not only did he publicly confirm Americans in their search for an authentic artistic vision equal to their sense of historical mission, but he offered them a possible solution to the dilemmas posed, on the one hand, by the breakdown of the tonal system and, on the other, by the modernist project of autonomy.

Ravel's emphasis upon sonority within relatively conventional classical and Romantic forms intensified the redundancy of those forms, in as much as they were inseparable from the mass commercialization of the arts and the reign of money. This sense of formal redundancy masked Ravel's perpetual reworking of the great modernist innovations, from Liszt to Schoenberg, by reanimating as though for the first time those sound worlds from which modernism had tried to break. Ravel thus cleared the way for artistic autonomy at the level of sonority, while emphasizing the deep continuities that existed between eighteenth-century classicism (and older forms of folk music) and twentieth-century modernism. To listen to the Sonata for Violin and Piano, *Tzigane*, or *Le Tombeau* was to experience the passage from one musical system to another: from the world of Couperin, Haydn, and Mozart, to that of Debussy, Schoenberg, and Gershwin.[74] Such a passage was essential to the process by which artists in the United States began to revise and re-evaluate their relation to the past, even as they acknowledged their debt to it. To paraphrase Virgil Thomson, Ravel's music was both a necessary inheritance from the nineteenth century and the means of liberation from it.[75] Just what that process meant in practice would preoccupy American musicians for decades to come.

---

[73] Orenstein, *Ravel*, 98.
[74] That Ravel requested Debussy's *Prélude à L'Après-midi d'un faune* to be played at his funeral should be evidence enough of this.

[75] Virgil Thomson, 'Looking Forward', *Musical Quarterly*, 31/2 (1945), 157–62: 161.

Appendix: Itinerary for Ravel's tour

Compiled by Deborah Mawer

Date	Venue/city	Event/auspices
31 December 1927	Boat journey to New York	Soirée on board the ocean liner *France*
4 January 1928	Langdon Hotel, New York	Ravel is met by French Consul General and E. Robert Schmitz (President, Pro Musica Society)
6 January	New York	[Unsigned interview], 'Ravel Says Poe Aided Him in Composition', *New York Times*
8 January	Carnegie Hall, New York; train to Boston	Concert: Boston Symphony Orchestra – all-Ravel programme; Ravel appears on stage, audience of 3,500, standing ovation; also private concert
12 January	Sanders Theater, Harvard University, Cambridge	Ravel conducts Boston Symphony Orchestra (American debut); programme, in order: *Le Tombeau de Couperin*; Debussy (orch. Ravel) – *Sarabande* and *Danse*; *Rapsodie espagnole*; *Shéhérazade* (Lisa Roma: voice); *La Valse*; this programme is repeated on 13 January
13 January	Symphony Hall, Boston	Ravel conducts Boston Symphony Orchestra; programme is repeated on 14 January
15 January	Gallo Theater, New York	Chamber programme (Pro Musica Society; Ravel, pf.; Joseph Szigeti, vn.), in order: String Quartet, *Sonatine*, *Histoires naturelles*, Violin Sonata (US premiere),

Ravel's main itinerary is reconstructed from a combination of correspondence, interviews, and reviews. I am indebted to several sources: Arbie Orenstein (ed.), *A Ravel Reader: Correspondence, Articles, Interviews* (New York: Columbia University Press, 1990); Arbie Orenstein, *Ravel: Man and Musician* (New York: Dover Publications, 1991); Norman Vance Dunfee, 'Maurice Ravel in America – 1928' (DMA dissertation, University of Missouri – Kansas City, 1980); and Gilles Potvin, 'Maurice Ravel au Canada', in John Beckwith and Frederick A. Hall (eds.), *Musical Canada* (University of Toronto Press, 1988), 149–63. See also 'Maurice Ravel *Frontispice*: Travels': http://www.maurice-ravel.net/travels.htm (accessed 3 January 2009).

Date	Venue/city	Event/auspices
		Chansons madécasses, *Introduction et allegro*; encores: 'Habanera', *Pavane*; reception with Bartók, Varèse, Gershwin, Fritz Kreisler; African-American dancing and spirituals (at Ravel's request)
16 January	Train from New York to Chicago (arrives on 17 January)	Olin Downes review, *New York Times*
18 January	Gold Room, Congress Hotel, Chicago	Recital (auspices of Pro Musica; Ravel, pf.; voice; vn.): programme includes Violin Sonata, *Histoires naturelles*, *Sonatine*
20 January	Orchestra Hall, Chicago	Ravel conducts Chicago Symphony Orchestra; programme includes *Daphnis et Chloé* (Suite No. 2); this concert is repeated on 21 January
22 January	Museum of Art, Cleveland	'Contemporary Music' lecture is read by Arthur Quimby; recital
26 January	Masonic Auditorium, Cleveland	Ravel conducts Cleveland Orchestra; programme includes *Valses nobles et sentimentales*, *Ma mère l'Oye*
3 February	Curran Theater, San Francisco	Ravel conducts San Francisco Symphony Orchestra (programme as that of 12 January); this concert is repeated on 5 February
4 February	Colonial Ballroom, St Francis Hotel, San Francisco	Recital (Ravel, pf.; voice; vn.): programme includes Violin Sonata
7 February	Los Angeles Biltmore Hotel, Los Angeles	Hollywood visit; meets Douglas Fairbanks
8 February	Biltmore Hotel Ballroom, Los Angeles	Afternoon visit to Metro-Goldwyn-Mayer film studio; evening lecture-recital (Los Angeles Pro Musica chapter) 'Contemporary Music' lecture; programme (Ravel, pf., cond.) includes Violin Sonata ('Blues' encore), *Introduction et allegro*

Date	Venue/city	Event/auspices
13 February	Spanish Ballroom, Olympic Hotel, Seattle	Afternoon lecture-recital (Ravel, pf.; voice) includes 'Rigaudon' and 'Menuet' (from *Le Tombeau*)
14 February	New Auditorium, Vancouver, Canada	Canadian recital debut (Ravel, pf.; Lisa Roma, voice), including four movements of *Le Tombeau*, *Cinq mélodies populaires grecques*
15 February	Multnomah Hotel ball-room, Portland	Lecture-recital includes *Introduction et allegro*
19 February	Scottish Rite Cathedral, Denver (leaves 20 February)	Ravel is interviewed about jazz (*Rocky Mountain News*); lecture-recital of piano and vocal items
21 February	En route to Minneapolis, via Omaha	Ravel hears jazz in Omaha during evening; continues on Overland Route, Union Pacific System
22 February	Art Institute, Minneapolis	Recital includes Violin Sonata, String Quartet, aria from *Myrrha* (encore)
26 February	Century Theater, New York	Olin Downes, 'Mr Ravel Returns' [interview], *New York Times*; recital (Ravel and E. Robert Schmitz, pf.; Lisa Roma, voice; plus vn., vc.) includes 'Habanera', 'Chanson hébraïque', Trio
7 March	Biltmore Hotel, New York	Eva Gautier (mezzo-soprano) gives dinner for Ravel's 53rd birthday; Gershwin among guests
8 March	Carnegie Hall, New York	Ravel conducts New York Symphony Orchestra; programme includes *Tzigane* (Samuel Dushkin, solo vn.)
11 March	Mecca Temple, New York (leaves on 12 March)	Programme as 8 March
14 March	Hotel Muehlbach Ballroom, Kansas City	'Contemporary Music' lecture; recital (under the auspices of Pro Musica) includes 'La Vallée des cloches' (as encore)
18 March	Arrived Toronto, Canada	Ravel is interviewed by local press; visits Niagara Falls during his stay

Date	Venue/city	Event/auspices
22 March	Margaret Eaton Hall, Toronto	Programme as 14 February, but also including Quartet
28 March	Institute of Arts, Large Hall, Detroit	Ravel (pf., cond.); members of Detroit Symphony Orchestra play *Introduction et allegro*
4 April	New York to New Orleans (arrives on 5 April)	Crescent Limited (railway route): New York–New Orleans
6 April	Rice Institute, Houston, Texas	Recital (Ravel, pf; Esther Dale, voice; Barbara Lull, vn.) includes 'Sainte', 'Nicolette', 'Air de l'enfant', *Deux mélodies hébraïques*, Violin Sonata
7 April	Rice Institute	Lecture-recital: 'Contemporary Music'; recital (Ravel, pf; plus voice, vn.) includes *Menuet antique*, *Berceuse*, *Tzigane*
8–13 April	Gulf of Mexico; Phoenix and Grand Canyon, Arizona	Automobile trip to Gulf of Mexico; Grand Canyon excursion
17 April	The Ballroom, Hotel Statler, Buffalo	Local press interview; recital (under auspices of Buffalo Musical Foundation; Ravel, pf.; voice) includes 'Nicolette'
19 April	Théâtre Saint-Denis, Montréal	Local press interview; recital programme (Ravel, pf.) includes *Ma mère l'Oye* (pf. duet version)
21 April	Boat journey from New York to Le Havre (arrives back on 27 April)	Ravel returns on board the ocean liner *Paris*

6   Crossing borders II: Ravel's theory and practice of jazz

Deborah Mawer

Within the contexts of popular musics and European modernist eclecticism, this chapter considers Ravel's reading of jazz through study of his writings and letters, followed by analytical exploration of selected works. It argues that Ravel translated an American jazz into his vernacular, creating a French-accented and personalized practice, and that this was an important aspect of his aesthetic–musical identity in the later 1920s. The topic may be viewed as part of a larger quest by various twentieth-century French musicians to revitalize their national music; paradoxically, it is a reinvigoration of French identity through the foreign.

To this end, and cued by Ravel's crossing of borders between America and France on his 1928 tour, I probe an intriguing double relationship that embodies transformative processes across a spectrum from minor to major change. The first relationship is between Ravel's 'theory' or views of early jazz – especially the associated blues – and the historical actualities, as interpreted by jazz scholars past and present (with the benefit of hindsight). Although there is much congruity, a modulation between actuality and theory is underpinned by intricate 'dynamics' which relate to broader processes of Gallicizing jazz, as in Jeffrey Jackson's *Making Jazz French*,[1] and to Ravel's artistic aesthetic and experience. While not underplaying the very real challenges in defining early jazz, which has meant different things to different people and even to the same people across time,[2] I claim that idiosyncrasies within Ravel's positioning can be revealed. The second relationship is between Ravel's theory and his practice across the 'Blues'

Earlier versions of this chapter were presented at 'Musique française: esthétique et identité en mutation, 1892–1992', Université Catholique de l'Ouest, Angers, France (April 2008) and at the joint conference of the Society for Musicology in Ireland and the Royal Musical Association, Dublin (July 2009). I am grateful for feedback and suggestions from Carolyn Abbate, Andy Fry, Jacinthe Harbec, Julian Horton, Barbara Kelly, Danièle Pistone, Jan Smaczny, and others.

[1] Jeffrey H. Jackson, *Making Jazz French: Music and Modern Life in Interwar Paris* (Durham, NC and London: Duke University Press, 2003).

[2] These problematics are confronted in many jazz histories; see, for instance, Gunther Schuller, *Early Jazz: Its Roots and Musical Development* (New York: Oxford University Press, 1968, reprinted 1986), 4: jazz is 'a hybrid that evolved through many stages of cross-fertilization over a period of more than a century'.

movement of the Sonata for Violin and Piano (1923–7), the 'ragtime' from *L'Enfant et les sortilèges* (1920–5), *Boléro* (1928), the Piano Concerto for the Left Hand (1929–30), and the Piano Concerto in G (1929–31). Again, this process is marked by complex dynamics: although theory and practice relate closely, one is not synonymous with the other. I suggest that more occasional idiosyncrasies emerge and that Ravel's compositional stance (the *poietic* – to use Jean-Jacques Nattiez's terminology) is not in any case synonymous with our analytical (*esthesic*) stance in seeking to understand his music.

Initially it is useful to outline topical research on the American–French jazz background: Jackson's influential text is part of a larger investigation and celebration of African-American culture in Paris by Glenn Watkins, Tyler Stovall, Jody Blake, and others.[3] This geographical transformation is mirrored by another: that of jazzing the classics, or indeed classicizing jazz, with its own rich literature. Mervyn Cooke's writing provides a fine illustration while, more historically, the incisive if eccentric views of André Hodeir (b. 1921) still hold some merit and offer a provocative foil.[4] Other resources include a fascinating article by Carine Perret who compares American jazz and French compositions, concentrating upon expressivity and spirituality, and treatment of Ravel's 'Blues' by Robert Orledge and by Mark DeVoto, the former making comparisons with Jerome Kern (1885–1945), George Gershwin (1898–1937), and Joe Venuti (1903–78).[5]

Although some records were imported during World War I, essentially early jazz arrived in Europe towards the end of the war, courtesy of American troop entertainment by James Reese Europe and others. And since much has been written on this topic I shall confine myself to summarizing matters relevant to Ravel.[6] Many white and a few African-American bands were

[3] See Glenn Watkins, *Pyramids at the Louvre: Music, Culture, and Collage from Stravinsky to the Postmodernists* (Cambridge, MA and London: Harvard University Press, 1994); Tyler Stovall, *Paris noir: African Americans in the City of Light* (Boston, MA: Houghton Mifflin, 1996); Jody Blake, *Le Tumulte noir: Modernist Art and Popular Entertainment in Jazz-Age Paris, 1900–1930* (University Park, PA: Pennsylvania State University Press, 2003); Petrine Archer-Shaw, *Negrophilia: Avant-Garde Paris and Black Culture in the 1920s* (London: Thames & Hudson, 2000).

[4] Mervyn Cooke, 'Jazz among the Classics, and the Case of Duke Ellington', in Mervyn Cooke and David Horn (eds.), *The Cambridge Companion to Jazz* (Cambridge University Press, 2002), 153–73; André Hodeir, *Hommes et problèmes du jazz* (Paris: Portulan, 1954);

Eng. trans. as *Jazz: Its Evolution and Essence*, trans. David Noakes (London: Jazz Book Club, 1958).

[5] Carine Perret, 'L'Adoption du jazz par Darius Milhaud et Maurice Ravel: l'esprit plus que la lettre', *Revue de musicologie*, 89/2 (2003), 311–47; Robert Orledge, 'Evocations of Exoticism', and Mark DeVoto, 'Harmony in the Chamber Music', in Deborah Mawer (ed.), *The Cambridge Companion to Ravel* (Cambridge University Press, 2000), 27–46: 42–3; 97–117: 115–16.

[6] For detail see Jackson, *Making Jazz French*, 19, 20, 111, 120–1; Carine Perret, 'L'Adoption du jazz', 311–20; and Deborah Mawer, '"Parisomania"? Jack Hylton and the French Connection', *Journal of the Royal Musical Association*, 133/2 (November 2008), 270–317: 280–4.

heard in Paris – or the 'Transatlantic Terminus' as it was known[7] – including Louis Mitchell's Jazz Kings which was resident at the Casino de Paris in 1918. Revues included *Pa-ri-ki danse* (1919), *Paris qui jazz* (1920–1), and *Laissez-les tomber!*, experienced by Jean Cocteau and Darius Milhaud, while more spontaneous jazz permeated the nightclubs of Montmartre (Bricktop's, Chez Florence, and the Grand Duc) and Montparnasse (The Jockey). Billy Arnold's white band featured in the Concerts Wiener in December 1921 and was much enjoyed by Ravel: the musicians were 'marvellous'.[8]

In Le Bœuf sur le toit, whose convivial atmosphere appealed to Les Six, Ravel most likely first heard Gershwin numbers,[9] including perhaps 'The Man I Love', the opening verse of which Perret proposes as a model for Ravel's practice.[10] Léon-Paul Fargue offers an attractive image of the composer as 'a sort of debonair wizard, buried in his corner at the Grand Ecart or Le Bœuf sur le toit, telling me endless stories which had the same elegance, richness, and clarity as his compositions'.[11] By contrast, in uncharitable and disdainful fashion, Hodeir talked of Ravel's 'jumping on the latest thing, regardless of where it came from, eager to exploit this novelty, slightly shopworn though it may have been, after he had followed Debussy and flirted a moment with Schoenberg'. He continued: 'There is no dearth of anecdotes in some of which he is shown applauding Jimmie Noone, in others the orchestra at the Moulin Rouge'.[12] A better balance is achieved by Arbie Orenstein, who notes that, although Ravel was intensely private when composing, 'he enjoyed Parisian nightlife, the conversations, the lights, the jazz, and the crowds'.[13]

In 1925, the remarkable Josephine Baker starred in *Revue nègre*, and the following year saw the first French tour by Paul Whiteman, who had premiered Gershwin's *Rhapsody in Blue*. But there was always a time lag in American fashions arriving and being reinterpreted in Paris: Louis Armstrong was not heard until 1932 and Duke Ellington a year later. On his American tour, however, there is evidence that Ravel visited the still-segregated Cotton Club in Harlem where Ellington appeared on stage,[14] though Ravel's priority seems

[7]   Sisley Huddleston, *Back to Montparnasse: Glimpses of Broadway in Bohemia* (Philadelphia, PA and London: J. B. Lippincott, 1931), 47.
[8]   Jean Wiener, *Allegro Appassionato* (Paris: Editions Belfond, 1978), 48.
[9]   See Maurice Sachs, *Au temps du Bœuf sur le toit* (Paris: Editions de la Nouvelle revue critique, 1948).
[10]   Perret, 'L'Adoption du jazz', 323–34. Ravel's practice echoes more obviously Gershwin's dotted figuration that begins the chorus (bar 21ff.).
[11]   Quoted in Arbie Orenstein (ed.), *A Ravel Reader: Correspondence, Articles, Interviews*

(New York: Columbia University Press, 1990), 15.
[12]   Hodeir, *Jazz*, 246–7. Jimmie Noone (1895–1944) was a New Orleans clarinettist, taught by Sidney Bechet, who from 1927 led a band at the Apex Club, Chicago. His style, blues-influenced yet lyrical and polished, would likely have appealed to Ravel.
[13]   Orenstein (ed.), *A Ravel Reader*, 15.
[14]   Joseph Roddy, 'Ravel in America', *High Fidelity Magazine* (March 1975), 58–63, quoted in Perret, 'L'Adoption du jazz', 322. The Cotton Club was for 'whites' only, though there were African-American performers.

to have been to play and hear Gershwin's renditions of 'Tea for Two', *Rhapsody in Blue*, '"My Blue Heaven", and other jazz tunes [*sic*]'.[15] Indeed Ravel and Gershwin met several times and much admired each other's work, to the extent that, according to the singer Eva Gautier, Gershwin sought composition lessons from Ravel.[16] At New York's Liederkranz Hall, Ravel heard Paul Whiteman's Orchestra recording with Bix Beiderbecke.[17]

Within his record collection Ravel amassed a diverse repertory, including occasional jazz numbers such as 'Tiger Rag', numerous chansons or music-hall songs: Gaston Claret's 'Si petite', Vincent Scotto's 'Tu m'fais rire', Mireille's 'Le Petit Chemin', and Maurice Yvain's 'Pourquoâ' (sung by the 'chansonnier montmartrois' or cabaret singer Paul Colline), together with popular piano music, notably that by the British musician Billy Mayerl.[18] For many modernist composers, to jazz up their classical style, as one type of eclecticism, enabled a significant means of inflecting their authorial voice; in addition to Ravel, Milhaud especially wrote about the impact of jazz upon his practice.[19] Archetypal products of this relationship include Stravinsky's *Ragtime for 11 Instruments* (1918), George Auric's *Adieu New York!* (1919), and Milhaud's *La Création du monde* (1923).

Relations between Ravel's theory and the actualities of early jazz

Ravel's theory of jazz is evidenced primarily from his notated lecture / pamphlet entitled *Contemporary Music* of April 1928 for the Rice Institute in Houston, rehearsed in his article 'Take Jazz Seriously!', and supplemented by interviews and correspondence.[20] Certain ideas recur across several years and sources and have been abstracted as themes in my constructing and

[15] Marie Dunbar, 'Maurice Ravel, Napoleon of World Music, Plays Popular Numbers', *Seattle Post Intelligencer* (13 February 1928), quoted by Perret, 'L'Adoption du jazz', 320. 'Tea for Two' was the hit from the New York musical *No, No Nanette* (1925), with music by Vincent Youmans and lyrics by Irving Caesar.

[16] Eva Gautier, 'Reminiscences of Maurice Ravel', *New York Times* (16 January 1938). Ravel's enthusiastic account about Gershwin is given in a letter to Nadia Boulanger (8 March 1928), in Orenstein (ed.), *A Ravel Reader*, 293. On the matter of teaching Gershwin compositional technique, Ravel asks Boulanger, 'Would you have the courage, which I wouldn't dare have, to undertake this awesome responsibility?'

[17] See Ravel seated at the piano with Whiteman standing, in Thomas A. DeLong, *Pops: Paul Whiteman, King of Jazz* (Piscataway: New Century Publishers, 1983), plate at 272–3.

[18] Bruno Sébald's listing in Orenstein (ed.), *A Ravel Reader*, 601–11.

[19] See Darius Milhaud, 'Les Ressources nouvelles de la musique (jazz-band et instruments mécaniques', *L'Esprit nouveau*, 25 (July 1924); *Etudes* (Paris: Editions Claude Aveline, 1927); *Ma vie heureuse* (Paris: Editions Belfond, 1974, reprinted 1987).

[20] Maurice Ravel, *Contemporary Music*, Rice Institute Pamphlet 15/2 (1928), 131–45; 'Take Jazz Seriously!', *Musical Digest*, 13/3 (1928), 49, 51.

presenting of this theory. On the one hand, a substantial part of the writing reveals Ravel as a connoisseur of American–French jazz, reflecting contemporary realities (so that criticisms by the early critic Hodeir may seem grudging and unfounded) and presenting, up to a point, an untransformed perspective.

Theme 1: Americans are urged to appreciate jazz as a cultural asset rather than something to be taken for granted. Interviewed by Olin Downes early in 1928,[21] Ravel declares how much he admires jazz, claiming that he values it more than many American contemporaries. Witness to this is the title of his article 'Take Jazz Seriously!' in which he chides Americans for regarding jazz as 'cheap, vulgar, momentary'.[22] We may argue that it is all very well Ravel being indignant and slightly self-righteous, but he is late on the trail in comparison with Milhaud, or Auric. Nonetheless, he feels justified in contrasting American lack of interest with a European perspective, whereby '[jazz] is influencing our work'. His knowledge of early jazz and French colonialism is such that, in a letter to Mme Fernand Dreyfus, he talks of his intention to look in affectionately on jazz's birthplace, New Orleans.[23] (By this point, he had seemingly had fleeting contact with Harlem jazz, and had written to his brother Edouard about experiencing African-American theatre in New York and jazz in Omaha, en route to Minneapolis.)[24] On the topic of the Gallicizing of jazz, Ravel paints a lively picture of New Year's Eve entertainment aboard the liner named the *France*, which took him literally and figuratively from Europe to New York. Writing to French friends, he exclaims, in anticipation of William Shack's *Harlem in Montmartre*: 'We are supping joyously in a dance hall which is hardly level: jazz, paper streamers, balloons, champagne, a Russian quartet, drunk Americans – all the local color of Montmartre.'[25]

In writings that postdate his tour, Ravel generally upholds the value of jazz for himself and fellow classical composers.[26] He presents a typical *Zeitgeist* stance in which jazz is seen to embody the modernist age: 'In jazz

[21] Olin Downes, 'Mr Ravel Returns', *New York Times* (26 February 1928), section 8, 8.
[22] Ravel, 'Take Jazz Seriously!', 49.
[23] Letter to Mme Fernand Dreyfus (4 April 1928), in Orenstein (ed.), *A Ravel Reader*, 294.
[24] See Orenstein (ed.), *A Ravel Reader*, 293n, 288, 293. Omaha has long been a jazz centre, frequented by Armstrong, Ellington, and others; the Omaha Riverfront Jazz and Blues Festival continues this tradition. See, Appendix to Chapter 5 of this volume.
[25] Letter to Nelly and Maurice Delage (31 December 1927), in Orenstein (ed.), *A Ravel Reader*, 287; William A. Shack, *Harlem in*

Montmartre (Berkeley, CA: University of California Press, 2001).
[26] See [unsigned interview], 'Factory Gives Composer Inspiration', *Evening Standard* (24 February 1932), in Orenstein (ed.), *A Ravel Reader*, 490–1: 490. The exception occurs in [unsigned interview], 'Problems of Modern Music, From a Conversation with Maurice Ravel', *Der Bund* (19 April 1929), in Orenstein (ed.), *A Ravel Reader*, 465–6: 466, where Ravel purportedly exclaimed: 'Jazz might serve many of us as entertainment, *but it has nothing in common with art.*' No other source expresses negativity, which may raise questions of authenticity.

rhythms, it is often said, the pulsation of modern life is heard.' Such a view echoes Robert Mendl: 'The energy, industry, the hurry and hustle of modern American methods find their counterpart in the [...] jazz orchestra.'[27] Ravel qualifies his position, saying that jazz is not the only influence, and should be seen in conjunction with that exerted by machines, industry, and technological endeavour: this alignment with a machinist aesthetic, especially following *Boléro*, reflects another popular Parisian cult from the early 1920s. Although by 1931 Ravel suspects, as had Milhaud five years earlier, that 'jazz influence is waning', he still credits it as a major factor in his late music, including the Concerto in G.[28] And he does not want to let go, reasserting, 'It is not just a passing phase [...] It is thrilling and inspiring'; as late as August 1932, in a little-known interview for *Rhythm* magazine entitled 'Jazz – Democracy's Music!', he reaffirms the influence of jazz and popular music.[29]

Theme 2: ragtime is credited as a specific entity, and is the first style or genre on which Ravel comments, aptly given its role as a precursor of jazz. As Terry Waldo cautions however, '*Ragtime* [...] is a much more eclectic term [than *rag*] and could be said to apply to almost any music that is syncopated.'[30] Nevertheless, Ravel's usage of foxtrot characteristics within ragtime in *L'Enfant* makes apparent his familiarity with a technique dating from around 1913. In a letter to Colette (27 February 1919), he asks her view of 'the cup and the teapot, in old Wedgwood – black – singing a ragtime?' His appreciation of raglike forms is evident from his remark that 'the form – a single couplet, with refrain – would be perfectly suited to the gestures in this scene: complaints, recriminations, furor, pursuit'.[31] An unconventional, politically savvy approach is highlighted in his good-humoured intention for a vocal ragtime to be given by two African-American singers at the then somewhat stuffy Paris Opéra. Ravel's use of the word 'nègres', while troubling, is typical of its time. (The first so-called jazz-band performance at the Opéra did not happen until Jack Hylton and his Boys appeared in February 1931, and this performance featured white players only.) Ravel also makes mention in *Contemporary Music* of the 'rags',[32] with perceptive quotation marks, of composers such as Hindemith and Casella.

[27] [Unsigned interview], 'Problems of Modern Music'; Robert W. S. Mendl, *The Appeal of Jazz* (London: P. Allen & Co, 1927), 97–8.

[28] [Special correspondent], 'A Visit with Maurice Ravel', *De Telegraaf* (31 March 1931), in Orenstein (ed.), *A Ravel Reader*, 472–5: 473.

[29] [Unsigned interview], 'Factory Gives Composer Inspiration', 490; the interview in *Rhythm* (not listed by Orenstein) was drawn to my attention by John Watson,

a music historian who researches into 'rhythm and novelty' pianists of the interwar years: personal communication (21 April 2008).

[30] Terry Waldo, *This is Ragtime* (New York: Da Capo Press, 1976, rev. 1991), 4.

[31] Orenstein (ed.), *A Ravel Reader*, 188. On the Ravel–Colette exchange, see Chapter 2.

[32] Ravel, *Contemporary Music*, 140; Waldo, *This is Ragtime*, 4: 'A *rag*, strictly speaking, is an instrumental syncopated march.'

Theme 3: in Ravel's theory, the blues deserves a special status, though as today's jazz scholars caution this term has no one concrete definition.[33] (Unlike ragtime, blues has continued in parallel with various jazz styles through to the present. But although authors such as Alyn Shipton consider the interrelationship between early jazz and blues, and although Cooke classifies blues, with ragtime, as a precursor to New Orleans jazz,[34] the relationships are not straightforward. While the blues is 'widely assumed' to have impacted on early jazz, more documentary research is necessary to clinch the case.)[35] In a further interview with Downes, Ravel demonstrates his earnest intent, stating, 'I take this "blues" very seriously,' and questioning: 'Why have not more of the important American composers turned to this "blue" material [...]?'[36] This stance is stressed in *Contemporary Music*, where he extols the inherent expressivity and emotional content of the blues, and reveals his deep enthusiasm for the genre: 'the "blues" is one of your greatest assets, truly American, despite earlier contributory influences from Africa and Spain'.[37] The Spanish connection resonates strongly with Ravel's own background and compositional practice (his writing of blues focusing the second part of my essay).

Theme 4: jazz should relate to larger questions of national identity. Ravel has a subtle understanding of such issues, influenced by his French identity. On various occasions,[38] he talks of the typically mixed sources of national musics arguing that, whatever its strict and varied origins, jazz is unequivocally American. A perceptive, detailed discourse is developed on American identity, with Ravel looking forward to experiencing more of 'those elements which are contributing to the gradual formation of a veritable school of American music'.[39] He debates 'high' versus popular art and American versus European music, perceiving two camps: those who believe folklore to be essential to national music and those who think that a national music will emerge from the music of the day. His tone is, however, disparaging when referring to the first group's agonizing over exactly which folklore, indigenous Indian traditions, spirituals or blues are authentically American 'until nothing is left of national background'. Nevertheless, French traditions and background remain crucial to Ravel. Ravel talks of the lure of European

---

[33] Paul Oliver and Barry Kernfeld, 'Blues', in Barry Kernfeld (ed.), *The New Grove Dictionary of Jazz*, second edition, 3 vols. (London: Macmillan, 2002), vol. I, 247–55: 247.

[34] Alyn Shipton, *A New History of Jazz* (London, New York: Continuum, 2007), 47–8; Mervyn Cooke, *Jazz* (London: Thames & Hudson, 1998), 192–3. See also Lewis Porter, 'The "Blues" Connotation in Ornette Coleman's Music – and Some General

Thoughts on the Relationship of Blues to Jazz', *Annual Review of Jazz Studies*, 7 (1994–5), 75–99.

[35] Oliver and Kernfeld, 'Blues', 248.

[36] Olin Downes, 'Maurice Ravel, Man and Musician', *New York Times* (7 August 1927), X6.

[37] Ravel, *Contemporary Music*, 145, 140.

[38] For example, Downes, 'Maurice Ravel', 49.

[39] Ravel, *Contemporary Music*, 142–3.

tradition versus the criticism faced by American composers whose music is seen as overly European. For him, the answer to this conundrum is to revisit the past and see how so-called nationalist composers held true to their individual conscience, surprisingly singling out Wagner.[40] His prediction is that, whatever the origins of 'negro [*sic*] music', it will have a significant role in establishing an 'American school'; the final rhetoric exhorts, showing seeming familiarity with the differences between jazz, blues, and spirituals, that a new American music should contain much of 'the rich and diverting rhythm of your jazz […] the emotional expression of your blues, and […] the sentiment and spirit characteristic of your popular melodies and songs'. [41]

On the other hand, and more interestingly, distortions and oversimplifications sometimes justify Hodeir's criticisms, and reveal transformation of actuality in Ravel's theory. The reasons for this include Ravel's entitlement to his own aesthetic and his role as a Frenchman in espousing his national identity. He is already selecting what he wants and reading jazz in relation to his artistic (and scholarly) needs. But perhaps the most significant reason is that, for much of the 1920s, his experience of jazz was indirect. Although we find in his record collection the classic 'Tiger Rag',[42] by 1927 Ravel, unlike Milhaud, had still not heard jazz on American soil. In a letter to Henry Prunières of September 1927, Ravel exclaims in slightly contrived fashion: 'As for my feelings about America, it would be better to limit yourself to the strict truth: never having been there, I would be happy to see it […] you may add that I like jazz much more than grand opera.'[43] So Hodeir has something of a point when he says of Ravel, as of Stravinsky and Milhaud, that errors of understanding stem from 'an insufficient acquaintance with authentic jazz'.[44] Conversely, current scholarship would argue for a more inclusive definition of jazz and regard claims of exclusivity or authenticity with suspicion.

Theme 5: Ravel's discussion of jazz can be rather vague and generic; 'Tiger Rag' apart, it is unclear which rags or types of ragtime (cakewalk, two-step, 'coon' song, or folk ragtime) he was familiar with. While he must have known well Debussy's reading in his early 'Golliwogg's Cake-Walk', Ravel never mentions Scott Joplin (1868–1917)[45] with his classics such as 'Magnetic Rag' (1914), or Irving Berlin with his vocal 'Alexander's Ragtime Band' (1911) (though this is not a true rag). There is no acknowledgement of those we now regard as the leading exponents of early, New Orleans jazz: Joe 'King' Oliver (1885–1938), the composer of 'West End Blues', or the young Louis Armstrong (1901–71). In fact Ravel explains that his thematic

---

[40] *Ibid.*, 143–4.
[41] *Ibid.*, 145.
[42] 'Tiger Rag' (Pathé X 94428), coupled with 'Tyrolian Song', sung by the Kentucky Singers.

[43] Orenstein (ed.), *A Ravel Reader*, 280.
[44] Hodeir, *Jazz*, 250.
[45] See Edward A. Berlin, *King of Ragtime: Scott Joplin and His Era* (New York: Oxford University Press, 1994).

inspiration for the Violin Sonata came from Parisian cabaret, though perhaps wisely he gives no more away;[46] elsewhere he refers to 'jazz idioms' which remain unspecified.[47]

Theme 6: Ravel's usage of the term 'picturesque' lays him open to Hodeir's criticisms of superficiality. Obvious comparisons may be drawn between his childlike utterance that 'It is to me a picturesque adventure in composition,' and Hodeir's accusation that the foxtrot of *L'Enfant* exhibits a mere 'picture-postcard exoticism'.[48]

Theme 7: there are issues of seeming oversimplification and misconception. Ravel suggests that jazz is synonymous with 'American popular music',[49] though to be fair he later qualifies his response, alluding to the influence of 'so-called' popular music, and referring in *Contemporary Music* to the blues as 'this popular form of your music'.[50] A revealing misconception – or perhaps a statement of preference – is about Gershwin's status as somehow representative of jazz, when his position was much more of a 'middle man', rather like Tin Pan Alley itself. In making the valid point about being attracted to melody, Ravel juxtaposes Gershwin and jazz, announcing: 'Personally I find jazz most interesting: the rhythms, the way the melodies are handled, the melodies themselves. I have heard some of George Gershwin's works and I find them intriguing.' (His expression, 'the melodies themselves', may refer to notated jazz standards.) Just as tellingly, if we can trust the source, Ravel is quoted as saying: 'The best jazz is *written* by good musicians.'[51] We may then understand Hodeir's disparaging attitude to what he saw as indiscriminate attraction to 'commercial counterfeits', and his exclamation, 'The surprising thing is that someone like Ravel was able to take even as much interest as he did in such obvious trash.'[52] But in a sense Hodeir too misses the point since Ravel was not aiming for any real portrayal of jazz, rather to use his 'take' on an inspirational source to develop his own voice. Furthering Ravel's defence, as mentioned above it is well recognized these days that the term 'jazz' was applied very loosely in the 1920s to a range of musics. And as a creative artist Ravel was perfectly entitled to favour what he perceived as Gershwin's refined stance: one that accorded well with his own aesthetic, including the centrality of writing for the piano which would be asserted ultimately in the concertos.

Finally, theme 8: African-American origins are sometimes downplayed. While there is no evidence that Ravel was in any way racist, indeed his views were distinctly left-wing, this occasional understatement does present as a

[46] [Unsigned interview], 'Ravel Says Poe Aided Him in Composition', *New York Times* (6 January 1928).
[47] Downes, 'Mr Ravel Returns'.
[48] *Ibid.*; Hodeir, *Jazz*, 256.
[49] Downes, 'Mr Ravel Returns'.

[50] Ravel, 'Take Jazz Seriously!', 49; *Contemporary Music*, 140.
[51] [Unsigned interview], 'Famous French Composer in London', *The Star* (16 October 1923), in Orenstein (ed.), *A Ravel Reader*, 428–30: 429 [my italics].
[52] Hodeir, *Jazz*, 251.

distortion.[53] There was an unfortunate expression in a British newspaper interview of 1923, where Ravel apparently damned jazz with faint praise, though it is unclear what, if any, editorial control he had: 'Jazz from America is not wholly to be despised.' More concerning is a comment about jazz harmonies: 'They come from the Negroes, no doubt, but I'm not sure their real origin is not partly English and partly Scotch.'[54] Apropos mixed origins, Ravel's thinking is consistent with the likes of Gunther Schuller, for whom jazz 'developed from a multi-colored variety of musical traditions brought to the new world in part from Africa, in part from Europe'.[55] Nonetheless, in relation to Ravel's special concern with the blues, more recent jazz scholarship is clear where the lion's share of credit should go: 'Blues is in essence an African-American music, with its roots in African-American culture'; crucially, 'its most profound expression' results from the oppressed position of its people, existing like a minority group within 'a dominant white society'.[56] In 1928, hints of Ravel's partial denial of origins persist as, overplaying his national quest, he presents a curious claim about an ostensible jazz from nineteenth-century France. This line of argument could be misconstrued, although Ravel's point about extensive syncopation and the ability of material to mutate whilst retaining a sense of its origin is well made.[57]

Relations between Ravel's theory and practice of jazz

So, even in spring 1928, Ravel's theoretical stance was a little removed from a first-hand experience of improvised jazz, but, importantly, his writings also advocate a set of transformational principles. His sophisticated engagement is plain, questioning the extent of influence and necessary reshaping needed for his compositional purposes. Here I find a little inconsistency in the argument of Perret, who talks rightly of the desirability of 'a marriage between jazz and western music, two musical worlds that one is more accustomed to oppose', but later claims that 'Ravel's step is constantly driven by a desire for confrontation between a foreign cultural language and his own style'.[58] Such a view perhaps overplays opposition and downplays *mélange*,[59] a point

---

53 The attitude was taken to extremes by contemporary critics such as Arthur Hoerée and André Suarès, whereas for Ravel it seemingly arose through considering national identities and musical mutations.
54 'Famous French Composer in London', 429.
55 Schuller, *Early Jazz*, 3.
56 Oliver and Kernfeld, 'Blues', 249.
57 Ravel, 'Take Jazz Seriously!', 49. He also makes a pertinent point about common ground between classical and popular musics.

58 Perret, 'L'Adoption du jazz', 313: 'une cohabitation entre jazz et musique occidentale, deux mondes musicaux que l'on a plutôt coutume d'opposer'; 335: 'La démarche de Ravel est constamment mue par un désir de confrontation entre un langage culturel étranger et son propre style.'
59 *Mélange* is achieved partly through Ravel's noting of an important commonality in national identity, whether from an American or a French perspective.

that will be clarified through analysis below. The following principles derive from Ravel's account of his ultimate jazz-inspired piece, the slow 'Blues' of the Violin Sonata.

Firstly, some borrowed elements are 'adopted'.[60] Within the eclectic approach there has to be assimilation of, or allusion to, the chosen external source(s), but such elements usually act simply as initial 'materials of construction'. Despite Ravel's problematizing of folklore in relation to national musics mentioned above, Perret considers that he still upholds the blues as folklore to be drawn upon.[61] (Her thinking matches that of Paul Oliver, who argues for this music as 'the creation of the people and not separate from the whole fabric of living'.)[62] In this context, we can reasonably assert that paradigms likely to be invoked are a scale with bended pitches,[63] especially at the third and seventh degrees, and the twelve-bar blues form. On the wider importance of certain fixities or predetermined elements which await melodic inspiration, we learn that Ravel's Violin Sonata 'was clearly outlined in his mind before the themes of the first and third movements had taken shape'.[64]

Secondly, materials must be subjected to 'minute stylization' and 'manipulation'.[65] In 'Take Jazz Seriously!', Ravel refers to a 'stylized jazz, more French than American in character, but nevertheless influenced by your so-called "popular music"', and here Hodeir's limitations surface in his naïve surprise that composers 'betray a desire to adapt and stylize it [jazz]'.[66] Back in *Contemporary Music*, Ravel explains that the artwork requires gestation to create a 'mature conception where no detail has been left to chance'; concurring with Perret, we could argue that Ravel's approach opposes at least one fundamental feature of jazz: its improvisatory nature. Such improvisation is itself, however, a complex, finely nuanced matter. Barry Kernfeld recognizes various contexts and types: 'solo'; 'collective', as employed in New Orleans style by the 'front line' players typically of trumpet, clarinet, and trombone; 'paraphrase improvisation' or thematic ornamentation, as explored by Hodeir; a wide-ranging 'formulaic improvisation' with personalized hallmarks or 'licks'; and lastly 'motivic improvisation'.[67] Furthermore, the notion of a completely spontaneous improvisation, without any predetermined framework or embedded harmonic knowledge, is itself a myth.[68]

[60] Ravel, *Contemporary Music*, 140.
[61] *Ibid.*, 143; Perret, 'L'Adoption du jazz', 335.
[62] Paul Oliver, *The Story of the Blues* (London: Barrie & Rockliff, 1969), 6.
[63] For an early, perspicacious study, see Winthrop Sargeant, *Jazz: Hot and Hybrid* (London: Jazz Book Club, 1959).
[64] 'Ravel says Poe Aided Him in Composition'; see too Ravel, 'On Inspiration' (1928), in Orenstein (ed.), *A Ravel Reader*, 389.

[65] Ravel, *Contemporary Music*, 140.
[66] Ravel, 'Take Jazz Seriously!', 49; Hodeir, *Jazz*, 251.
[67] See Barry Kernfeld, 'Improvisation', in *What to Listen for in Jazz* (New Haven and London: Yale University Press, 1995), 119–58; Hodeir, *Jazz*, 161–7.
[68] For a detailed perspective, see Paul F. Berliner, 'Introduction: Picking Notes Out of Thin Air?', *Thinking in Jazz: The*

Finally, 'national characteristics' and 'individualities' are imposed upon the borrowed material,[69] which is enveloped within a larger whole. (On 'individuality', see too Chapter 5, under 'Ravel received: 1928'.) In February 1928, Ravel stresses that 'my musical thinking is entirely national', and in *Contemporary Music* he develops this idea, hypothesizing about other composers, American and European, utilizing the same material, yet emerging with very different results.[70] In this extension of Ravel's notion of origins, the composers' national identities are privileged over those of the sources; in shaping ideas to their own ends, the 'individualities' of Milhaud or Stravinsky outweigh any debt to the 'materials appropriated'. Indeed, as Ravel noted elsewhere, faithful copying would be impossible but, fortuitously enough, originality often emerges through 'unintended unfaithfulness to a model'.[71] And beyond his most obvious exemplar, it is worth summarizing Ravel's assessment of the impact of jazz: 'No one can deny the rhythms of today. My recent music is filled with the influence of jazz. The "fox trot" and "blue" notes in my opera *L'Enfant et les sortilèges* are not the only examples'; in the Concerto in G too: 'one can recognize syncopation, although it is refined'.[72] So, according to Ravel's theory, his compositional techniques involve a mixture of adoption (appropriation) and adaptation (distortion), followed by incorporation within individualized forms. Still viewed within that early jazz context, these principles may now be tested analytically across the parameters of instrumentation, timbre, and texture; ragtime rhythm and form; blues form and melody.

Instrumentation, timbre, and texture

'A pliable set of sounds is at the heart of jazz,'[73] and on these instrumental and textural fundamentals Ravel's practice demonstrates well his idea of assimilation combined with adaptation. Although ragtime is often associated with piano (as immortalized on piano rolls), instrumental and sung versions were also created: so in *L'Enfant*, Ravel's ragtime-foxtrot is introduced by a small bandlike ensemble (Fig. 28ff.). Three trombones, bass clarinet, contrabassoon, bass drum, percussion, voice, and piano are supplemented by upper wind (flutes, clarinet, trumpet, and horns), before the orchestral palette expands to embrace strings with their banjo or guitarlike plucked chords (Fig. 31ff.). Similarly, in the 'Blues', a banjo or guitar sound is adopted, then adapted, as the violin's opening pizzicato triads (developed at Figs. 7

Infinite Art of Improvisation (Chicago and London: University of Chicago Press, 1994), 1–17.

[69]   Ravel, *Contemporary Music*, 140.

[70]   Downes, 'Mr Ravel Returns'; Ravel, *Contemporary Music*, 140.

[71]   Quoted by Roland-Manuel, 'Des valses à *La Valse* (1911–1921)', in Colette et al., *Maurice Ravel par quelques-uns de ses familiers* (Paris: Editions du tambourinaire, 1939), 141–51: 145.

[72]   'A Visit with Maurice Ravel', 473.

[73]   Kernfeld, *What to Listen for in Jazz*, 159.

and 10) are transferred to piano with increased percussive edge (Fig. 1ff.). Fixity and precision in the piano are contrasted by pitch fluidity and timbral variety in the violin: glissandos, 'sul tasto', 'sul ponticello', and 'sul Sol'. As Ravel pointed out, 'What I wanted to do in the violin sonata was to accentuate the contrast between the percussive piano accompaniment and the weaker violin melody.'[74] (The ultimate expression of this articulation is *Boléro* where the 'front line' melody players become consumed by a rhythm section which finally destroys the work.) But while the piano simulates a rhythm-bass section, this does not preclude its exploring subtle timbres, notably the '[con] sord.' indications (Fig. 3ff.): thus this rereading also confounds expectation. In the Concerto in G, Ravel felt he had addressed the same issue through different means. Orenstein observes the enactment of orchestral/solo contrast in the first movement through the presenting of harp and woodwind cadenzas – in jazz parlance, 'breaks' – before the pianist finally gets his turn.[75] Additionally, a jazz-influenced instrumentation is used to reiterate the main theme (Fig. 2ff.): trumpet, supported by trombone (plus horns), and percussion, supplemented by pizzicato strings. The second subject group also foregrounds a jazzlike ensemble of E♭ clarinet, muted trumpet, piano, and percussion (Fig. 5ff.), while subjugated strings sustain a chord beneath. Instrumental combinations apart, Ravel revels in characterizing sound, such as the flutter-tonguing effects on winds in the recapitulation (Fig. 24ff.).

Ragtime rhythm and form

In contrast to Hodeir's dismissive view of Ravel as carried away in *L'Enfant* by 'picture-postcard exoticism', Orledge finds this work to be 'the most successful eclectic amalgam of jazz with different types of "otherness".'[76] Certainly Ravel's rich fantasy vision was not a purist one, but there are, nonetheless, allusions to ragtime and foxtrot (Figs. 28–37). Similarly, Hodeir's further comments seem unduly negative, though conversely they point up Ravel's personalization: 'Maurice Ravel seems to have assimilated the rhythmic procedures of jazz [only] in a very elementary way.'[77] Granted that those distinctive dotted rhythms in *L'Enfant* derive from foxtrot rather than the syncopated patterns of a classic rag and so denote some transformation of the source, nevertheless foxtrot was an accepted variant in later rags from around World War I. Elsewhere, syncopated rhythms do find a place in the 'Blues' of the Violin Sonata, the first movement of the Concerto in G (Figs. 1, 4, 7, and 10), and the opening of the Left Hand Concerto (Fig. 1ff.). Within *L'Enfant*, at the 'Allegro non troppo' (Figs. 28–9; introduction) a striking rhythmic locus

[74] [Unsigned interview], 'Ten Opinions of Mr Ravel', *De Telegraaf* (6 April 1932), in Orenstein (ed.), *A Ravel Reader*, 492–5: 494.

[75] *Ibid.*, 495.
[76] Hodeir, *Jazz*, 256; Orledge, 'Evocations of Exoticism', 43.
[77] Hodeir, *Jazz*, 257.

occurs which serves to mark time, to feature a vamping on the lugubrious tones of the contrabassoon, third trombone, and bass drum, and to create a backing for the casual banter between the Teapot (black Wedgwood) and the Cup (Chinese). In correspondence with Colette, Ravel wondered: 'Perhaps you will object that you don't usually write American Negro slang. I, who don't know a word of English, will do just like you: I'll work it out.'[78] The result is a delightfully zany few bars whose English stresses are reversed and set against the metre, but whose nonsense declamation approaches the spirit of a 'Satchmo' scat, combined as Colette observed with the world of music hall. Benjamin Ivry suggests that the neat inclusion of 'How's your mug?' may have been courtesy of Victor de Sabata, *L'Enfant*'s original conductor.[79] (For more on the textual genesis, see Chapter 2, under 'Musical and poetic interplay'.)

Formally, instrumental rags, operating in a 2/4 or 4/4 march-like metre, tended to be built up in units as AABBCC et cetera comprising at least three different sixteen-bar themes or strains, each consisting of four four-bar phrases. Their themes were subjected to repetition and later reprise, and might feature introductions and brief interludes (both elements adopted by Ravel); extended patterns yielded formulas such as 'AABBAACC, AABBCCDD, and AABBCCA', starting in the tonic before moving to the subdominant for a 'trio' section.[80] While Ravel's raglike conception was a free one, he theorizes nevertheless about 'a single couplet with refrain'[81] to which he adheres closely in practice. In miniaturist fashion, he halves the quantities of a standard raglike recipe and brings expected modulations forward; in fact, the small-scale lyric patterns may be seen as quartered, creating a hierarchy of relations as illustrated in Table 6.1. A truncated fifteen-bar section for the Teapot (Figs. 29–31) is portrayed literally as a 'black' A♭ minor – the minor key being much rarer in ragtime – with the maximal seven flats. Theme A (Fig. 29), with its antecedent focused initially upon B♭ minor, is balanced by a modified repeat (Fig. 30) on its subdominant major, E♭ (for the pitch detail, see under 'Blues form and melody' below). Other subtle customization includes the overlaying of a lyric couplet, 'nose/chose', across a musical articulation. The ensuing Theme B for the Chinese Cup occupies a twenty-bar trio section (Figs. 31–3: sixteen bars, plus a four-bar interlude), which again is characterized literally as a much paler F major with one flat – effectively a semitonal misreading of classic rag theory that would favour the subdominant of the relative, i.e. F♭. After Ravel reaches the expected relative: C♭ major, as the dominant of F♭ (Fig. 30^{+3}), he pushes up a further chromatic step to C[7]

[78] Orenstein (ed.), *A Ravel Reader*, 188.
[79] Benjamin Ivry, *Maurice Ravel: A Life* (New York: Welcome Rain, 2000), 130.
[80] See Edward A. Berlin, 'Ragtime', in Stanley Sadie (ed.), *The New Grove*

Dictionary of Music and Musicians, 29 vols. (London: Macmillan, 2001), vol. XX, 755–9: 756.
[81] Orenstein (ed.), *A Ravel Reader*, 188. (See 'Theme 2' above.)

Table 6.1 Comparison of raglike forms

(a) Typical rag form	(b) Ravel's form in L'Enfant (Figs. 29–32)		
Music	Fig.	Music	Lyrics
A (16 bars – occasional minor key)	Fig. 29 (8 bars)	Theme A: Antecedent – melody on B♭ minor; A♭ minor: V⁷	a: Black, and costaud, Black and chic,
		A♭ minor: [V⁷]–i	a: Black, black, black, jolly fellow, jolly fellow, black,
		Consequent; V⁷–i	b: I punch, Sir, I punch your nose,
		[i]	b: I punch,
A (16 bars – exact repetition)	Fig. 30 (7 bars)	Theme A': Antecedent – melody on E♭ major; A♭ minor: i	b: I knock out you, stupid chose!
	.	C♭ major: I (relative)	a': Black, black and thick, and vrai beau gosse,
		Consequent; shifting	b': I boxe you, I boxe you,
		C major: V–I⁷	b': I marm'lad' you.
B (16 bars – relative major)	Fig. 31⁻¹	Trio: Theme B – pentatonic (F major: V⁷ – raised subdominant of relative)	c: Kengçafou, Mahjong, c: Kengçafou, Puis'kongkongpranpa, d: Çaohrâ, Çaohrâ, d: Çaohrâ, Çaohrâ …

(Fig. 31⁻²), as the dominant of F. His extended reprise offers a nice twist in combining the main themes bitonally (Figs. 33–7), ultimately favouring the tonality of F. Tellingly, a similar black/white musical conceit is played out in 'Aoua!', from *Chansons madécasses* (1925–6), to denote the tensions between black and white peoples, which remain sadly irreconcilable in de Parny's text presented from a black perspective.

Blues form and melody

On the large scale, Ravel's 'Blues' movement employs a ternary, or modified sonata form,[82] but might there be evidence of localized blues form? Although Orledge perceives 'no signs of the conventional chord progressions associated with the twelve-bar negro blues', I want to test this idea further in relation to the introduction. Certainly there is profound manipulation, but the opening

[82] Unlike Perret ('L'Adoption du jazz', 344), I do not perceive a separate development section at Fig. 5 (bar 63ff.), but this point still marks a B section on the dominant(s). Section A' (Fig. 9; bar 110) then recapitulates ideas from both earlier sections.

Table 6.2 Comparison of blues forms

(a) Standard 12-bar blues					(b) Ravel's 10-bar blues			
|I	|(IV)	|I$^{(7)}$	|—	|	|I	|I IV	|I V	|
|IV$^{(7)}$	|—	|I$^{(7)}$	|—	|	|I	|—	|—	|
|V$^{(7)}$	|(IV)	|I$^{(7)}$	|V$^{(7)}$	||	|I	|I IV	|I	|I V ||

violin strumming does provide a kind of blues harmonic structure in simple crotchet pulses, as a paradigm, or primed canvas on which to paint. Kernfeld offers a model here in relating a basic blues structure to customized versions by Charlie Parker ('Blues for Alice', 1951) and Charles Mingus ('Goodbye Pork Pie Hat', 1959).[83] Thus Table 6.2 compares a standard, schematic twelve-bar blues form[84] with Ravel's truncated ten-bar structure. Standard four-bar phrases are contracted to three-bar ones and, while the main I–IV–I–V–I progression is maintained, initially without added sevenths, the rate of harmonic change ebbs and flows. But Ravel's reading still employs a common blues-form variation known in the trade as the 'quick to four' – an early move to the subdominant – in bar 2 and ends with a dominant (bar 10), to effect what is aptly called a 'turnaround'.

By contrast, across bars 11–26 (Figs. 1–2), Orledge privileges a sixteen-bar 'verse' structure more akin to the songs of Gershwin or Kern, with a gentle rhythmic syncopation 'in the character of Gershwin's sanitisations of authentic rough jazz'. But consistent with Ravel's interventionist theory, Orledge identifies the end of this passage as classic Ravel: 'a cycle of fifths pattern typically spiced up with sevenths, ninths and judiciously spaced bitonality',[85] in the keys of A♭ and G. So we have more evidence of transforming and individualizing those 'constructive materials'; we shall return to these bars presently.

On the crucial expressive and fluid blues melody, Hodeir's observation, apropos the concertos, of 'appreciable melodic borrowings from the language of blues and spirituals' still holds sway.[86] Incipient blues third gestures, linear but spatially separated, are found in *L'Enfant* in the Teapot's line: a dotted minor phrase: B♭–C, D♭–C, B♭–C, D♭ (Fig. 29; 'Black, and costaud, Black and chic') is balanced by a major phrase a fourth higher: E♭–F, G–F, E♭–F, G (Fig. 30; 'I knock out you, stupid chose'), anticipated in the second half of the first phrase. Rag/blues theory is closely played out – as major/minor mixture

83 Barry Kernfeld, 'Blues Progression', in Kernfeld (ed.), *The New Grove Dictionary of Jazz*, vol. I, 255–6: 256.
84 See Kernfeld, 'Blues Progression', 255, and Richard Middleton, *Studying Popular Music* (Milton Keynes and Philadelphia, PA: Open University Press, 1990), 197–8.

85 Orledge, 'Evocations of Exoticism', 42. Even here, Ravel creates three phrases as a reconfigured blues form: A (1 + 5 bars), B (5½ bars), B (4½ bars), rather than AAB.
86 Hodeir, *Jazz*, 252.

Example 6.1 Ravel, Piano Concerto in G: blues third treatment
(a) Start of second subject, solo piano (I, Fig. 4, bars 1–5)
(b) Second subject group (continued), solo piano (I, Fig. 8, bars 1–4)

and partitioning between lower and upper scalic segments – and is therefore less transformed. Similarly, in the Left Hand Concerto, an opening minor idea on contrabassoon is balanced by a major reinflection (Fig. 2; see Example 6.2a and 6.2b). Later, we find a neat reworking of blues third combined with scalic partitioning, noted as 'one of the melodic lines most frequently used by old-time singers and players of the blues'.[87] Above a plucked string pedal on C, with oscillating major–minor third: E–D♯ (on viola), an 'espressivo' bassoon repeats the lower scalic segment: E♭–D–C (Fig. 28ff.), followed by the upper segment which emphasizes the flattened seventh: (G) B♭–A–G. But a double melodic/harmonic emphasis of the flattened seventh (Fig.1) shows Ravel effectively outdoing, or transforming, any blues model: the ending of the contra's theme outlines a seventh chord, C, E, G, B♭, the root of which is the flattened seventh of the tonic, D. Meanwhile, in the Concerto in G, a 'vertical' blues third occurs near the start of the poignant second subject on solo piano (first movement, Fig. 4; Example 6.1a): based harmonically upon the seventh degree, F♯, the major third, A♯, is asserted in the bass arpeggiation and pitted against melodic A within a Phrygian collection on F♯ (i.e. F♯, G, A, B, C♯, D, E). But a more 'authentic' linear expression is adopted with the resumption of the piano texture (first movement, Fig. 8ff.; Example 6.1b): in A major, set beneath an exquisite, accented seventh degree which falls to the sixth, G♯–F♯, the bass arpeggiation presents the minor blue note resolving onto the major third: B♯–C♯.[88]

[87] *Ibid*. Ravel commented on 'this jazz music' being brought to the fore in the scherzo: Michel-Dimitri Calvocoressi, 'M Ravel Discusses His Own Work', *Daily Telegraph* (11 July 1931).

[88] This idea was rehearsed in the Left Hand Concerto (Fig. 8^{+4}), where an F♯ arpeggiation features a major third falling to the minor: A♯–A, a gesture replayed on D♯–D within a B^7 harmony (Fig. 9^{+2}).

The ultimate locus is, however, the 'Blues', to which we return. Ravel surely understands the flexible melodic bending of seventh and third scalic degrees (horizontally, within a phrase), as demonstrated in the main theme (Figs. 1–2). We could categorize linear blue notes as an element 'adopted' (perhaps as Orledge suggests after Venuti and, following transfer of the bending to the piano, after Paul Whiteman's Orchestra), then 'stylized' and controlled. Pitch bending is particularly effective on violin, akin to the voice, where Ravel details the use of the A string and the playing of F–F♯–G (bars 12–13) with the second finger alone, the gesture then reiterated and balanced on A–B♭–B (bars 15–16). Still aligned with Ravel's theory, further manipulation and personalizing is revealed when the bitonal violin and piano parts are combined (bars 11–18; see Example 6.5a). The antecedent part of the melodic phrase: G–F–F♯–G, may be read as 8–7–7♯–8 in an upper modality on G. Alternatively, F♯–G might be heard as G♭–G: an expressive, lingering blues seventh gesture in the lower modality of A♭, which is after all the key signature. The 'nostalgico' marking, apt given the innate melancholy and seriousness of the blues, also indicates something elusive or unattainable – 'real' jazz?[89] The consequent of this phrase (bars 14–16) emphasizes the minor seventh, F, via upper and lower neighbour notes (i.e. G and E♭), thence to the A–B♭–B gesture, which does feel to be a blues minor–major third inflection in G, supported by the repeated G/B in the central texture. Of course, B may also be heard as C♭, a flattened third in terms of the bass on A♭. So in a clever transformation, and with deceptive economy, Ravel achieves a blue effect with a single pitch: B/C♭, in relation to tonics on G and A♭.[90] Similarly, in the second phrase (bars 17–22), a major–minor third: C♭ [B]–B♭, in G (bars 17–18) coexists with a minor–major gesture: C♭–C, in A♭. A distinct blue-note complex emerges: see Table 6.3.

On a larger scale, malleability of material is pursued through five variant readings of the main 'Blues' theme,[91] as a composed-out improvisation – a contradiction in terms, yet implying a greater heeding of this fundamental jazz concept in Ravel's practice than in his theory (as discussed above). Varied

[89] Carolyn Abbate has questioned why Ravel used 'nostalgico' here if his motivation in adopting jazz was essentially modernist. Ravel's music is temporally complex and invariably engages with the past in some way. Despite his claim that the 'Blues' was more Parisian than American, the very title might reasonably indicate empathy with the history of an oppressed people (as in the *Chansons madécasses*, composed concurrently). The music also layers the serious and the more frivolous.

[90] Harmonically, Ravel's use of combined fifths a semitone apart (A♭–E♭; G–D) apes that of the typical flattened fifth in jazz (albeit notated as A♭–D). I am grateful to Julian Horton for this point.

[91] Perret too discusses 'variation thématique': 'L'Adoption du jazz', 344. As for a blues-form complex, we might view the first three variants of the main theme that comprise section A as a medium-scale rereading of blues form (or indeed the complete ternary structure in the same way).

Table 6.3 Ravel's melodic/harmonic blue-note complex

Blue notes:	Minor–major thirds		Minor–major sevenths	
Pitches:	B♭–B	B[C♭]–C	F–F♯	F♯[G♭]–G
Tonality:	G	A♭	G	A♭

Example 6.2 Ravel, Piano Concerto for the Left Hand: thematic variation
(a) Introductory theme – minor (bars 2–4; contrabassoon);
(b) Introductory theme – major (Fig. 2, bars 1–2);
(c) First subject proper (Fig. 4⁺³; piano)

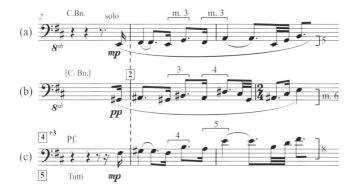

repetition also occurs in the Concerto in G (I), where a higher profile is afforded to improvisatory notions courtesy of the harp's *Quasi cadenza* designation (Fig. 22), followed by the *Cadenza* proper (Fig. 26). It is a special factor in the Left Hand Concerto, where the thematic material only gradually becomes focused. Until confirmed by a forthright orchestral repetition (Fig. 5), we wonder whether the piano's cadenzalike entrance (Fig. 4), as an early jazz 'break', denotes a more distant derivative of the contrabassoon's opening melody (with intervallic expansion through to an octave), or the arrival point of 'true' thematic identity. This variation process is illustrated in Example 6.2.

Discrepancies in practising jazz

Since Ravel's theory generally postdates his practice, extensive correlation is unsurprising, but interestingly elements of his practice are glossed over in theory: in particular several overt cross-references between his music and that of others, as straight 'adoption' – almost quotation. So, as with the first relationship investigated in the first half of this chapter (page 117–23) we find some untransformed aspects, although they are more exceptional here.

On predictable territory, there are striking similarities between Ravel's jazz practice and Gershwin's: one dimension in which Ravel's music is notably Americanized. We can compare a piano figuration in the 'Blues' (Fig. 5ff.),

Example 6.3 Comparison between Ravel, Concerto in G and Bruch, Violin Concerto
(a) Ravel (I, Fig. 5, bars 1–2); (b) Bruch (II, Adagio, bars 16–20)

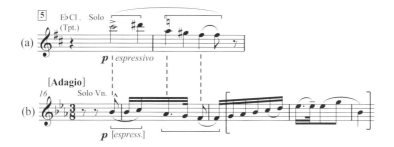

featuring reaccented three-quaver groupings as a melodic third progression: (F♯–G♯) A–G♯–F♯, with a repeated three-quaver accompaniment from *Rhapsody in Blue*: B♭–A–G; B–A–G (Figs. 9–11).[92] Ravel's dotted figure on piano – C♯, D♯–C♯, E[♮] (Fig. 6ff.) – echoes the refrain from Gershwin's 'The Man I Love' (or is it the opening verse of 'Fascinating Rhythm', or even Milhaud's 'Fugue' from *La Création*?). Equally, we could relate it back to the woodwind (bass clarinet, flute) and vocal figurations of the Teapot in *L'Enfant* (Figs. 28–31), or forward to the opening theme of the Left Hand Concerto: E, F♯–E, G (–F♯, A). These loci all derive from, or extend, a 'four-note figure' identified by Hodeir as 'particularly prized by composers "inspired" by jazz'.[93] Other close Gershwin references include the syncopated rising melody in E major, with a prominent sixth scalic degree, from the Concerto in G (first movement, Fig. 7) and an idea in A minor from *Rhapsody in Blue*, as compared by David Schiff.[94] Beyond their shared overall contour, both four-bar phrases are subdivided as 1 + 1 + 2.

We also find unexpected, untheorized similarities: the resemblance of the 'espressivo' imitative theme in the second subject group of the Concerto in G (first movement, Fig. 5ff.) to the powerful 'Adagio' theme from Max Bruch's Violin Concerto No. 1 in G minor; see Example 6.3. The main intervallic relations and stresses are very similar, with the tritonal descent around the apex of Ravel's melody suggesting an expressive exaggeration of Bruch's major third, 'jazzed' à la Gershwin.

Further unexpected correspondence exists between Ravel's 'Blues' and a light-hearted piano piece by Mayerl: his 'Marigold' (1927), an item held in Ravel's record collection in a performance by Carmen Guilbert.[95] Since

92 Ravel uses other three-note hemiola figures, ostinato-like, near the start of the Concerto in G (Fig. 1ff.): G, E–D, in even quavers on upper woodwind and: C, E–D(–C), in a counterpointed dotted augmentation on bassoons and horns. See too David Schiff, *Gershwin: Rhapsody in Blue* (Cambridge University Press, 1997), 18, 20.

93 Hodeir, *Jazz*, 254.
94 Schiff, *Gershwin*, 20.
95 Billy Mayerl, 'Marigold', from *Syncopated Impressions*; Carmen Guilbert, piano (Pathé X 98042). Guilbert also recorded Ravel's 'Alborada del gracioso' in 1935 (Pathé (Fr) PAT23); see Orenstein (ed.), *A Ravel Reader*, 611.

Example 6.4 Comparisons between Ravel, Sonata for Violin and Piano: 'Blues' and Mayerl, *Syncopated Impressions*: 'Marigold'
(a) Melodic comparison: Ravel (bars 43–5) and Mayerl (bars 5–7)
(b) Harmonic comparison: Ravel (bar 46) and Mayerl (bar 8)

Guilbert's Paris recording was not made until July 1931,[96] it is reasonable to assume that the similarities are effectively generic within a raglike mould, rather than connoting Mayerl's influence upon Ravel, though Ravel might conceivably have heard the former's music live in 1927. Whatever the cause and effect, from a hermeneutic stance, Ravel's raglike dotted, descending figuration (Fig. 3ff.: bars 43–5 of the piano part) may usefully be compared with Mayerl's main theme (bar 5ff., following a brief introduction), as demonstrated in Example 6.4. Apart from the general melodic-rhythmic contour, commonalities include an upper neighbour-note figure, the motive C, B♭, G, and dotted notes F–E♭ (amid a fondness for major seconds and fourths). Another instance concerns the harmonic gestures which follow: Ravel's E♭⁹ bass treatment (bars 46–7) and Mayerl's more characterized, fruity chromatic reading on B♭¹³ (bars 8 and 16). Both feature the chordal root in the bass (beat 1), followed by a tenor stepwise descent (beats 2–4), with inner pedal notes that span a major second: the two sets of bars could comfortably belong to the same piece.

As for possible setting of agendas, Ravel's main 'Blues' theme (Fig. 1ff.) cannily anticipates Gershwin's 'Summertime' aria from his opera *Porgy*

[96] Personal communication from John Watson (21 April 2008). Watson, who compiled the discography for Peter Dickinson, *Marigold: The Music of Billy Mayerl* (Oxford and New York: Oxford University Press, 1999), describes Guilbert's renditions of Mayerl's pieces as 'competent, if perhaps slightly cautious, performances'. Ravel's apparent appreciation of Mayerl was reciprocated by Mayerl on BBC Radio's *Desert Island Discs* in 1958 when he requested 'Laideronnette' from *Ma mère l'Oye*, plus works by Stravinsky and Milhaud.

Example 6.5 Ravel's apparent anticipation of Gershwin
(a) Ravel, Sonata for Violin and Piano: 'Blues' (bars 12–16)
(b) Gershwin, *Porgy and Bess*: 'Summertime' (Fig. 17^{-1})

and Bess (1935). This idea develops Orledge's suggestion of stylistic similarities between Ravel's 'Blues' and Kern or Gershwin songs, though it must be remembered that such songs were never strictly jazz or blues. We might argue for a more finely nuanced triangulation of similarity.[97] Undoubtedly, the melodic influence of songs from Gershwin's *Lady Be Good* (1924), including 'Fascinating Rhythm' and 'The Man I Love' – in fact discarded from the show – is felt in Ravel's 'Blues' (heard by Gershwin in 1928), which seemingly then acts as a catalyst for Gershwin in 'Summertime' (Example 6.5a and 6.5b). Ravel's marking of 'nostalgico' well befits the bittersweet recollections of summer, and is maintained in Gershwin's marking of Clara's lullaby 'with much expression'. The two loci share a quiet, spacious lyricism and gentle 'Moderato'. Melodically, both open with a sustained pitch, reinforced from beneath – by a second or third interval, respectively – to form the antecedent, which leads to a syncopated (or dotted) descending consequent. Portamentos act as final expressive gestures in each piece. Harmonically, both are supported by significant fifth intervals.

[97] One of the most respected studies of Gershwin's music, with a chapter on *Porgy and Bess*, does not mention this similarity: Steven Gilbert, *The Music of Gershwin* (New Haven and London: Yale University Press, 1995), 182–207. Gilbert does, however, note references in *Porgy* back to *Rhapsody in Blue*: 194, and so the triangulation continues.

As a second triangulation, while Ravel's guitarlike plucking in the 'Blues' surely betrays the influence of typical Spanish models, in turn it looks forward to the jazzed practice of Django Reinhardt. Balancing this, Ravel's violin treatment may, according to Orledge, reveal the influence of Venuti, but it neatly anticipates the young Stéphane Grappelli (1908–97). An American number by Walter Donaldson with lyrics by Gus Kahn entitled 'I've Had My Moments', recorded in September 1935 by Grappelli and His Hot Four, features a very similar punctuated rhythmic/chordal background on guitar which supports a floating, melancholic melody on violin.

Jazz Gallicized and 'Ravelized'

Scrutiny of Ravel's theory in relation to the complexities of early jazz has shown how the composer's impressive cultural grasp makes for close correspondence, coupled with some transformation: a few distortions may have been unintentional; other idiosyncrasies are in line with his argument for compositional 'individuality'. In the main theory–practice(–actuality) relationship, analysis of Ravel's compositional techniques has confirmed his stated transformative principles, amid some untheorized similarities between his music and potential sources. Ultimately, this sophisticated theory–practice of jazz (broadly interpreted) needs to be understood as part of a necessary response and contribution to modernism itself, and as one privileged form of eclecticism. It operates in a similar fashion to Ravel's fascination with machines, or his lifelong love of Spain and the Pays Basque. Despite, or perhaps because of, his strong attraction to Gershwin's example, Ravel was not looking to convey an 'authentic' jazz; instead he used his enthusiastic reaction to it as a way of accessing new 'exotic' colourings and timbral/textural finds to inflect his own voice.

The result of this border crossing, and the arrival point of Ravel's theory, is a further developed French music which retains its national core. It exists within what was already becoming, thanks to Milhaud, Auric, and other members of Les Six, a distinctly Gallic tradition of jazzed art music. Blues acts as an expressive vehicle for Ravel to pursue an archetypally French musical concern with 'la mélodie' while, harmonically, his seventh chords and certain textures owe much to Debussy, the violin pizzicati in his 'Blues' being reminiscent of 'Ibéria' from *Images*.[98]

As important, the jazz-inspired repertory maintains a personal core and so is 'Ravelized': the frequent harmonic fifth intervals in the 'Blues', A♭–E♭

[98] DeVoto, 'Harmony in the Chamber Music', 115.

combined with G–D, act as a hallmark in Ravel's musical language from *Daphnis et Chloé* (1912) onwards.[99] This versatile fifth object serves to connote the ancient and, even more widely, a blended otherness not only of the past and the exotic, but of the classical and the popular. (Ravel's literalism in *L'Enfant* and 'Aoua!' from *Chansons madécasses*, in portraying black/ white relations, is another stylistic hallmark.) And if we criticize Ravel for his unacknowledged near-quotation of others, we should at least recognize this as part of his own aesthetic of recycling – especially postwar, since he also quotes himself. In the 'Blues', both the effective strumming, which anticipates *Boléro*, and the raglike, melodic fifth 'tic' that begins and ends the piano part are rereadings of *L'Enfant* (Figs. 31–7).

Crucially, Ravel's engagement with jazz gives as much as it takes. While the American premiere of the Violin Sonata, played by Joseph Szigeti and the composer, at the Gallo Theater in New York offered a most convenient springboard for the 1928 tour, Ravel's invocation of jazz was of longer-term consequence. It created an impetus for, and a key to our understanding of, his late works from *Boléro* to the piano concertos. Arguably, it played a role in his final work before terminal illness silenced his creativity: the third song, 'Chanson à boire', from *Don Quichotte à Dulcinée* (1932–3) opens with a prominent melodic outline of a seventh chord that echoes the Left Hand Concerto (Fig. 1). Furthermore, aspects of Ravel's 'Blues' anticipate wider developments of the 1930s, both American and French: the main melody has been shown to resonate with Gershwin's 'Summertime', yet to come, and the combination of jazzed violin lyricism plus strumming accompaniment presages the captivating sound world of Grappelli and Reinhardt. But for all his adopting and adapting of elements of American jazz, the last word should be this: 'I venture to say that nevertheless it is French music, Ravel's music, that I have written.'[100]

---

[99] Other reminders of *Daphnis* in jazzed contexts include the rippling LH accompaniment of sextuplet semiquavers (down–up contour) in the cadenza of the Concerto in G (first movement, Figs. 26–8) and the primordial opening of the Left Hand Concerto, where a quartal harmony in cellos and basses, pitched as the bass open strings

(E, A, D, G), is 'horizontalized' as sextuplet semiquavers (up–down contour). With its foreboding start, the Left Hand Concerto continues a fatalistic strand in Ravel's writing, apparent in *Daphnis* and resurfacing in *La Valse* and *Boléro*.

[100] Ravel, *Contemporary Music*, 140.

Encountering *La Valse*: perspectives and pitfalls

David Epstein, completed by Deborah Mawer

In a *New York Times* review on 12 December 1997 of a concert in Carnegie Hall by the Boston Symphony Orchestra, the critic Paul Griffiths spoke with admiration of the brilliant performance of Ravel's *La Valse* that closed the programme.[1] He noted among other things the 'heroic work' done by the players in keeping to the conductor's 'dizzying tempo at the end'. Indeed *La Valse*, one of Ravel's most popular and often-played works, routinely closes in current performances with a tempo of great speed, be it 'dizzying', 'exciting', 'brilliant', or, as this chapter will suggest, a somewhat perverse distortion of a deep work for the sake of effect and easy success.

This chapter is thus concerned with performance, specifically with ways by which concepts of a work may be determined, and with the effect these concepts have upon interpretation. Not the least of these concepts is that of tempo, an element that in the view of one writer appears increasingly to play an overarching role in shaping the flow of musical ideas.[2] The focus here is Ravel's choreographic poem *La Valse* (1919–20), in its orchestral version. The perspective upon tempo, unlike the view that motivated my 1995 study, is not so much global as local – namely, what Ravel may have meant by the special score designation 'Pressez' as a clue to the music lying within the closing minutes of this work. Although the

This chapter is dedicated to the memory of David Epstein (1930–2002).

Beyond standard editing, the chapter has been completed by combining an 'expanded abstract' (in fact a nineteen-page typescript of text and footnotes, dated 13 April 1999), a series of analytical examples, and three pages of 'additional perspectives' and paragraphs intended for the development of this 'nascent' or 'quasi-article' (letter to the editor, 21 April 1999), which were entrusted to me. My intention in publishing these materials posthumously with the permission of David's family is to pay an affectionate tribute to David Epstein, who was keenly supportive of *The Cambridge Companion to Ravel* and this sequel, *Ravel Studies*. It was David's wish that his work should be included here (correspondence with the editor, 11

December 1999) – expressed in his inimitable fashion, 'So let's plan on it.' Now, a decade or so on from those well-laid plans, it is my honour and pleasure to attempt to realize it.

While endeavouring to produce a cohesive, complete piece of scholarship, I have been circumspect about introducing new material, and have clarified in footnotes where interpolations or reorderings occur; I have also reduced some potential duplication. I very much hope that the reader will find this a valuable and special inclusion.

[1] For more on Ravel, the Boston Symphony Orchestra, and Carnegie Hall, see Chapter 5. [Ed.]

[2] See David Epstein, *Shaping Time: Music, the Brain, and Performance* (New York: Schirmer Books, 1995).

focus is restricted, revolving around just one direction for speed, the concern is in fact a macro one. For how this direction is understood determines how the entire work will ultimately be seen – that is, as an essentially brilliant work exclusively of high-level 'entertainment', or as a statement that also contains darker implications of the tragic. As with many distinguished works of art, an amalgam of concepts pervades *La Valse*. This is no simple matter, however. Some of these concepts must be derived from evidence not necessarily explicit; some may obtrude from perspectives beyond the work itself. In addition, some may be hierarchic in import, overriding others in interpretative significance.

These views are hardly commonplace in interpretative thinking, guided as it often is by the pressures and pragmatic demands of performance. Yet these views bear critically upon the shaping of *La Valse*, particularly in the ways by which they determine tempos and their associated climaxes. Failure to perceive them often leads to readings that underplay, if not misrepresent, Ravel's important score.

Among the formative concepts underlying *La Valse* is certainly the notion of spectacle – a 'good show', as our media moguls would have it, in the sense of an exciting theatrical event. *La Valse*, after all, was planned as theatre – as ballet.[3] Furthermore, the work is laid out upon carefully structured dimensions. Significant among its factors are: a carefully scheduled tonal plan; an *étude*-like approach to its materials; and a structural unity among its numerous waltz themes that relies upon the prevalence of motivic intervals, a Ravelian compositional approach not unlike Schoenberg's concept of a *Grundgestalt*, or basic shape, although the association of these two names, so many poles apart in the spectrum of twentieth-century composition, may come as something of a surprise.[4]

Theatre and the tonal framework of *La Valse*[5]

The 'murky' beginning of *La Valse*, the gradual emergence of waltz rhythms from this obscurity (see Example 7.1 a–c), the eventual flowering of a full-scale waltz (Example 7.2) – these events, and the frenetic explosion that closes the work, are the stuff of theatre. It is not hard to imagine lighting, costumes, and choreography which in the initial conception of the work would serve to enrich this musical scenario. That beginning is more than theatre alone, however. Its seeming obscurity in fact rests upon a scheduled tonal plan

[3] It did not initially see life that way, however, due to a misunderstanding between Ravel and Diaghilev. See Arbie Orenstein, *Ravel: Man and Musician* (New York: Dover Publications, 1991), 77–8. (For more on ballet, see chapters 2 and 8 in this volume. [Ed.])

[4] On the concept of the *Grundgestalt*, with associated references, see David Epstein, *Beyond Orpheus: Studies in Musical Structure* (Cambridge, MA: MIT Press, 1979).

[5] Most headings in the text are editorial. [Ed.]

Example 7.1 Ravel, *La Valse*: gradual emergence of waltz rhythms
(a) Bass reduction (bars 1, 5, and 9)
(b) Bass reduction and chordal constructs (Figs. 1 and 3)
(c) Reduced score (Figs. 5, 7, and 8–9)

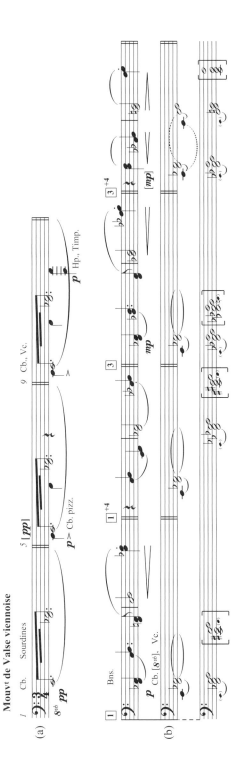

Example 7.1 (cont.)

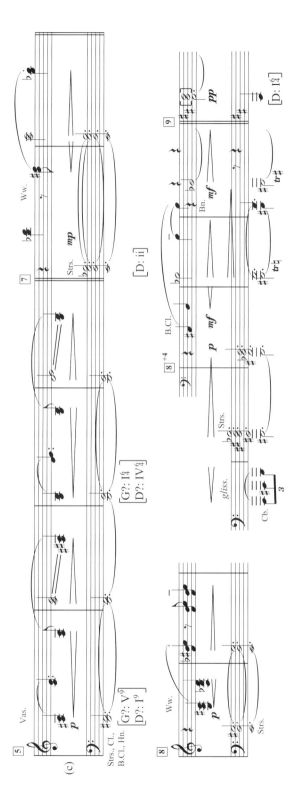

Example 7.2 Ravel, *La Valse* (Fig. 13, bars 2–8): reduced score

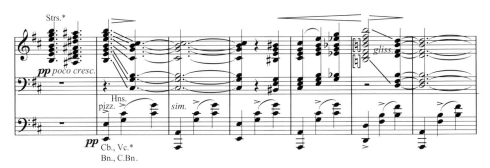

* Strs. - con sord. Mutes to be removed one by one.

whereby the music lies upon satellite degrees of the tonic, D major, arriving at the tonic only at Fig. 9,[6] some minutes into the music; see again Example 7.1. Chromatic harmony in this murky opening builds upon chords compatible with the bass note F, prolonging the 'floating' motion that delays the arrival in the tonic (Example 7.1b).

To expand on this point: the 'murkiness' involves more than merely deep and at times obscure sonorities, or soft dynamics and articulations.[7] It extends to ambiguities of harmonic structure in the passages that are shown in Example 7.1b. As seen in the harmonic summary below the sketch of the score in Example 7.1b, the 'simplest' harmonic context of these bars favours a low F as the structural bass note. In this first version, its adjacent pitch, E, functions as a lower neighbour note and is thus ornamental, despite the fact that it is metrically prominent because of its placement upon the first beat of each bar – indeed, an accented placement. A second reading is also feasible, and is shown in the bracketed chords of the harmonic summary. Here, E serves as the structural bass note, with F lying as an adjacent (and ornamental) upper neighbour note. The bassoon lines from Fig. 1 through to Fig. 3[+4] fit harmonically in this view as well. Hence the ambiguity, even if the two versions are not necessarily equal in their harmonic rationale. The notion of F as the structural bass is probably more convincing, not least for the greater simplicity with which it fits the overall harmonic paradigms, but also for the fact that F provides a stronger lower line from a melodic or contrapuntal perspective. F leads down to E as a structural bass at Fig. 4[+2] (in the cellos and lower line of the double basses, and, two bars later, the entry pitch of the harp). In turn, E leads downward to D at Fig. 5, where a more significant melody is

[6] Rehearsal figures are those given in Maurice Ravel, *La Valse* (Paris: Editions Durand, 1921). For copyright reasons, it has not been possible to include all the short score quotations that were envisaged by Epstein, but in any event the reader is directed to the full score to support most effectively the detailed discussion of the music which follows. [Ed.]

[7] This paragraph was originally an extensive footnote. [Ed.]

heard; see Example 7.1c. That melody is an outgrowth of the motivic fragment first heard in the bassoons at Fig. 1.

The first waltz allowed to appear in 'full bloom', so to speak (Fig.13^{+1}; Example 7.2), is set over a pedal tone on the dominant of D, coming to a full tonic resolution only at its close (Fig. 18^{-1}). D as tonic, therefore as the focal tonal centre, appears only at calculated places in the score – a tonal anchor in the midst of excursions to other centres. Thus the return to D at Fig. 54 carries with it a recall of the opening – significantly, at the opening tempo, and with the same 'murkiness' and tonal ambiguity as at bar 1; the return to D at Fig. 76 initiates the final section of the score.

The notion of étude

A conceptual perspective in *La Valse* slightly less obvious than that of theatre still embodies a characteristic modus operandi of Ravel: one whereby a work serves as an *étude*. *Le Tombeau de Couperin* (1914–17; orchestrated 1919), for example, is a study of dance forms of the French baroque: the 'forlane', 'rigaudon', and 'menuet'. The *Rapsodie espagnole* (1907–8), in its 'Malagueña', 'Habanera', and 'Feria', emulates, 'studies', and plays with Spanish dance idioms. *Alborada del gracioso* (from *Miroirs*, 1904–5; orchestrated 1918) embodies a broad spectrum of Spanish genres. In a manner similar to the beginning of *La Valse*, the 'Prélude à la nuit' of the *Rapsodie* studies the harmonic possibilities consistent with tonal harmony that are latent in the notes of its opening obbligato.[8] *Boléro* (1928) is a study in orchestration, as is Ravel's transcription of Mussorgsky's *Tableaux d'une exposition* (Pictures at an Exhibition, orchestrated in 1922). The *Tzigane* (1924) probes gypsy music, as the two piano concertos, of 1929–31, do American jazz. Additionally, numerous songs by Ravel emulate genres of French, Italian, Hebraic, Scotch, Flemish, and Russian music.

This *étude* approach is a subtext of *La Valse*. Elements of its studies generate subsequent events in the piece. The various tableaux touch upon nuances and character embodiments of the waltz idiom, all of them integral to the Viennese style that reigns throughout the work. (The overriding tempo direction of *La Valse*, unadorned by any quantified reference such as a metronome indication, is simply 'Mouvement de Valse viennoise'.) Thus the waltz is seen in its brilliant extrovert elegance, *fortissimo* brass and percussion being the salient instrumental sections (Fig. 26). Elsewhere the broad, sweeping phrases conjure images of ball gowns, glittering lights, and royalty

---

[8] On this topic, see Epstein, *Shaping Time*, 332–5.

Example 7.3 Ravel, *La Valse* (Fig. 46, bars 1–4): reduced score

(Fig. 30). At Fig. 41, the waltz is heard in muted voice, not unusual in the repertory of the Strausses. Equally Straussian are the waltz flourishes lightly played by supple woodwind (Fig. 50). Furthermore, the waltz appears as salon music, its tempo slightly slower ('Un peu plus modéré'), the upbeat bar of its phrase stretched to the extreme, the phrase endings poised – elegant, if also affected – by virtue of the string players' 'thrown' up-bows (Fig. 46; see Example 7.3). In particular, that extended first note of the melody for solo cello and two solo violas is the equivalent of a *fermata* – virtually a salon-music cliché.

Motivic coherence and the *Grundgestalt*

So far, these characteristics of *La Valse* are hardly obscure: the theatrical qualities are easy to discern, while the *étude*-like aspects follow closely behind. The formal structure, to be sure, demands analysis, but its components, though sophisticated, are not recondite. In fact, many of its sectional properties will be familiar to the experienced musician who undertakes the piece for the first time. The music is so ubiquitous in our concert halls that its oft-heard details form a reference frame, even if not a conscious one. A further factor for coherence lies in the motivic use of intervals, as suggested earlier. This is a particular necessity for *La Valse*, for its initial section (through to Fig. 54) contains a variety of waltz tunes, each of them of differing character. Without a unifying element the music would be of lesser import – a mere 'medley' of waltz tunes.[9]

---

[9] In fact, this portion presents almost 60 per cent of the work – specifically, 441 of its 755 bars.

Example 7.4 shows a number of these unifying motives, which utilize a *Grundegestalt*-like approach. Segment (a) of the example shows several themes in which the interval of a minor or a major seventh (and its inversion) is a prominent, in some cases defining, feature. Segment (b) depicts a number of themes in which the melodic sequence of tonal degrees: 8–7–8–3, or 8–7–8–5, is prominent – again, in some cases, definitive. The contents of segment (c) are not unrelated to elements in the prior segments: intervals seen in those earlier segments are here reworked to form a different motive – a chain of ascending semitones. This motive serves a subsidiary role in some cases, that of harmonic embellishment. In other instances it constitutes an inner contrapuntal voice in a theme where, as in the practice of J. S. Bach, the melodic line encompasses several voices. In yet another example, at Fig. 20^{-2}, the cadential segment of the melody is itself the rising chromatic line.

In developing and expanding this *Grundgestalt* perspective,[10] a music analyst might consider various things including: firstly, the frequency with which waltz themes begin on the sixth degree of the scale – often thereby upon the harmony of a dominant ninth;[11] and, secondly, the correlating of aspects of upbeat or downbeat orientations of themes and additional groupings of harmonic patterns of themes.[12]

It is also useful, at this juncture, to relate to and expand upon the formal design of the work. Essentially, *La Valse* has an introduction, an 'expository' section in which the various waltz themes (an apparent 'medley') are set forth, and a 'development' in which various themes are exploited, leading to the climactic ending section. The introduction extends until Fig. 9, the

---

[10] This interpolated paragraph and the one that follows are based closely upon 'perspectives' 1 and 2, as presented in Epstein's extended letter (21 April 1999), pp. 1–2. Epstein found that he had become so involved with this project that 'my view of *La Valse* has grown continually as I looked ever further into the piece from the standpoints that you will find here. This process continues.' He determined therefore that 'it would be best if I could provide you with the abstract as it now stands, and [...] suggest as well the additional perspectives that I envision incorporating in the article'. [Ed.]

[11] The most overt illustration is the luscious theme at Fig. 13^{+1}, commencing on B as part of a V^9 harmony in D – A, $C\sharp$, E, G, B – but the first prominent sixth actually occurs in the initial bassoon theme (Fig. 1): the emphasis upon $D/D\flat$ within a localized F minor modality (balanced, at Fig. 5, by the violas' E in terms of a localized G). See also Figs. 8 ($C\sharp$ over an E pedal, as '$V^{[13]}$' of V' in D), 16^{+6} and 17^{+4} (B as part of a Straussian

$V^9 – I^6_5$ in D), plus 34 and 35 (D within C^9 in F). Sixths apart, several themes favour the fifth degree, e.g. Figs. 9^{+3} (A as part of I^6_5 in D), 18 (A as part of a chromaticized V^9 in D), 23 ($B\flat$ in terms of $E\flat$), and 30 ($B\flat$ within IV^9 in $E\flat$). Epstein also contemplated 'the possibility of transposing all themes to the key of D, so that comparisons of formative shapes may be seen within one context of pitch and tonality'. On reflection, the original notation has been maintained to show the equally important tonal fluidity and inventiveness. [Ed.]

[12] Overall, there is a surprisingly even balance between upbeat and downbeat orientations of themes, sometimes featuring an immediate alternation, e.g. Figs. 1 and 3, with downbeat antecedent balanced by upbeat consequent: see again Example 7.1b. A similar principle of alternation occurs with themes at Fig. 8 (anacrusic) and 9^{+3} (non-anacrusic). The correlating of harmonic patterns of themes tends to privilege the $(II^{13})–V^9–I^6_5$ 'waltz' progression. [Ed.]

Example 7.4   Ravel, *La Valse*: *Grundgestalt* shapes within themes
(a) Melodic interval of a seventh (or second)
(b) Melodic sequence of tonal degrees: 8–7–8–3, or 8–7–8–5 (opening–Fig. 41)
(c) Sequence of ascending semitones (Figs. 4–34)

Example 7.4 (*cont.*)

(c)

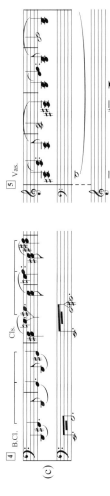

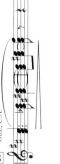

Example 7.4 (*cont.*)

primary feature there being harmonic/tonal: the move to a clear statement of D major which emerges from those somewhat 'murky' sojourns upon satellite harmonies of this key, as discussed above. The expository thematic section extends until Fig. 54 (where the 'murkiness' of the introduction returns as the initial means to extend and develop various ideas of the work). Its 'medley' of waltzes is very much suggestive of the nineteenth- and early twentieth-century tradition of 'light' dance music as it was played in summer concerts in the parks of Middle European spas and other small towns. This formal design just outlined further correlates with tempos within the piece, not least with the sparing use of the term 'Pressez', which first appears eight bars before Fig. 54, thereby helping to mark the arrival of this major section (the 'development').[13]

Issues of tempo and *La Valse* as metaphor

None of these perspectives, however, equips a conductor to deal with what may be the most subtle aspect of the piece: the tempo changes found well into the music.[14] They include the acceleration indicated late in the score (Fig. 82), the subsequent faster tempo ('Assez animé', at Fig. 88), and the direction 'Pressez' encountered at Figs. 86[+4] and 100, the latter exerted through to the close of the work. These instructions, particularly the accelerando and the 'Pressez', often lead conductors to drive the music to almost furious speeds, so much so that elements of the score fly by as a 'whoosh' of sound, their details unclear. For sure, the music arouses palpable excitement. The loud, aggressive phrasing at the close draws audiences to their feet. The 'bravos' fly. The performance is a triumph of virtuosity – and, thereby, a success.[15]

[13] One optional development that Epstein considered (letter, 21 April 1999, p. 2) as a way of relating concepts (his perspective 2.3) was 'a "time-line" schema, wherein the harmonic, tonal, thematic, and tempo elements are shown, together with their correlations with the large sections'. From an editorial perspective, it was felt, however, that the existing examples already conveyed their points convincingly and that an amalgamation might prove rather cumbersome. [Ed.]

[14] The text returns here to that of the main abstract. [Ed.]

[15] This overheated, rushed sense of the music toward the close is an observation drawn from numerous performances witnessed in the concert hall. It has also been pursued by way of recordings in preparation for this essay. The recorded performances include those of Ernest Ansermet/Orchestre de la Suisse Romande (Decca 468564 [*c*.1960]); Leonard Bernstein/New York Philharmonic (Columbia ML 5293 [1958]); Semyon Bychkov/Orchestre de Paris (Philips 04161[*c*.1990]); Pierre Dervaux/L'Orchestre des Concerts Colonne (ReDiscovery RD052 [1960]); Charles Dutoit/Montreal Symphony Orchestra (Decca 460214 [1981]); Bernard Haitink/Amsterdam Concertgebouw (Philips 438745 [1975]); Armin Jordan/L'Orchestre de la Suisse Romande (Erato B00004UJRK [*c*.1990]); Jean Martinon/Orchestre de Paris (EMI Classics 00892 [1973–4]); Charles Munch/ Boston Symphony Orchestra (RCA Victor Gold Seal 6522 [1962]); Sezi Ozawa/ Boston Symphony Orchestra (Deutsche Grammophon 4741722 [*c*.1974]); and Stanislaw Skrowaczewski/Minnesota

Or is it? The view from this corner is mixed. Who is to gainsay a cheering audience and a standing ovation? On the other hand, what may be the deepest aspect of the piece, the most profound level of its conception, is slighted if not destroyed by this headlong pacing. That perspective is the goal of this study. It stems from a musical concept formed of elements not exclusively musical, components drawn from a larger world, elements that must be grasped as much by intuition and a cultivated mind as by purely musical means.

On this deepest level *La Valse* serves as a metaphor. In its subject matter, the waltz, and in the elegant frame that surrounds that subject – the high Viennese style that reigned in the performance of the waltz – *La Valse* represents what Ravel and many Europeans of his generation regarded as a peak of refined European culture. In truth it was more than culture: it marked an era – an epoch marked by the attainment of high art, architecture, literature; an era that saw the flowering of science, theatre, music, and fashion. It was an era also underlain by social unrest, inequality, and nationalism, for those who cared to see them. Furthermore, it was an era that came to a crashing close via World War I. Postwar Europe was left in chaos – the old order upset, values changed or overthrown. Germany was numbed by inflation, depressed by defeat; Russia was in revolt; new nationalisms, new nations (then Czechoslovakia and Yugoslavia) had emerged. The once-elegant world of high culture was in dissolution, its adherents – artists and intellectuals among them – desolate, emotionally lost.

Ravel was deeply attached to prewar European culture, as his numerous letters and statements attest.[16] For instance, his brief scenario for *La Valse*, printed at the front of the orchestral score, was specific in its mid-nineteenth-century reference to 'Une Cour impériale, vers 1855' ('an Imperial Court, around 1855'); similarly, he expressed overtly his affection for the music of Johann Strauss: 'I admire and love his waltzes' (as well as for that of Chabrier, Mozart, Couperin, and so on).[17] He was left distraught by the violence and destruction he witnessed at the front lines while a lorry driver in the service of the French artillery. A personal aftermath of the

Orchestra (Mobile Fidelity 4002 [1974]). (Epstein had intended to supply the identifying record labels and numbers, which have been surmised and added editorially. The notion of virtuosity is also addressed in Chapter 5 under 'Orpheus in the New World'. [Ed.])

[16] Arbie Orenstein (ed.), *A Ravel Reader: Correspondence, Articles, Interviews* (New York: Columbia University Press, 1990), presents much of this evidence. (See too Orenstein, *Ravel*, Chapter 7: 'Musical

Aesthetics', 117–29, which references Baudelaire and Edgar Allan Poe, as well as Schubert, Mendelssohn, and Bizet; and Barbara L. Kelly, 'History and Homage', in Mawer (ed.), *The Cambridge Companion to Ravel* (Cambridge University Press, 2000), 7–26. [Ed.])

[17] [Unsigned interview], 'Viennese Impressions of a French Artist', *Neue freie Presse* (29 October 1920), reprinted in Orenstein (ed.), *A Ravel Reader*, 419–20: 420. [Ed.]

war was a depression that for a while inhibited his efforts to compose.[18] Some of this despair over the lost world of prewar culture seems intrinsic to *La Valse*.[19]

It is also worth signalling that, while *La Valse* definitely provides the most overt expression of the phenomenon in his music up to 1920, the matter of the dark side of Ravel's persona exists as a broader, underpinning concern.[20] This side of him seemed to manifest itself little in his associations with colleagues; it seems, rather, to have been a private part of his personality. Certainly it is found in his music, as many have observed. Arbie Orenstein has some pertinent points to make about this, referring for example to 'a less common but distinct thread of drama extending from *Un grand sommeil noir*, *Si morne!*, and *Gaspard de la nuit*, through *La Valse*, the *Chansons madécasses*, and the Concerto for the Left Hand'.[21] Although it is not necessary to go into great detail about this matter, it makes sense to flag it up here since my discussion of tempo and its bearing upon the 'self-destruction' of the music, as considered below, in part stems from this dark vision of life.

---

[18] This depression was exacerbated profoundly by the death of Ravel's beloved mother in 1917, leading to a virtual compositional paralysis of nearly three years. [Ed.]

[19] For all his undoubted affinity with high culture, Ravel was anxious (perhaps overly so) to deny any socio-political or added meaning behind *La Valse*. See, for example, his comments in C. v. W., 'The French Music Festival: An Interview with Ravel', *De Telegraaf* (30 September 1922), in Orenstein (ed.), *A Ravel Reader*, 423–5: 423: 'It doesn't have anything to do with the present situation in Vienna, and it also doesn't have any symbolic meaning in that regard.' Yet he adds, more ambiguously: 'It is a dancing, whirling, almost hallucinatory ecstasy, an increasingly passionate and exhausting whirlwind of dancers, who are overcome and exhilarated by nothing but "the waltz".'

Although Ravel mentioned the concept of *Vienne* (the initial title of *La Valse*) as early as 1906, its composition did not progress significantly until December 1919, and was emphatically a product of the immediate postwar period. Despite Ravel's equivocations, listeners and critics have found it illuminating to interpret *La Valse* at least partially in extra-musical terms for almost as long as the work has

existed. For a reading which also embraces the death of Ravel's mother and gender issues, see Deborah Mawer, 'Balanchine's *La Valse*: Meanings and Implications for Ravel Studies', *Opera Quarterly*, 22/1 (2006 ['Sound Moves' issue]), 90–116. [Ed.]

[20] This paragraph is developed from perspective no. 4 in Epstein's letter (21 April 1999), p. 3. [Ed.]

[21] Orenstein, *Ravel*, 121. As Epstein notes in perspective no. 4 (letter, 21 April 1999), there are also lesser-known testimonies of those who 'had a close personal relationship with Ravel' – in particular, 'Perlemuter/Jourdan-Morhange have some interesting things to say about this'. Vlado Perlemuter and Hélène Jourdan-Morhange, *Ravel According to Ravel*, trans. Frances Tanner and ed. Harold Taylor (London: Kahn & Averill, 1970), 6: 'the confession which releases all the passion of *Daphnis*, the fatal frenzy of *La Valse*'; 7: 'the piece [*Sonatine*: 'Final'] contains a violent passion'; 20: '"La Vallée des cloches", with its melancholy fervour'; 31: 'Already attracted to Edgar Allan Poe, Ravel was to be tempted by this tormented poet [Aloysius Bertrand] who took pleasure in the infernal visions of the Middle Ages'; and 31: 'Ravel has translated all the macabre resonance of the poem [in *Gaspard de la nuit*: 'Le Gibet']. [Ed.]

The idea of destruction

Like ancient Greek drama, *La Valse* carries within it the seeds of its own destruction.[22] This concept is certainly relevant to the metaphorical aspect of the work – namely, that *La Valse* mirrors the downfall of high European culture.

The idea of destructive elements lying within a work, often within the persona of a leading character, was a recurrent theme in much nineteenth-century literature and drama. It is seen in Emile Zola's *Germinal* (1885), in Gustave Flaubert's *Madame Bovary* (1857), or in Leo Tolstoy's *Anna Karenina* (1877) and *War and Peace* (1865–9). It can be seen as latent within the entirety of *La Valse*, hinted at in those 'murky' opening bars, although their potential meanings there are both manifold and obscure. It first appears specifically at Fig. 76, the place where the return to the key of D also marks the beginning of the final section. There is a significant though subtle change in the orchestration of the waltz metre. If we compare Figs. 1 and 76, the initial orchestration is mellifluous, including double bass pizzicatos and offbeat harp clusters; at Fig. 76, however, that orchestration is changed, effected through the introduction of snare drum and cymbals on the offbeats of the bars. These sonorities carry references of foreboding, fear, the unknown, and so on, from prior usage in the musical literature. We may think of Hector Berlioz's *Symphonie fantastique* (first published in 1845), or of Gustav Mahler in many of his symphonies, as well as in 'Revelge' (1899) and 'Der Tamboursg'sell' (1901) from the song collection *Des Knaben Wunderhorn*, with their terrors of death and execution …

The change of orchestration in the Ravel, moreover, affects interlocking perspectives in that the waltz metre changes continually in its instrumentation through the work. Some illustrations of this are provided in Example 7.5. Thus the snare drum/cymbal change can be seen as one of a number of ongoing, continual variations of sonority that embellish the waltz metre. From a different perspective, however, these unique sonorities effect the change of mood and content just outlined. Note, too, that in the earlier orchestral embodiments of the waltz metre the overall effect of the music is, at most, unclear, or mysterious. With the insertion of the percussion, the character modulates significantly in the direction of fear, or foreboding.

There is another aspect of destruction relevant to this discussion – namely, that we as the audience are forced to witness both the act of destruction and its inevitability, thereby resonating all the more with its horror and with our response to this horror – our inability to stop it. This sense is very much an

[22] The heading 'The idea of destruction' and the paragraphs which follow comprise perspective no. 3 (letter, 21 April 1999), pp. 2–3. On Ravel's destruction of dance, especially in *La Valse*, see too Deborah Mawer, 'Ballet and the Apotheosis of the Dance', in Mawer (ed.), *The Cambridge Companion to Ravel*, 140–61: 153–5. [Ed.]

Example 7.5 Ravel, *La Valse*: orchestration of waltz metre

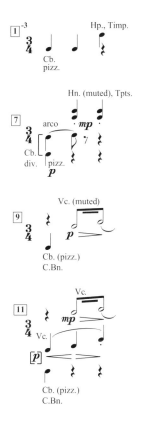

element in the literary works of the nineteenth century mentioned above. The act of witnessing slow destruction extended to subsequent experimental cinema in France as well. For example in 1932, roughly a decade after *La Valse*, Jean Cocteau, who knew Ravel, incorporated in his film *Le Sang d'un poète* a scene showing a brick chimney being dynamited. The sequence, which had a powerful impact upon the American composer Elliott Carter, is described by Carter in his article, 'String Quartets Nos. 1, 1951, and 2, 1959':

> the entire dreamlike action is framed by an interrupted slow-motion shot of a tall brick chimney in an empty lot being dynamited. Just as the chimney begins to fall apart, the shot is broken off and the entire movie follows, after which the shot of the chimney is resumed at the point it left off, showing its disintegration in mid-air, and closing the film with its collapse on the ground.[23]

As an integral issue, the greatest manifestation of despair also occurs at the close of *La Valse*, the first hint discerned at Fig. 82.[24] The acceleration there,

[23] Jonathan W. Bernard (ed.), *Elliott Carter: Collected Essays and Lectures, 1937–1995* (Rochester, NY: University of Rochester Press, 1997), 233.

[24] The text now returns to that of the main abstract. [Ed.]

underlain by a chromatically rising bass line, leads to an abrupt cut-off at Fig. 85 and to subsequent music of ever more heated temperature. The passages begin an emotional crescendo that yields music slightly frenetic (Fig. 94), and ultimately, from Fig. 98 onwards, music that virtually destroys itself, driving its motives to fury, injecting foreign elements into the mix, compounding harmonies by complexities that threaten to annihilate tonality itself.

These latter passages (Fig. 98ff.) themselves amount to dissolution. Certainly they destroy the character of the piece. In a metaphorical sense they can be seen as a dissolution of the waltz genre itself, as that genre is represented by *La Valse*. The metaphor has yet greater horizons. Seen as an analogue of that civilized European culture with which Ravel so identified, the dissolution of *La Valse* projects the dissolution of an era. That perspective leaves us as interpreters under no small obligation: it is not enough just to bring out the excitement of this score, or its theatrical and *étude*-like properties alone. *La Valse* in performance must project its world-view as well – the aspects of the score that build, indeed create, the dissolution that so enmeshed Ravel's perspective.

Those aspects are brilliantly conceived. Ravel's structures of dissolution, from Fig. 98 onwards, involve trombone and tuba glissandos upon second-inversion triads, answered by descending trumpets also in second inversion. Opposing the trumpets are the ascending woodwind (flutes, piccolo, oboe, cor anglais, and clarinets) and violins set in root-position triads; see Example 7.6.[25] The effect is chilling. The dark, slithering trombone and tuba sonorities can be terrifying, the trumpet versus woodwind/violin lines icy, the dissonances of these clashing parts evocative of chaos, if not horror. The import of it all is driven home by four calculated repetitions of this paradigm. Yet more, these events are overlain by percussion – the tam-tam colouring the trombone glissandos,[26] the cymbal crescendo intensifying the woodwind/string sonorities,[27] the effect in both cases being a heightening of the fearsome elements of the passages.

These events, and those that follow from Fig. 100, require time – time to be shaped in their playing, time to be perceived to the full effect that this destruction and dissolution, in their increasingly chaotic, clashing sonorities, convey. Done thus, the horror we experience is analogous to a terror

---

[25] Some of Ravel's note spellings have been altered enharmonically in Example 7.6 [and 7.4] to show most readily the parallel triadic structures.

[26] Care must be taken that the tam-tam plays *fortissimo* only, so that it does not cover the other instruments. Note that the trombones begin *ff*, and that the bass line of woodwind and strings reaches *fff* when the tam-tam sounds. Ravel, characteristically, takes great care with instrumental balances here – something not always observed in performance.

[27] Again, note the percussion dynamics, with the cymbal crescendo beginning at *p* and increasing only to *f*. A blend of colours is clearly indicated, not a 'drowning' of sounds by the percussion.

Example 7.6 Ravel, *La Valse* (Figs. 98–9): reduced score

we have witnessed in World War II newsreels showing the bombings and destruction of buildings in Warsaw during the early attack on Poland as Nazi forces invaded the country: elegant apartment house façades, models of architectural style in cities aged and eminent, undergo transformation. As we view them, cracks appear in the masonry. Slowly, inevitably, against our disbelief, the fissures spread like spiders' legs. The façades disintegrate as the buildings tumble. Icons of an era are reduced to rubble.

This horrendous disintegration embeds itself in our consciousness, in part because of the seeming 'slow motion' with which it happens. In like fashion, and for similar reasons, Ravel's calculated disintegration requires deliberate pacing. Hence arises the all-important question of tempo (and tempos) in *La Valse*, a question made all the more urgent since the passage from Fig. 100 onward has the instruction 'Pressez jusqu'à la fin' (Press forward until the end), with the further advisory note that the penultimate bar, with its four crotchets to be played in the space of the usual 3/4 bar, should be 'Sans ralentir' (Without slowing down).

Focusing on 'Pressez' and avoiding pitfalls

What does Ravel communicate by 'Pressez'? What are its implications? Are we to understand the term as a synonym for the more usual 'accélérez', thus demanding simple acceleration? Or are there more complex aspects to the direction, implications resonant with the process of disintegration just discussed?

It is notable that *La Valse* moves essentially in one tempo: that indicated at its beginning. As Table 7.1 shows, there are but two slight deviations from this central pace. One, connected with the 'Salon music' waltz (Fig. 46), advises 'Un peu plus modéré' (A little more moderate). The other (Figs. 88, 97) advises 'Assez animé'. The latter is the more subtle direction of the two. 'Animé', suggesting an animated, perhaps lively tempo, is modified by that complex French qualifier 'assez', which implies 'somewhat', 'rather', 'controlled', or 'in good measure'. In no way, thereby, can this sense of liveliness be light, or carefree. That Ravel envisioned 'Assez animé' as a very small change from the prevalent tempo (Tempo I), moreover, is clear at Fig. 97, itself marked 'Au Mouvement (assez animé)'. For, only two bars earlier, the tempo instruction is 'A peine retenu (1er Mouvt)', which tells us essentially that the music should be 'barely' or 'scarcely' held back (i.e., it should be at Tempo I).

The music thus moves predominantly at a steady pace. Where the tempo changes, that change underlies some special structural purpose: the *étude* view of the waltz as salon music (which, significantly, is followed by a return to the prevalent tempo at Fig. 50); an initial step towards the coming disintegration of the waltz itself. Two further instructions add complexity to the mix. Ravel issues the instruction 'Pressez' in three places: firstly, at Fig. 53^{+1} ('Pressez un peu' for a short passage of eight bars); secondly, at Fig. 86^{+4} (again, a short passage, this time of six bars); and thirdly at Fig. 100 ('Pressez jusqu'à la fin' – the significantly longer stretch with greater structural consequence). By contrast, he issues a different order at Fig. 82: 'Accélérez jusqu'à 85' (Accelerate until Fig. 85).

This careful use of terminology implies a distinction in meaning – indeed, a critical distinction. To accelerate is to increase velocity with respect to time. The concept concerns speed (the psychological transformation of velocity) *per se*. By contrast, to press (forward) is to move ahead as the consequence of a driving force. Pressure, be it physical or emotional in nature, lies behind this process, in fact seems to be its driving force. The result is most likely to be a change in velocity, but the cause of the change is different from that of

Table 7.1 Ravel, *La Valse*: tempo indications

Location in score	French tempo marking	English tempo equivalent (and comments)
Bar 1	Mouvᵗ de Valse viennoise	Tempo of the Viennese waltz
Fig. 46	Un peu plus modéré	Tempo a little more moderate ('Salon music' *étude*: extended phrase upbeat. The first note of the melody is the written-out equivalent of a long-held *fermata*.)
Fig. 50⁻⁴	Revenez au Mouvᵗ	Return to the [primary] tempo (Over this four-bar period make a gradual return to Tempo I.)
Fig. 50	1ᵉʳ Mouvᵗ	Initial tempo (The return to tempo indicated four bars earlier is reached here.)
Fig. 53⁺¹	Pressez un peu	Press the tempo forward a little
Fig. 54	Iᵉʳ Mouvᵗ	Tempo I (Suddenly, after the eight-bar passage of forward-moving tempo. The music at Fig. 54, which recaptures Tempo I, is a recall of the opening passages.)
Fig. 82	Accélérez jusqu'à 85	Accelerate until Fig. 85
Fig. 85	Mouvᵗ du début	Tempo of the beginning (Tempo I)
Fig. 86⁺⁴	Pressez	Press the tempo forward (The passage lasts six bars.)
Fig. 88	Assez animé	Somewhat more lively (Assez animé is the goal tempo of the preceding passage.)
Fig. 97⁻²	A peine retenu (1ᵉʳ Mouvᵗ)	Barely held back (i.e., Tempo I)
Fig. 97	Au Mouvement (assez animé)	Return to the previous tempo [Assez animé of Fig. 88] (The tempo indications at Figs. 88, 97⁻², and 97 reveal that Ravel regarded Assez animé as very close in speed to Tempo I.)
Fig. 100	Pressez jusqu'à la fin	Press forward until the end

acceleration. Likewise, the feeling engendered by 'Pressez' is different; it is more intense, more driven – driven, perhaps, by *Angst*. Conversely, the result will probably be a new velocity that is less than that attained by pure acceleration. For, to move as fast as (or faster than) the product of acceleration would serve to dilute the complex pressures that underlie the very sense of pressing forward.

The distinction makes musical sense in the context of *La Valse*. The acceleration from Figs. 82 to 85 carries to a climax the excitement of a forward-moving 'rush', ending in that brassy phrase at Fig. 85 (which, we should note, is marked: 'Mouvt du début', i.e. at Tempo I). The 'Pressez' passages (Figs. 53^{+1} and 86^{+4}) each have about them an anxious quality, reinforced in each case by an underlying crescendo, while the final 'Pressez jusqu'à la fin' defines a passage of ultimate anxiety.

La Valse appears in a different interpretative light as a consequence of this perception. To be sure, it remains 'good theatre' – exciting 'entertainment' on the level of high art. But it is, moreover, sophisticated in that unique Ravelian sense of an *étude* – a study of its sources, its materials. Certainly it is a *tour de force* of structural design.

All of these contexts will ply their functions, however, no matter how the music is scaled in its tempos. And, indeed, the performance that accelerates its final passage to a rousing if hurried finish will probably bring an audience to its feet – the tam-tams crashing in reverberation, the closing bars an explosion of sound. Beware, however. This kind of excitement comes easily. But it does so at a price – a substantial price: the negation of the deepest level of the piece. Ravel's metaphor – exquisitely detailed, carefully worked out – of a culture in dissolution is itself destroyed. That is more than just mindless performance. It is nothing less than misrepresentation, in this case misrepresentation of a concept which the composer has gone to considerable lengths to specify, to portray, and to establish.

Thus this is artistic deformation, exerted in the face of careful, deliberate distinctions in language – depictions precisely indicated to communicate nuances of tempo by which this special perspective is carried. Ravel's fastidiousness in crafting orchestral sound is reflected in his fastidious use of language.

A brief survey of Ravel's orchestral output makes clear this distinction in the use of language, particularly with respect to the term 'Pressez'. Used in the most sparing way within *La Valse*, as just outlined, 'Pressez' occurs even more rarely in the rest of Ravel's orchestral repertoire.[28] Throughout the *Rapsodie espagnole*, both piano concertos, the suite *Ma mère l'Oye* (Mother Goose), the *Pavane pour une infante défunte*, *Une barque sur l'océan*, *Boléro*, *Tzigane*, *Le Tombeau*, *Valses nobles et sentimentales*, and the song cycle *Shéhérazade*, the designation 'Pressez' is used not at all. In the *Alborada del gracioso* it is found only once, and in that instance for only one bar. The moment occurs in the bassoon solo, three bars before Fig. 12. The term there indicates a nuance in a characteristically flamenco type of flourish; see Example 7.7.

---

[28] Some of this repertoire also appears in versions for piano and/or piano with other solo instruments. The analysis here is confined exclusively to Ravel's orchestral music in order to provide a standardized basis for this survey of tempo indications.

Example 7.7 Ravel, *Alborada del gracioso* (Fig. 12⁻⁶): occurrence of 'Pressez'

In only one other work is 'Pressez' to be found – in *Daphnis et Chloé*: both in the ballet score and at parallel places in the orchestral suite drawn from the ballet. (The discussion here is confined to the ballet.) In all instances, the music in its gestural character shares the psychological sense of an emotional pressure that drives the tempo forward, very much as described and considered earlier. The places where this occurs are shown schematically in Table 7.2.[29] Relating to Part II of the ballet, Table 7.2a contains three occurrences of the term. The initial two, found between Figs. 142 and 143, are similar in both character and phrase structure. Each lasts only a half-bar, and is marked by a somewhat impassioned 'up-beat breath', the gesture at its conclusion reverting to music of a slower tempo. The third place, which begins at Fig. 143⁺², presses a reiterated motive forward over four bars, the passage closing into a slow tempo ('Lent') at Fig. 144. As with the other cases, the psychological sense of a driving force seems to lie behind these bars, suggested in part by a crescendo marking across the first half of the phrase. Table 7.2b relates to a brief segment from Part III of the ballet where the 'Pressez' phrase resembles the earlier segments from Part II (Table 7.2a). The forward-driven passages are similar, the first 'Pressez' lasting only a bar, the second, initially of similar music, carrying the motion further across five bars until the 'Vif' (Lively) at Fig. 180.[30] The final passages similarly marked (Table 7.2c) occur later in the piece (at Fig. 189 and briefly thereafter; only the first occurrence is noted). Again, 'Pressez' occupies merely a half-bar, the musical character similar to that identified for Table 7.2a.

The argument is yet more extensive. Not only do all the 'Pressez' passages share the unique character discussed above. In addition, throughout

29 This tabulation is editorial. For the full effect, the reader is directed to the orchestral score: Maurice Ravel, *Daphnis et Chloé* (Paris: Editions Durand, 1913). [Ed.]

30 The tempo relationship given in the Durand orchestral score at Fig. 180 (crotchet equals the preceding semiquaver) seems wrong (a printing error, or possible miscalculation) since it calls for 'Vif' to be four times faster than the previous bar. At the prior tempo of ♩ = 66, given at Fig. 176 as 'Lent', the new tempo at Fig. 180 translates to ♩ = 264. This seems frankly unplayable, and so fast, if it were playable, as to be out of character.

Table 7.2 Ravel, *Daphnis et Chloé*: occurrences of 'Pressez'

(a) Figs. 142–4

Figure	Bar/beat (2/4 metre)	Tempo indication
142	1/beat 1	Moins animé
	(2)	————
	3/beat 2	Pressez
	4/beat 1	Un peu moins
	(5)	animé
	6/beat 2	Pressez
143	1/beat 1	Un peu moins animé
	(2)	————
	3/beat 1	Au Mouv^t et en
	(4)	pressant
	(5)	————
	(6)	————
144	1/beat 1	Lent

(b) Figs. 179–80

Figure	Bar/beat (2/4 metre)	Tempo indication
179	1/beat 1	au Mouv^t
	2/beat 1	Pressez
	3/beat 1	au Mouv^t
	4/beat 1	Pressez
	(5)	————
	(6)	————
	(7)	————
	(8)	
180	1/beat 1	Vif

(c) Fig. 189

Figure	Bar/beat (3/4 metre)	Tempo indication
189	1/beat 1	♩ = 80
	(2)	————
	3/beat 1	Cédez très peu
	4/beat 2+	Pressez
	5/beat 1	Plus lent

the ballet Ravel uses a wide variety of tempo terms to describe the character of the accelerations that the music requires. Within Parts I and II are found the descriptions 'Vif', as already seen, 'Moins lent' (Less slow), 'Revenez au mouvt' (Back to tempo), 'Accélérez' (Accelerate), 'Très libre' (Very free), 'Animez progressivement jusqu'au très modéré' (Animated progressively until [the indication] 'very moderate'), 'Plus animé' (More lively), 'Modérément animé' (Moderately lively), 'Animez un peu' (A little lively), 'Animez peu à peu' (Little by little become more animated), 'Très animé (Very lively), 'Très agité' (Very agitated), 'Agité et très rude' (Agitated and very rough), and a number of other refinements upon the term 'Animé'. With so large a number of fine-spun descriptions of forward-moving tempos, and with so few and such special uses of the term 'Pressez', the indications are strong that Ravel means the latter term to denote a particular mode of tempo increment – one to be suggested both rarely and in particular places.

This careful use of tempo terminology is found in other works as well, though it does not concern the designation 'Pressez'. The fourth movement of *Rapsodie espagnole*, its wild finale entitled 'Feria', indicates 'De plus en plus animé' (Fig. 31) at its close. In actual fact, 'Pressez' is not to be found, even though its meaning is not that remote from what Ravel does indicate. But in the composer's mind there appears to have been a difference. In the second movement of the same work ('Malagueña'), the imperative 'Animez' is marked (Fig. 11), and both before and thereafter through into the finale 'Animé', either modified by additional adjectives or found alone, is a common term – again communicating differences of nuance. In the late Piano Concerto for the Left Hand, the term 'Accelerando' is found for brief passages of a half-bar to two bars' duration, each instance reverting to the prevailing tempo (i.e. 'a Tempo'); see for instance the four occurrences across Figs. 4–5. Conversely, 'Accelerando' toward a goal (Allegro) is found at Fig. 14^{-3}, and 'Più vivo ed accel.' is placed at Fig. 43 – again, subtle distinctions in meaning and nuance. Meanwhile, the early song cycle *Shéhérazade* uses a variety of terms for slowing tempo with equally careful distinction: for example, 'Cédez', 'Rall[entando]', 'Ralenti', 'Ralentissez' (all first occurring in 'Asie'), and 'Rit[ardando]'. In a similar way, in the *Alborada* (Fig. 13), Ravel advises 'Revenez au … Plus lent'.

The supporting perspective of Vlado Perlemuter

So much evidence suggests that we must take seriously the musical refinements and distinctions communicated by Ravel's usage of words. That thought is confirmed by another source entirely: the book *Ravel According to*

Ravel (1970).[31] Its origins lie in a series of programmes for Radio Française, broadcast from Paris in 1950, in which the pianist, Vlado Perlemuter, played all Ravel's works for solo piano and discussed them with Hélène Jourdan-Morhange. In his youth, Perlemuter had studied Ravel's solo piano *œuvre* with the composer, while Jourdan-Morhange, a violinist, had given the premieres of some of Ravel's music in 1922, and had a close and enduring friendship with the composer over the last two decades of his life. The transcript of the broadcasts, initially published in French, formed the basis for the book. Excerpts from these broadcasts speak powerfully to the point under consideration here. As an initial example, Jourdan-Morhange declares: 'I have never known a composer so sure of himself with regard to the markings in his music,' hearing in Perlemuter's playing the idiosyncrasies and qualities that Ravel wished, among them 'strict time in expression and rigour even in rubato'.[32]

In contemplating Ravel's *Sonatine*, Jourdan-Morhange observes that she has often heard the first part of the work played too fast, to which Perlemuter replies, 'Indeed, it is nearly always played too fast. Ravel insisted that the tempo should not be too hurried'; moreover, he states that Ravel always wanted the tempo 'to be strict and without rubato'.[33] Tellingly, with respect to tempo Jourdan-Morhange comments that, 'as always with Ravel, there is an indication on the score'.[34] Subsequently Perlemuter states: 'Ravel insisted on absolutely strict tempo. The grandeur of the piece [in this case 'Le Gibet' from *Gaspard de la nuit*] depends on the rhythmical structure.'[35]

Later exchanges further indicate Ravel's sensitivity to tempo. Apropos the Left Hand Concerto another interviewer, Pierre Maylan, asks Perlemuter what tempo he takes in the opening Lento. Perlemuter replies:

> You must follow Ravel's indication: 44 to the crotchet, which sometimes is not done by some young pianists who take this movement too fast. Using his intuition Ravel solved the melodic problem, posed by the fact that there is only one hand, by playing the top note of the chord with the thumb, which is strong and carries more weight from the hand.[36]

The implication is that if the music is played faster, it is difficult to manipulate the hand so as to create this accent. Later in this discussion Maylan asks Perlemuter how he conceives the Allegro, which with some interpreters becomes a 'cavalcade devoid of expression'. The pianist responds: 'In my opinion Ravel's markings must be followed. He indicated 138 for the dotted crotchet; on no account must you exceed 144 [an increment of 4.2 per cent,

31 See n21. [Ed.]
32 Perlemuter and Jourdan-Morhange, *Ravel According to Ravel*, 3.
33 *Ibid.*, 11
34 *Ibid.*
35 *Ibid.*, 33.
36 *Ibid.*, 84.

probably imperceptible].[37] In the second theme of the *Allegro* […] the rhythm is more intense, more tragic. Played too quickly, this theme […] cannot be given all its depth.' If played too fast, 'Too often the orchestral accompaniment is weak' and, as a consequence, the staccato notes in the violas and cellos (Fig. 28ff.) 'sometimes lack rhythmic nervosity'.[38]

Much the same advice applies to the Concerto in G: in the first movement, for example, Perlemuter stipulates that

> *Allegramente* does not mean *presto*! One must take into account Ravel's marking: ll6 to the minim. If you play it too quickly you lose wind instruments and the whole display of the piccolo. The repeat is often taken too fast (Fig. 10 in the score), to the detriment of clarity and neatness. The performance of the pianist is affected by this and becomes strained. The same applies to the *Finale*.[39]

A further comment is fascinating for what it says about important rhythmic figures and the small modifications of tempo necessary to let these figures speak. In discussing with Jourdan-Morhange the opening piece of *Miroirs*, entitled 'Noctuelles', Perlemuter refers to the 'poco rubato' (bars 33–5) which precedes the 'Pas trop lent' found at bar 37 of the score. Apropos this rubato, he remarks that, 'Ravel asked me to bring out the accents in the left hand'. '[T]hat', says Perlemuter, 'is why the rubato is necessary […] so that the triple rhythm takes its place calmly beneath the duple rhythm of the right hand, a subtle way of introducing the rubato.'[40]

This statement seems relevant to *La Valse* as well, specifically to the places after Figs. 98 and 99 in the score where the trombones and tuba make their frightening interjections of second-inversion triads in glissando; see again Example 7.6. As studied above, these events occur at the place where the waltz begins most violently to break up. If, as this chapter argues, this portion of the music is related metaphorically to the destruction of European culture in the aftermath of World War I, then it is important that these moments should be brought out, and the choice of tempo affects vitally their audibility. Here, too, there seem to be places where, if anything, the tempo should not be rushed, but should, like the passage from 'Noctuelles', be unhurried, perhaps by means of a subtle rubato, so that the events sound to the fullest.

In sum, Ravel's *La Valse* has literary, social, and interdisciplinary associations and affects. In this respect it is something of a pioneering musical step forwards – certainly a serious work, in my view ultimately a tragic one.[41] Not the least disturbing aspect of the current vogue for rushing the close of *La Valse* is what it indicates of our current concert life and what it portends. The concert world of Ravel has undergone vast changes across a period of some

---

37 *Ibid.*, 85. On this matter, see Epstein, *Shaping Time*, 157–70.
38 Perlemuter and Jourdan-Morhange, *Ravel According to Ravel*, 85.
39 *Ibid.*, 88–9.
40 *Ibid.*, 20.
41 This sentence is transposed from Epstein's letter (21 April 1999), p. 3. [Ed.]

eighty years.[42] We exist today in the media age, our products of art and music manipulated and promoted by massive commercial interests,[43] our time pressured, often consumed, in families with two working partners, by computerized data banks and processes, by new pastimes and fads of a short half-life that attract a younger and seemingly ever greater audience. It is within this world that concerts and recordings must compete, and that classical music must contend with the ever-changing developments of a rock-, pop-, and video-orientated youth culture.

Can the art of Ravel (and other serious composers) survive in this climate? The question is beyond the scope of this contribution. One thing seems clear, however: it is doubtful whether classical music can survive the modern media world if the focus that drives its performances is geared continually towards 'excitement' gained at the cost of deeper content. That kind of excitement quickly wears thin. What we do must be done at its best, and thereby at its most compelling. We cannot breast the competition of the media world if the contest is waged by the standards of the media world itself. It is that prospect which frames the issues raised in this study: the essential properties of *La Valse*, and their interpretation.

---

[42] 'Seventy' years in the original typescript. [Ed.]

[43] A decade or so on, Epstein's observations still seem highly pertinent. For further consideration of commercialism in music, see Chapter 5. [Ed.]

8   Ravel dances: 'choreomusical' discoveries in Richard Alston's *Shimmer*

Stephanie Jordan

The curtain rises on a man and woman waiting in a bright light, their short cobweb-lace tunics speckled with crystals. The sound of a piano behind them in the gloom sets them in motion, a singing melody over a glittering, rippling accompaniment. The two figures cling to each other, and to what they hear – she folds her leg over his arm and tucks herself up against his side; they wind around each other; a high note like the crest of a wave cues her to fall back flat, a sharp exhalation, and he saves her, once, twice. Then, when a big musical wave breaks, he swings her up on to his hip.

The lively accompaniment halts, a signal for her to break away and continue on her own, carving circles and curves through the air – a series of breath impulses without such tight attention to the music – leading, watching him watch and follow her.

Returning to him, she stretches over his back in arabesque, her left leg rising high behind. Then, slowly, easing into the music again, she curves her leg around him in an embrace and he reaches for it with his opposite hand, completing the shape of the circle and the act of enclosure. The musical phrase comes to an end (bar 19; see Example 8.1). Now, to a simple, sighing motive ('Un peu retenu'), he draws her arm over his breast: further enclosure, further intimacy. But does this extend from the initial embrace, or is it a new action to the new sighing motive? The motion continues in the same direction and it is as if the man and woman are held within the same emotional moment – despite the seam in the music. A second musical sigh … and off they go again…

The piece I have described above is the much praised *Shimmer* by Richard Alston (b. 1948), a leading British contemporary (modern) dance choreographer since the 1970s, and the music is the first movement of Ravel's *Sonatine* (1903–5) for piano. Jonathan Goddard and Ino Riga are the dancers, captured on DVD during a performance of the Richard Alston Dance Company given at the Joyce Theater in New York on 16 May 2004; see Plates 8.1 and 8.2. These details are important because timing and impressions often shift from one performance to the next – in another performance, for instance, the man, not the woman, seems to lead the middle section of the work. Premiered earlier in 2004, *Shimmer* progresses to include selections from Ravel's *Miroirs* (1904–5) and to involve a cast of seven dancers.

165

Example 8.1   Ravel, *Sonatine* (I, bars 17–21); Alston, 'Sonatine': *seam* and *sighing motive*

Yet this movement vocabulary, described by Alston himself as 'strange, flowing', and 'animal',[1] is not what one would normally expect as a setting of Ravel. Ravel's music has been used regularly for dance: there are scores actually written for dance such as *Daphnis et Chloé* (1912), *La Valse* (1920), and *Boléro* (1928), not to mention the numerous movements, and orchestrations of movements, with dance titles and rhythms: for instance, *Le Tombeau de Couperin* (1919) and *Pavane pour une infante défunte* (1899). But, almost without exception, it is the world of ballet, with a movement vocabulary very different from Alston's, which rushed to absorb Ravel. It all began in Paris in 1912, with *Ma mère l'Oye*, choreographed by Jeanne Hugard for the Théâtre des Arts, and then *Daphnis et Chloé* by Mikhail (Michel) Fokin(e) for Diaghilev's Ballets russes. Later examples are the 1920 setting of *Le Tombeau de Couperin* by Jean Börlin for the Ballets suédois, Bronislava Nijinska's *La Valse* of 1929 for the Ballets Ida Rubinstein and, later still, Frederick Ashton's *Daphnis and Chloë* (1951) and *La Valse* (1958), Maurice Béjart's *Boléro* (1961), and George Balanchine's *Le Tombeau* (1975).[2]

Ravel's music has been variously admired for its detail, delicacy, and quintessential refinement, and for the perfection of the musical mechanism: Alston himself, in Stravinskian tradition, has likened listening to the music to

[1] Richard Alston, interview with the author (5 January 2008). Unless otherwise indicated, this is the source of material quoted from Alston in this chapter.

[2] For an overall account, see Deborah Mawer, *The Ballets of Maurice Ravel: Creation and Interpretation* (Aldershot: Ashgate, 2006).

Plate 8.1 Jonathan Goddard and Ino Riga (in arabesque) in Richard Alston's *Shimmer* (2004). Photograph by Chris Nash. Reproduced by kind permission of the Richard Alston Dance Company, London

looking 'inside a clock'.[3] Consider the most obvious dance equivalent and ballet vocabulary is certainly most likely to come to mind, and one aspect of it as much as any – *pointe* work, with its diamond precision, together with classical ballet's attention to the short phrase or step pattern. A good example is Balanchine's *pas de deux* setting of the *Sonatine* for the New York City Ballet's Ravel Festival in 1975.[4] Balanchine cast the French dancers Violette

[3] Richard Alston, lecture-demonstration on *Shimmer* at 'Sound Moves' Conference, Roehampton University (5 November 2005). (On the 'Swiss clockmaker' analogy, see too Chapter 1, under 'Artist and artisan'.)

[4] George Balanchine, *Sonatine*, danced by Violette Verdy and Jean-Pierre Bonnefous of

Plate 8.2 Jonathan Goddard and Ino Riga in Richard Alston's *Shimmer* (2004). Photograph by Chris Nash. Reproduced by kind permission of the Richard Alston Dance Company, London

Verdy (b. 1933) and Jean-Pierre Bonnefous (b. 1943), dressed in simple practice clothes, and he featured Verdy on *pointe* to an unusual degree, walking, presenting, and sometimes literally looking at her feet. 'I speak with my feet!' she told me,[5] referring to her tiny runs, detailed rhythms, and response to the short–short–long musical patterns. On a few occasions, during the first movement of the *Sonatine*, we see a *battement* or *cabriole* drawing attention to a high note.[6] There is a much faster rate of events here than in Alston's style.

the New York City Ballet, filmed by Amram Nowak Associates (Jerome Robbins Archive of the Recorded Moving Image, New York Public Library, 14 January 1976).

[5] Violette Verdy, interview with the author (14 May 2008).

[6] The *battement* here is a swing of the leg upwards and forwards. Bonnefous lifts Verdy

Pointes can create the image of lightness – and Verdy emphasizes this, sometimes picking up her feet as if she has trodden on something very precious and fragile. But *pointes* also have a hardness that is literally heard as they hit the floor, and which shuts off the sensuality of the foot, its soft pad and pliant sole: a sensuality that contemporary dance (including Alston's) usually celebrates. There is a hard side to Ravel too: the piano is, after all, a percussion instrument. I will return to Balanchine's *Sonatine* later on.

Alston's style is more obviously three-dimensional than that of ballet: elastic, using the metaphor of breath, and concerned with giving in to the full weight of the body. There is a physical immediacy that draws our own bodies readily into his work, and perhaps it is significant that he often sings an accompaniment to the dancers in rehearsal, embodying the music rather than merely counting in relation to its metrical framework. He once spoke in interview about classical ballet being 'so relentlessly concerned with shape', and that he wanted 'to know more about the person […] what comes from inside […] it's not a look that I want – it's a feeling'.[7] He is also the master of the long, continuous phrase – he creates the image of a 'figure-of-eight' – often built up from the overlapping phrases of more than one dancer in conversation. And, as he says, there is always in his work 'a flow of energy'. 'I think of the body as a book that opens and closes really from the spine. I'm very often taking one side out and then the other side out and then folding over like a continuous moebius strip so that the flow of energy is going: rising, falling, rhythmic steps, long big sweeping movements.'[8] Yet, as I will illustrate, there are also times during the progress of *Shimmer* when Alston finds detail and concentrates on the individual moment.

A strong reason for focusing upon Alston here is his widely acknowledged 'musicality' – and that is not to deny the many confusions and inaccuracies which surround that often-used term. Over his forty-year career as a choreographer he has explored a wide range of musical styles, both classical – representing many historical periods – and popular; he would be the first to say that his work is prompted primarily by music. He also reads music – not all choreographers are by any means fluent enough to work with scores – although, naturally, the look of the score does not drive his analysis as much as it does for many musicians. We might even claim that his choreography is primarily *about* the music, that relations between music and dance are, more than anything else, what make his choreography interesting. Perhaps there is a particular balance of power here, as in much of Balanchine's work: a

in the *cabriole*, which is a beating of the legs in front of the body.
[7] Richard Alston, interviewed on 'Just Dancing Around? Richard Alston', television documentary, director Mark Kidel, producer

Debra Hauer (Euphoria Films, Channel 4, 1996).
[8] Siobhan Davies and Richard Alston, 'Siobhan Davies and Richard Alston in Conversation', *Dance Theatre Journal*, 15/1 (1999), 16–20: 18–19.

shift towards a concert-based genre of dance, in which dramas emerge from 'choreomusical' relations rather than the other way round.[9]

The route to Ravel was logical, though not straightforward. There was a fleeting interest in his music when Alston was a teenager. Years later, two components of his life came together. He developed a collaboration with the pianist Jason Ridgway, making two works in the genre of 'piano ballet' with Ridgway on stage: settings of Brahms's *Klavierstücke* Opp. 118 and 119 (*A Sudden Exit*, 1999), and Robert Schumann's *Davidsbündlertänze* (*Strange Company*, 2001). (Alston was following in the piano ballet tradition of Balanchine's *Duo Concertant* (1972) to Stravinsky, and Jerome Robbins's pieces to Chopin, *The Concert* (1956) and *Dances at a Gathering* (1969).) Alston then noted that his friend the distinguished broadcaster and art critic Bryan Robertson (to whom *Shimmer* is dedicated) listened increasingly to Ravel during his final, long battle against illness; the *Sonatine* was played at his funeral. So Robertson, as it were, brought the choreographer back to the composer. Alston decided to use the *Sonatine* score himself and to add three of the *Miroirs*, which are very different in spirit from the *Sonatine*. The scores had been written in rapid succession, and both were early pieces, completed in 1905 and premiered in 1906. (The first movement of the *Sonatine* was written separately, in 1903, for a competition that failed to materialize.) With the exception of the middle movement of the *Sonatine*, designated 'Mouvement de Menuet', none of the music is conventional dance music.

Alston removed the third, virtuoso movement of the *Sonatine*. This happened by chance after he had begun to choreograph *Miroirs* and had reached the point when he felt that the whole piece lasted long enough[10] – normally, he never tampers with scores. But, unknown to him, there was a musical history behind this editing, for Ravel usually omitted the last movement in his own concert performances, because he felt unable to play it well enough.[11] Likewise, the five *Miroirs* are not always performed as a set. Again, Ravel made selections when he performed the work,[12] and the Spanish-inspired 'Alborada del gracioso' has been used independently for ballet on at least four occasions.[13] Each of the *Miroirs* is dedicated to one of Ravel's brother Apaches ('Ruffians'), a group of renegade artistic contemporaries who included, if briefly, the young Stravinsky. Alston chose the following three numbers: 'Oiseaux tristes' (written for the pianist Ricardo Viñes), 'Une barque sur l'océan' (for the painter Paul Sordes), and 'La Vallée des cloches' (for the composer and pianist Maurice Delage).

[9] Stephanie Jordan, *Stravinsky Dances: Re-Visions across a Century* (Alton, Hants: Dance Books, 2007), 7–15 and 256.

[10] Alston, interview.

[11] Richard Dowling, Preface to Maurice Ravel, *Sonatine* (February 2003), www.richard-dowling.com/SonatinePreface (accessed 20 August 2009).

[12] Arbie Orenstein, *Ravel: Man and Musician* (New York: Dover Publications, 1991), 95.

[13] Mawer, *The Ballets of Maurice Ravel*, 284–5.

'Choreomusical' relations: methodological issues

Before embarking upon detailed analysis of *Shimmer*, it is useful to address some issues of method. The first is concerned with how relationships between music and dance can be conceptualized. Ravel's own view of this conformed with the ideal of synaesthesia, drawing upon the widely held early-twentieth-century theory of equivalence between one art medium and another and a belief in the possibility of translation between media: 'For me, there are not several arts, but one alone. Music, painting [add dance], and literature differ only as far as their means of expression. There are not therefore different kinds of artists, but simply different kinds of specialists.'[14]

This synaesthetic principle governed the early period of Diaghilev's Ballets russes and related to the aesthetic of symbolism, the theory of correspondences stemming from poetry, while the concept of *Gesamtkunstwerk*, or fusion of the arts, was associated with the music dramas of Richard Wagner. For dance, music was often the primary source, to be matched, or rather visualized, through movement. We see this in the work of the American modern dance pioneer Isadora Duncan (1878–1927) – highly influential in Europe, she promoted the *Geist* or spirit of music as basis for dance – and in that of Ruth St Denis and Ted Shawn (Denishawn), through their so-called 'music visualizations'.[15] Within the Ballets russes, we find these principles informing the choreography of Fokin and of Nijinsky in his *Le Sacre du printemps* (1913). It is important that Nijinsky was strongly influenced by the eurhythmics system of the Swiss music pedagogue Emile Jaques-Dalcroze (1865–1950), who again promoted the concept of equivalence between music and dance. The credibility of these principles was soon questioned by work that foregrounded dissociation and disunity of semantic content, such as early surrealism and cinema, as well as through devices of structural independence or counterpoint. Mid-century, Merce Cunningham (1919–2009) and the composer John Cage (1912–92) took the radical step of proclaiming extreme independence and a resultant coexistence between music and dance, both strands conceived entirely (or virtually entirely) separately in their collaborations together. Along the way too, there have been dances in silence, proving the autonomy of movement, that dance can function without any music whatsoever. Alston, who studied with Cunningham during his early career, soon became aware of the wide range of musical possibilities that had opened up across the century.

---

[14] Maurice Ravel, 'Mes souvenirs d'enfant paresseux', *La Petite Gironde* (12 July 1931), 1: cited and trans. in Mawer, *The Ballets of Maurice Ravel*, 22.

[15] [Uncredited article], 'Music Visualization', *Denishawn Magazine*, 1/3 (1925), 1–7.

The theorizing of relationships between the arts has changed correspondingly. Increasingly in recent years, scholars dealing with relationships between music and dance have used fluid conceptual models, theories of dynamic interaction between the media, which view the two juxtaposed media of dance and music as subject to change (rather than as static entities), operating within a mechanism of mutual implication and interdependence.[16] Rapidly disappearing are the old, hard binaries of parallelism and counterpoint. We are dealing with a composite form: music and dance. While we might still be able to trace their separate development during a piece, especially in the case of music that already exists outside the dance and that might preserve something of its original identity, these two sensory planes now meet to affect each other and to create a new identity from their meeting.

A number of theorists from outside dance have been directly useful to the development of this thinking about dynamic interaction between media. The film theorist Claudia Gorbman queries whether 'the music "resembles" or [...] "contradicts" the action or mood of what happens on the screen [...] Is there no other way to qualify film music which does not lie between these opposites but outside them? [...] It is debatable that information conveyed by disparate media can justifiably be called *the same* or *different*.'[17] Ultimately, it is essential to go to precise examples within precise contexts in order to address relationships between music and dance in any meaningful way, to go beyond the question of *whether* music and dance meet each other or not, to ask *where* or *how* they meet.[18]

It is important to realize that, in the particular instance when an existing score is used by a choreographer, its effect will change accordingly. Ravel is no longer just what we hear in a concert or a recording. Through the shifting mechanisms of interdependence and mutual voicing, movement changes musical perceptions. We can actually hear new notes, or a particular instrumental line suddenly emerges more strongly. Movement seems to seek out related properties in the music, and vice versa, and new meanings emerge from their points of contact. The consequence of, or underside to, this is that other aspects of the music and dance are hidden from view or perhaps even erased, and the two media combined might, for instance, create a new shape through time.

Furthermore, different choreographic settings highlight and hide different components of the music. The Ravel of Alston's *Sonatine* is different from the Ravel of Balanchine's, and the act of comparison emphasizes

[16] For more on notions of interdependence, see Stephanie Jordan, *Moving Music: Dialogues with Music in Twentieth-century Ballet* (London: Dance Books, 2000). [Ed.]

[17] Claudia Gorbman, 'Narrative Film Music', *Yale French Studies*, 60 (1980), 183–203: 189.

[18] Barbara White, '"As If They Didn't Hear the Music", Or: How I Learned to Stop Worrying and Love Mickey Mouse', *Opera Quarterly*, 22/1 (2006 ['Sound Moves' issue]), 65–89: 73.

the distinctiveness of their approaches. But this is not simply a question of different interpretations or perceptions of the same music by different choreographers. Whether or not Alston heard the music differently from Balanchine, he became an audience to his own work as he made it and had, like any of us, to engage with a new, composite form.

It is useful to touch on Alston's own account of his working process, what he has chosen to give away in interviews and lectures. For some time now, he has been consistent in his statements, for instance, about his overall approach: 'I have a real passion for accident. Everyone thinks that my work is about structure. Actually, I'm totally intuitive and I don't work out structures, never have. A lot of the work that I do now – in terms of dancers working with each other – is looking at "happy accident".'[19]

Yet, throughout his career, Alston has also held to some important principles about the balance between challenge and 'legibility' for his audiences, and these principles do relate to structure. In terms of challenge, 'I have an allergy to repeats,' he once said in a lecture-demonstration on *Shimmer*. 'They're comforting, but I like keeping people on the edge of their seats.'[20] Then, on the question of repetition: 'See the same movement; change the music so you see it differently.'[21] But, in terms of legibility: 'I've discovered that I can articulate difficult rhythmic phrases if the sound echoes them.'[22] And 'A lot of my work is about the play between imitating a vocal or melodic line and leaving it.'[23]

Such imitation is a good deal more subtle than we might first imagine and, moreover, Alston sometimes works in quite another way, virtually guaranteeing no imitation of a musical line. In a lecture-demonstration given at the Purcell Room in London on 4 October 2008, he choreographed a long strand of double-work (i.e. material for two dancers), in silence and without settling its rhythms. Then, he simply put on a recording of Brahms's *Intermezzo* Op.116, No. 2, while he and the dancers literally found their way alongside, gradually fixing timing and synchronization as they repeated the sequence. Most important, however, whatever he says about his early processes, Alston's explanations suggest that a useful analytical approach to his work is to check its structural subtleties and, for what they can evoke, the ebb and flow between closure and uncertainty and the pleasures and anxieties of both.

Like most choreographers – but rather fewer composers – Alston emphasizes the role of his performers. His 'collaboration' with them during the

[19] Davies and Alston, 'Siobhan Davies and Richard Alston in Conversation', 16–17.
[20] Alston, lecture-demonstration.
[21] *Ibid.*
[22] Stephanie Jordan, *Striding Out: Aspects of Contemporary and New Dance in Britain* (London: Dance Books, 1992), 123.
[23] Alston, lecture-demonstration; see also Alston interviewed on 'Working with Bodies – Richard Alston' (*The South Bank Show*, London Weekend Television, 1982).

creative process extends to the occasion of performance itself and an interest in seeing his own work change – he mentions enjoying how that early '*fall back flat*' (see the opening description), which was choreographed to happen *on* the high note, began to happen *after* it.[24] There was too the 'double whammy' of the musical performance changing in the hands of his pianist, Ridgway again. Alston based his early dance rehearsals on two music recordings: one by Pascal Rogé (1974) and, for the final 'La Vallée' solo, one by Louis Lortie (1989).[25] Ridgway too was at first guided by these recordings but, as we shall see, Alston was open to him negotiating his own musical interpretation as well as his relationship to the choreography and dancers. Here, the pianist's presence on stage raises issues about leadership, initiation and response, the conversation between him and the dancers, the opportunities for them to give to and take from each other, while we are also invited to consider his visible physicality.

In addition to all this, there is a personal process, which has defined as well as opened up my viewing and listening: watching the choreography in performance and rehearsal, as well as the invaluable lecture-demonstration on *Shimmer*, watching it both with and without the sound being present, trying out dance and musical material on myself and at the piano. It was inevitable that I would draw upon my experience of watching and writing about a number of Alston's dances over the years, and the recollection of the 'feel' of his movement in the body through any number of dance classes taught by him in the 1970s and 1980s. But it was a stroke of excellent fortune that Alston elected to revive Martin Lawrance's 'La Vallée' solo for his sixtieth-birthday London Dance Umbrella performances of 2008,[26] during my own writing process for this chapter, thus enabling me to pay extra-concentrated attention to 'liveness' for this particular dance.

Different readers may wish to take different routes through the analysis that follows. Some, for instance, might prefer to ride rapidly over the more technical analysis. A priority is to convey something of the spirit of the work.

Performing the analysis

Alston 'constructed' his *Shimmer* (score and choreography) as if to allow the work to become more strange and mysterious as it progressed. If, at the start, during the movement that he labelled 'Sonatine', we glimpse the sophistication of a couple in jewelled costumes (designed by Julien Macdonald), there

---

24   Alston, lecture-demonstration.
25   Pascal Rogé, *Ravel: Piano Works* (Decca 440836 [1994; recording dates: *Sonatine*, 1973; *Miroirs*, 1974]); Louis Lortie, *Ravel: Piano Music*, vol. II (Chandos 8647 [1989]).

26   Martin Lawrance was a member of the Richard Alston Dance Company and is now its Rehearsal Director. Dance Umbrella is an annual dance festival.

Table 8.1 Alston, *Shimmer*: structural chart indicating the original casting

[*Sonatine*]

Movement	Dancers/action	Cast
'Sonatine'	Black/red couple	Jonathan Goddard, Ino Riga
'Minuet'	White couple	Luke Baio, Francesca Romo

[*Miroirs*]

Movement	Dancers/action	Cast
'Oiseaux tristes'	Blue couple	Martin Lawrance, Sonja Peedo
'Une barque sur l'océan'	Group; Woman in blue: short 'seagull' solo (which becomes a duet with the Man in blue); Black/red couple: duet	Full cast of seven onstage together near the end
'La Vallée des cloches'	Man in blue	Martin Lawrance

is also, even then, a suggestion of bonding with natural forces in the duet's 'animal' qualities and 'wave' imagery. Later, there are images of birds, still more waves, the portrayal of fitful weather, and the framing by stage lighting of dark nights and warm, glowing sunny days and evenings. The 'Mouvement de Menuet' (Alston's 'Minuet') is as far as Alston goes within this work in the direction of the chic and conventional civility of social dance: he created it as a homage to Ashton, recalling his use of gloves in the party piece *Les Rendezvous* (1933) – side by side, the couple take a walk down the diagonal, and the choreography stresses hands, gesturing and touching. This is the only section that begins with a rise in the signature melody line, while the absence of the hint of melancholy that falling intervals introduce elsewhere might be of note. For a formal outline of *Shimmer*, which also details the original dancers, see Table 8.1.

By contrast, the *Miroirs* pieces seem especially dark.[27] Ravel knew it. In an autobiographical sketch, he said that they 'mark a change in my harmonic development pronounced enough to have upset those musicians who till then had had the least trouble in appreciating my style'.[28] Alston senses a

---

[27] The reader is referred to the score: Maurice Ravel, *Miroirs* (Paris: E. Demets/Editions Max Eschig, 1906); see too *Miroirs*, Urtext edition ed. Roger Nichols (London: Edition Peters, 1995). [Ed.]

[28] Roland-Manuel, 'Une esquisse autobiographique de Maurice Ravel' [1928],

La Revue musicale, 19 (December 1938 [special issue]), 17–23: 20. 'Les *Miroirs* […] marquent dans mon évolution harmonique un changement assez considérable pour avoir déconcenancé les musiciens les plus accoutumés jusqu'alors à ma manière.'

'magical' quality here. But there is also a much freer, more unpredictable sense of form – Ravel was interested in writing music that sounded like improvisation.[29] The composer includes a wider range of timbre and register than in the movements of the *Sonatine*, notably introducing the lower levels on the piano. In the same autobiographical sketch, Ravel explained that 'Oiseaux tristes' 'evokes birds lost in the oppressiveness of a very dark forest during the hottest hours of summer'.[30] The music is suffused with bird calls. Alston reads it as 'nocturnal', and, in a duet that he describes as 'claustrophobic', his two dancers reference 'birds roosting, huddling together, tucking their heads under their wings'.[31] Rather differently, within 'Une barque sur l'océan', individuals disappear into ensemble waves, although a couple of times, a solo or duet emerges: for the woman in blue (one of the 'birds' from 'Oiseaux tristes'), he now uses the image of a seagull staying close to the waves. Contrast the 'La Vallée' solo for the man in blue, exquisitely alone, but now very human after the earlier submergence of the individual. The sound of bells evokes space, distance, and his isolation.

In terms of what Alston refers to as 'legibility', his *Miroirs* is far more testing than *Sonatine*, and 'Une barque' most of all. Yet there is a kind of musical *ritornello* here from which other material spins off in unexpected ways. Evoking as it does a sea that heats up to boiling point, calms, and erupts angrily all over again, and drawing from a fresh palette of piano thunder and rattle, most of 'Une barque sur l'océan', according to Alston, is 'music that you have to ride [...] so many notes!'[32] A scribble on his copy of the score says 'let rip!' On several occasions, the dancers simply dash through a canon sequence, a cascade of action that fills the stage, leaving a virtual, arclike, trace. Halfway through this dance (marking proportions very clearly; end of bar 73), the group suddenly coalesces into a tight circle, a focal point: 'It's Doris Humphrey!' says Alston,[33] recalling the American modern dance pioneer's famous *Soaring* (1920) to Schumann, when five women rush together, a cloud of silk billowing over their heads.

The musical *ritornello* becomes a relatively stable choreographic section, though differently cast when it returns, at one point turned around by ninety degrees, and finally fragmented, like the music. The initial movement starts on the second note of the melody, emphasizing the end of the falling intervallic gesture. This is not obvious *dancing to* music, yet it turns out to be a useful way of cueing the beginning of a dance. (The 'Sonatine' movement begins likewise.) The second time that we hear/see this section (bar 61), there

[29] Roland-Manuel, *Maurice Ravel*, trans. Cynthia Jolly (London: Dennis Dobson, 1947), 41.

[30] Roland-Manuel, 'Une esquisse autobiographique', 20. '[J]'y évoque] des oiseaux perdus dans la torpeur d'une forêt très sombre aux heures les plus chaudes de l'été.'

[31] Alston, lecture-demonstration.

[32] *Ibid.*

[33] *Ibid.*

is a canon: a couple and a trio, one dance count apart. Alston felt that each group nuanced the melody line differently, which pleased him – perhaps one of his 'happy accidents', but I also hear a second, inner part or voice in the music: accented notes emerging from the rumbling accompaniment that suggest, but never quite evolve into, a line. It is the two groups in canon that seem to bring this second part into consciousness: each group has a musical voice. The later, 'seagull' solo music (from bar 83) also carries more than one voice, and again, the fact of a person in view on stage enhances the effect of music as representing a subject or subjects. The woman in blue seems to belong to the plaintive fragments from the pianist's left hand (bars 83–5; 90–1); a low striding bass theme suggests an outside presence (bars 86–8; 92–4). Nature, the sea, is haunted.

A comparison between the Alston and Balanchine settings of *Sonatine*

The 'Sonatine' and 'Minuet' movements of *Shimmer* make the point most clearly about choreography offering a second structural layer, creating a new composite shape together with the music. The point is especially well made here as we can compare Alston's setting of these two movements with Balanchine's.

Ravel's *Sonatine* first movement is a kind of sonata form, using the familiar classical model but with the twists of an early twentieth-century rereading; see Table 8.2.[34] The first subject of the exposition (bars 1–10) has the '*rippling accompaniment*', the second emerges after the '*accompaniment halts*' (bar 13), and we could make a case for a third, with the '*sighing motive*' ('Un peu retenu') derived from part of the first subject (bars 20ff.), before a short codetta, marked *a tempo* (bars 24ff.). The exposition repeats, according to the strict model, after which there follows a middle section or development based upon what we already know, and a recapitulation with a six-bar coda.

Alston's dance structure has nothing like the thematic or material organization of musical sonata form, far less large-scale repetition. Instead, he creates what he calls a 'chorus', or 'nuggets' of movement that recur. The chorus starts as Riga '*curves her leg around him*' (Goddard) '*in an embrace*', as the '*musical phrase comes to an end*' (bar 19). After the first '*musical sigh*', she starts to pull away, and then drops sideways to the floor. Later, as they stand together, he gently pushes her arm up to the upper-voiced (offbeat) E of the codetta (bar 24; see Example 8.2).

---

[34] In Table 8.2 and elsewhere, the designation *bis* (twice) is used to distinguish the bars of a musical repeat which have been set to through-composed choreography.

Table 8.2 Ravel, *Sonatine* (I); Alston, 'Sonatine': diagram of structure (indicating the choreographic repetition patterns)

Music	Choreography
Exposition (bars 1–25, 1st-time bars)	Lift and '*fall back flat*' (bars 6 and 8); 'Chorus' material (bars 19–25)
'Repeat' (4 *bis* – 25 *bis*, 2nd-time bars)	'Chorus' material repeated at bars 19 *bis* – 25 *bis*, with variation (from bar 23 *bis*)
Development (bars 31–55)	
Recapitulation, with short coda (bars 56–84)	'Chorus' material (bars 74–84; from bars 19–25), with variation (from bar 80) Opening lift and '*fall back flat*' (bar 84; from bars 6 and 8)

Example 8.2 Ravel, *Sonatine* (I, bars 20–6); Alston, 'Sonatine': 'chorus' passage

We see/hear this phrase of movement three times in all (to the musical exposition, repeat of exposition and recapitulation); see again Table 8.2. The music remains the same, but Alston's ending develops. The second time, the man crouches to the floor before the woman takes her arm (and leg) up, on the E (bar 24 *bis*), of her own accord. The third time he lies on the floor (bars 79–81), she holds still and delays her gestural completion for two bars.

There is one other repeated nugget, but to different music: the beginning of the dance becomes the very end, in compressed form (bars 6, 8, and 84) – '*she folds her leg over his arm and tucks herself up against his side*', which is now followed straightaway by the '*fall back flat*', a dangerous act and ambiguous point of closure. All these moves are consistently angled the same way towards the audience, so the repetition is simple to perceive. The effect of this dance structure next to the musical structure is of an unforced interlocking. Or, remembering that Alston's creative act followed Ravel's, it is as if Alston has lightly pinpointed certain stages within the musical form. The procedure is like laying a transparency over a piece of paper so that we can see where the marks on them both match up. And there is no special signalling of the main dance repetition – no musical phrase starting and confirming the structural point in the choreography – the moment when she *curves her leg around him in an embrace* seems to arrive out of nowhere.

Balanchine's approach to form is very different. Verdy and Bonnefous start onstage just listening to the pianist, then they prepare themselves in a courtly fashion, and the dance proper begins with the '*sighing motive*'. Now they articulate the detail of the music much more than Alston does, the rise and fall of the *sighing motive*, three times, thus making us hear it more clearly: she steps up, *posé*, he turns her around, and then she steps down, presenting her foot in *tendu* (i.e. stretched, with toes touching the floor). Next, she highlights the upper E (in both bars 24 and 25) with a quick upward *battement* of the leg and, when the music repeats in the recapitulation, with a *cabriole*. But the overall form of the Balanchine duet is more open, with even less regular repetition than in the Alston setting; Balanchine said that the dance should 'look like an improvisation'.[35] At the end, both dancers leave the stage with the music (Alston's dancers leave in the silence, after the music).

The musical form of the 'Minuet' movement is more like ABA, with varied harmonic treatment for the second occurrence of section A. Appropriate to the conventions of social dance, there is much greater symmetry here in Alston's choreography than in his 'Sonatine' setting, a long recapitulation of twenty-two bars of dance material (bars 53–74, taken over from bars 1 *bis* – 22: effectively the whole of section A without its repeat), emphasizing the sameness in the music rather than its difference through reharmonization or, looked at another way, allowing the choreography to be perceived slightly differently because of changes in the music (see Table 8.3). Again, as in his setting of the 'Sonatine', Balanchine's approach is more open, and the dance steps dissolve eventually into a kind of meditation during which Verdy drifts offstage. Again, his 'Minuet' starts with listening, no dancing to the first twelve bars. To the musical repeat (bars 1 *bis* – 12 *bis*), there is a solo for Bonnefous in a taut, percussive czardas style, including a thigh-slapping jump. Bonnefous pulls slightly incongruously against Ravel's genteel legato, forcing his position a little. Verdy's softer version of folk style looks more lovely and liquid by contrast (bars 13–22). For their shorter recapitulation, they simply put their two phrases alongside each other (bars 53–64). The coda is a strange, conventionally virtuoso outburst for the man, which demands a response – the joyous, unrestrained, 'Animé' third movement of the *Sonatine*

---

[35] Verdy, interview with the author (14 May 2008).

Table 8.3 Ravel, 'Mouvement de Menuet'; Alston, 'Minuet': diagram of structure (indicating the choreographic repetition patterns)

Music	Choreography
Section A (bars 1–12; repeated 1 *bis* – 12 *bis*)	Long diagonal across the stage (through-composed: bars 1–12, 1 *bis* – 12 *bis*)
Continuation (bars 13–22)	She curls around him (bars 13–14)
Section B (bars 23–52)	
Section A′ (bars 53–78)	Repeat of material (bars 53–74; from bar 1 *bis* – 22); she curls around him (bars 65–6; from 13–14)
Coda (bars 79–82)	She curls around him (bar 82; from 13–14)

which ends with the pair racing offstage in opposite directions. Alston's coda ends with another of his nuggets: he (Luke Baio) curves her (Francesca Romo) round to lay her across his thigh (bars 13 and 65 – marking the same musical moment; bar 82 – to different music), and again they leave in silence.

Alston's 'Minuet' turns out to be the most pulse-based, rhythmically detailed section of *Shimmer*. During its long threads of movement, we enjoy a range of unpredictable rhythm patterns and accents counterpointing those of the melody line, and it is the melody line that leads the ear. A good example is the second dance phrase to the repeat of the first musical section (bars 1 *bis* – 12 *bis*; see Example 8.3). In both music and dance, there is a shared tendency towards weighting the second beat of the bar. But we immediately sense independent articulations as well. For instance, as at the opening of the 'Sonatine' and 'Une barque sur l'océan', this dance phrase begins on beat 2, after the music, with two hand gestures on the last two beats. Again, hand gestures are delayed until beats 2 and 3 (bar 8 *bis*), then a pause in motion respects the tied-over note on beat 1 (bar 9 *bis*). But a step *on* a melodic tied note begins a bar (bar 6 *bis*). And the dancers make another striking accent of their own on beat 3 (bar 11 *bis*), anticipating the bar line, not corresponding to any movement in the melody, but creating a final piquant 'dissonance'.

Mostly, the dance accents are movements downwards into *plié* (bending the supporting knee or knees) which gives a cushioned, slightly bouncy quality; the woman's stressed step *up* on to the toes (right foot, bar 10 *bis*) adds an extra sense of depth to the final accent *down* (bar 11 *bis*). Clapping the dance rhythm line alongside the music, feeling within the body the alternating sinking and rising as the arrows in Example 8.3 point downwards or upwards, we get a sense of the choreomusical rhythm and flow. Alston rarely visualizes changes in musical pitch in a way that stands out especially, but the dancers seem to relish the occasional linkage (bar 5 *bis*): stepping, bending the knee with the drop in the melody at the beginning of this bar, and then picking themselves upright with the music (bar 7 *bis*). At the end of the final

Example 8.3 Ravel, *Sonatine* (II, bars 1 *bis* – 12 *bis*); Alston, 'Minuet' (indicating dance steps, accents, major changes in movement level (arrows up and down), and hand gestures; the combined rhythm of both dancers is notated, reflecting their double-work)

phrase, two closing steps draw our attention away from the melody line to the two notes in the bass accompaniment (bar 12 *bis*). So it is as if, with the play between movement and sound, Alston creates a new 'shape' of his own with this twelve-bar phrase.

Alston's *Miroirs*

The 'Minuet' is a contained, tender prelude to the more disturbing other world of the *Miroirs*. Now, the interlocking forms are much less straightforward and, in 'Oiseaux tristes' (see Plate 8.3) and 'La Vallée', Alston's nuggets of movement are often just a single image rather than a phrase. But this is in

Plate 8.3 Martin Lawrance and Sonja Peedo in Richard Alston's *Shimmer* (2004). Photograph by Chris Nash. Reproduced by kind permission of the Richard Alston Dance Company, London

keeping with his particular attention here to the musical moment. In both pieces, single notes are important, and they seem to hang, like objects that have been frozen, or turned to stone. Alston makes them key reference points. He helps us to register them by allocating them plenty of time, fixing them, as though willing them more permanence.

In 'Oiseaux tristes' there is just one recurring dance phrase for the man and woman, when they fall sideways across the stage: she (Sonja Peedo) stops in a crossed-leg position looking down to one hand, and he (Martin Lawrance) raises a flexed foot and swings his arms, before arriving close behind her.

We see this phrase in truncated form later (bars 21–3), 'as if without the prepositions', Alston suggests,[36] and it is with this material that the dancers finally leave during the musical silence. Twice there is a cadenza-like passage (bars 15ff. and 25ff.) – and a rush of motion. But the most memorable moments are those when the dancers 'mark' the pronounced single notes. Here, the notes characteristically appear in pairs: high B♭, B♭, at the beginning, followed by E♭, E♭, a fifth below (bars 3ff.), back to the B♭ pairings (bar 7), while, later, those on E♭ (or D♯) start to take over (bars 10ff.). The dancers show the continuity between the paired notes. Near the beginning, she slowly curves over forwards and he lifts her up, hanging 'dead' with arms and legs suspended below. Later, he stands and tilts gently backwards towards her supporting arms, again very slowly, again showing the link between the notes (two pairs of two notes). To a single F♯ (bar 13), the woman suddenly strikes a powerful sickle-shaped arm gesture over the man's back. Later, we hear the same note accented again (bar 20) – our pitch memory might well refer us back to the earlier occasion – and both dancers send their arms flying upwards, cutting through the air. Is this initiation or response? Do the dancers 'make' or 'move' the sound, or do they react swiftly, adding their own confirmation? Alston always instructs his dancers to maintain the continuity of their movement: 'Never *wait* for a sound.'[37] It seems that this moment was 'found' by chance in rehearsal and that both Ridgway and the dancers decided to accent the note regularly, and more than they might normally, like a sudden highlight.

The voice of the performers

On several occasions, dancers 'found' moments when they could connect with the music. Perhaps it was the innate urge to connect that encouraged the couple in the 'Sonatine' to delay their dangerous '*fall back flat*'. Hearing and feeling the high C♯ (bars 6 and 8; 84), they wanted to stay up *with* it, at least momentarily, rather than marking the descent that moves in opposition to the direction of pitch.

In 'La Vallée', the single (though paired) notes of 'Oiseaux tristes' are now bells: bells everywhere and echoes of bells, tolling ominously and ringing out brightly. Apparently, Ravel had been inspired by the noontime sound of the many church bells in Paris.[38] The single notes now reverberate freely and Lawrance's dance is as much about listening to them in stillness and opening his body to their sound as about moving. Since, in 2008, Lawrance was given an opportunity to revisit this solo, I have incorporated his thoughts alongside those of Ridgway into the following discussion.

---

[36] Alston, interview.   [38] Orenstein, *Ravel*, 160.
[37] Alston, lecture-demonstration.

The dance had been inspired by the image of Prospero left alone on his island at the end of Shakespeare's *The Tempest*:

> *Our revels now are ended; these our actors,*
> *As I foretold you, were all spirits, and*
> *Are melted into air, into thin air:*
> *And, like the baseless fabric of this vision,*
> *The cloud-capp'd towers, the gorgeous palaces,*
> *The solemn temples, the great globe itself,*
> *Yea, all which it inherit, shall dissolve,*
> *And, like this insubstantial pageant faded,*
> *Leave not a rack behind: We are such stuff*
> *As dreams are made of, and our little life*
> *Is rounded with a sleep.*[39]

Prospero's tone is dark but, as Alston says, he was also 'magical, a sorcerer, and very powerful'. Thus, Alston wanted to show 'someone in his domain […] marking out territory'; Lawrance becomes the most austere figure in *Shimmer* and, after all the other dancers cluster around him, he too is left behind. Yet meanings are left open, and there is no exaggerated sense of a character: Lawrance told me that the overriding image for him was of the deeply felt *hommage* to Bryan Robertson.[40]

Lawrance explores a range of vocabulary, sometimes fragmentary utterances, as simple as a couple of steps, sometimes long convoluted sentences that involve the full three-dimensional body travelling boldly across the stage. The dance is like a thought process, coming to terms with inner voices, and the emergence of an individual personality. Signature ideas in 'La Vallée' are modified in different ways next to different music: like a perilous fall, literally a stumble over the front of the foot – 'almost tripping myself up' – from which Lawrance stretches his body flat across the floor. With his left arm following across in front, as if shielding him from view, this is a devastating image, unannounced, emerging from nowhere (bar 20), then sustained as if for ever (bars 36–9 and 46–7). As spectators we feel suddenly closed off from him, as if no longer seeing him. Lawrance rather senses himself as a still centre, 'like a stone stopping under water', amidst waves at the surface. Then there is a luscious rolling movement, from kneeling, when he uncurls his spine to swing himself around and down into a fleeting, precarious halt, right hip poised just off the floor (bars 10, 30, 53–4). We see this once, twice, and at the very end, always within a compelling light beam from downstage left: 'it's like there is another world outside that you return to after private time, like

[39] William Shakespeare, *The Tempest* (4.1. 148–58), from *The Complete Works of William Shakespeare*, with an introduction by St John Ervine (London and Glasgow: Collins, *c*.1923), 19.

[40] Martin Lawrance, interview with the author (28 September 2008).

someone opened the door and caught me doing something'.[41] A questioning discord is the final statement.

The choreography touches only obliquely the arch form of the music, yet it remains very close to the sounds and rhythms. When Lawrance falls still, we listen more. Or, when he raises his arms and listens, looking up and out into the space, it is as though he is searching to make contact with the bells. There are further highlighted connections. Just once, he treads the ground gently, as if treading literally three notes in the melody (the beginning of bar 26), his feet like the paws of a cat, after which he bends over to extend the effect of the fall in the melody line. Two focal points occur within the diagonal beam when, to a choralelike passage, marked *très calme* (at bars 12ff. and 42ff.), Lawrance circles his arm and presents his right hand, then steps sideways and sinks to a distinctive falling motive (from the pianist's right hand). These are like moments of transcendence, and Ridgway catches his initial hand gesture down in the bass. At the start of the final trajectory towards the light (bars 50ff.), Lawrance twists back on the first of four bass discords and looks at Ridgway close by: 'as if I'm almost predatory but asking – "is it right?"'

Is Lawrance playing or being played by the music? The effect can change from performance to performance. These are moments of precise, staged connection and Ridgway watches out eagerly for them. (He also knows the dance as a spectator acquainted with video recordings.) Lawrance notes his own tendency to go slow: 'but I love chasing the music too'. Ridgway acknowledges his role here as the accompanist, fitting in with a choreographic conception of the music, and of choreomusical relations. But he is also aware of his power to drive the dance: 'Live music will differ from one performance to the next in small musical details. And this will, in turn, challenge the dance.'[42] He responds to Alston's concern that relations should not be too consistently close and that each performer should have her/his own freedom. Ridgway borrows an image from music to capture Alston's particular choreomusical style: 'it's like creating a polyphony rather than being very vertical'.

In short, Alston gives us a less familiar vision of Ravel as a dance composer, acclaiming his humanity and qualities of yielding and permeability rather than the mechanistic aspects that gave rise to Stravinsky's famous 'Swiss clockmaker'[43] metaphor. Perhaps Alston brings back to us the particular qualities of volatility and sensuality with which early Ravel recordings, including those by the composer himself, were imbued.[44] Certainly, the

---

[41] *Ibid.*

[42] Jason Ridgway, interview with the author (5 October 2008).

[43] José Bruyr, 'En Marge… d'un premier chapitre', *La Revue musicale*, 19 (December 1938 [special issue]), 279–80: 279.

[44] Ronald Woodley, 'Performing Ravel: Styles and Practice in the Early Recordings', in Deborah Mawer (ed.), *The Cambridge Companion to Ravel* (Cambridge University Press, 2000), 213–39: 218, 220–1, 231, 235.

liveness of dance performance – the release of the dancers' and pianist's personal musicalities – contributes to the perception of these other qualities. Indeed, this very point might be seen as the manifesto of *Shimmer*, which increasingly as it progresses emphasizes performer power.

Shimmer also shows us that even Ravel's non-dance music can dance. Alston's style does not need the step rhythms of waltzes and boleros; arguably, the discovery of the twentieth century was that dancers did not necessarily need to be motorized. Here, through Alston's special approach to music, not only do we hear the music very clearly, but we also hear it modified and moved by the dance – guided by the choreographer, the dancers, and the pianist – and there is a good chance too that we might hear the dancers as musicians.

9 The longstanding medical fascination with 'le cas Ravel'

Erik Baeck

The tragic death of Maurice Ravel, who lost his creativity to a debilitating progressive brain disorder in his last years when he was regarded as one of Europe's most distinguished composers and had, in his own words, 'still everything to say',[1] has long aroused medical fascination. Cases involving famous composers have, of course, always been particularly intriguing.

Scientists have also tried to define musical receptivity and musical talent: the former being an aptitude possessed by the majority of humans although rare cases of so-called congenital amusia (tone-deafness) have been known since 1878, the latter a specific quality expressed in musical performance or composition. Both aspects of musicality are research topics that open interesting windows on brain function. In the nineteenth century, autopsies of musicians including Beethoven and Schumann had already been undertaken, and in 1894 much attention was paid to the discovered skull of J. S. Bach.[2] Later, investigators set out to find the psycho-organic cerebral substrate of musical perception,[3] and knowledge of the relationship between brain and music has increased enormously in the late twentieth century by means of neuropsychological and imaging techniques.[4]

In attempting to unravel the genetic defects, neurobiochemical abnormalities, and morphological features of congenital amusia, degenerative dementia or so-called *idiots savants*, scientists may also provide further insight into the cerebral substrate of music. While local cerebral hypertrophy can be correlated with professional musical practice, degenerative diffuse or segmental brain atrophy may impair musical pursuits, even making them impossible. In all these respects the case of Ravel is exemplary.

---

[1] Hélène Jourdan-Morhange, 'Mon ami Ravel', *La Revue musicale*, 19 (December 1938 [special issue]), 192–7: 195; 'j'ai tout à dire encore'.

[2] W. His, *Anatomische Forschungen über Johann Sebastian Bachs Gebeine und Antlitz nebst Bemerkungen über dessen Bilder* (Leipzig, 1896).

[3] Macdonald Critchley and Robert A. Henson (eds.), *Music and the Brain* (London: Heinemann, 1977).

[4] Erik Baeck, 'The Neural Networks of Music', *European Journal of Neurology*, 9/5 (2002), 449–56.

Facts and uncertainties in Ravel's disease history

In 1927, following the completion of his Sonata for Violin and Piano, Ravel complained of 'great tiredness', 'cerebral anaemia', and 'amnesia'.[5] But he had often had such symptoms. He was a frail man who had been exempted from military service at the age of twenty and who, throughout his life, had shown what might be seen as a psychological vulnerability, despite his pronounced character. As early as 1912, he had written to Ralph Vaughan Williams exclaiming that 'My various works which were performed last season, and, above all, *Daphnis et Chloé*, left me in pitiful condition. I had to be sent to the country in order to take care of an incipient neurasthenia.'[6] In 1913 he apologized to the sick Mme Casella for his late answer since 'I myself was in pitiful shape, because my work began to resemble a grave illness: fever, insomnia, lack of appetite.'[7] Enlisted as a volunteer during the Great War, he underwent abdominal surgery in 1916 and was discharged from military duty in 1917. In autumn 1918 he remarked upon 'an unbelievable state of exhaustion and weakness. It strongly resembles neurasthenia,'[8] and in 1919 'a slow tuberculosis' was feared as he again complained of extreme tiredness and hours of depression in which he despaired of ever being able to resume work again.[9]

Significantly, after a performance of the Violin Sonata in 1927, Hélène Jourdan-Morhange, worried by Ravel's strange attitude at the piano, called Dr Pasteur Vallery-Radot (1886–1970).[10] Indeed Ravel did then go to see this famous Parisian physician who prescribed a year's rest. But in spring 1928, neglecting the advice, he undertook a successful but demanding American tour of four months' duration and, on his return, composed *Boléro*. Some postcards which Ravel sent from America do, at certain points, reveal an unsteady handwriting that some scholars consider to be the first sign of dysgraphia (impaired writing),[11] though others regard the unsteadiness merely as provoked by the jerkiness of the train on board which they were written.[12]

In November 1928, Ravel made a tour of Spain with the singer Madeleine Grey who later recalled that he had had to play his *Sonatine* at the French ambassador's residence in Madrid. Unsettled by the loud conversations of the public, 'he became nervous, lost the thread, and, being in a hurry to finish, coupled the coda of the Finale to the exposition of the first movement'; despite

5 Hélène Jourdan-Morhange, *Ravel et nous: l'homme, l'ami, le musicien* (Geneva: Editions du milieu du monde, 1945), 242.
6 Arbie Orenstein (ed.), *A Ravel Reader: Correspondence, Articles, Interviews* (New York: Columbia University Press, 1990), 132.
7 *Ibid.*, 134.
8 *Ibid.*, 182.
9 A.-Ferdinand Hérold, 'Souvenirs', *La Revue musicale*, 19 (December 1938 [special issue]), 198–9: 199.
10 Jourdan-Morhange, *Ravel et nous*, 242.
11 Marcel Marnat, *Maurice Ravel* (Paris: Fayard, 1986), 663.
12 Bernard Mercier, 'Biographie médicale de Maurice Ravel', PhD dissertation, Université Paris Nord (1991), 66.

this, the listeners expressed their admiration to the pianist who was elated about 'this involuntary mystification' of his audience.[13] As with the incident with the American postcards, opinions diverge as to whether this was a memory lapse,[14] or indeed a so-called mystification.[15]

Between 1929 and 1931 Ravel worked concurrently on his two concertos for piano and orchestra: he interrupted work on the Piano Concerto in G when Paul Wittgenstein, an Austrian pianist who had lost his right arm during World War I, commissioned a Piano Concerto for the Left Hand, a project which Ravel completed in some nine months before resuming the Concerto in G.[16] A further full year was necessary to finish the latter. On 20 November 1931, Ravel wrote to Henri Rabaud: 'Kindly excuse me for the Osiris competition: my concerto is finished, and not far from being so myself, I would risk falling asleep at the first candidate. I have been ordered complete rest, and am being treated with injections of serum.'[17]

The world premiere of the Left Hand Concerto took place on 5 January 1932 in Vienna, performed by Wittgenstein and conducted by Robert Heger. The first performance of the Concerto in G was given in Paris on 14 January 1932, with the composer conducting and Marguerite Long playing the solo part; thereafter both made a European tour which lasted until April. In the summer, following a commission for the film *Don Quichotte*, Ravel started to compose *Don Quichotte à Dulcinée*, a cycle of three songs for voice and piano. Then on the night of 8–9 October 1932, he was hurt in a taxi accident in Paris and subsequently assessed by Dr Abel Desjardins.[18] By Ravel's own admission to Manuel de Falla, three months later, the accident 'was not very serious: a bruised thorax and some facial wounds. And yet, I was unable to do anything but sleep and eat.'[19] On 17 January 1933, he nonetheless managed to conduct the Parisian premiere of his Left Hand Concerto with Wittgenstein as soloist. But shortly afterwards, he merely attended another performance in Monte Carlo and had to decline an invitation for a Russian tour.

Two episodes signified, poignantly, a notable downturn in Ravel's health. While holidaying, Ravel apparently wanted to demonstrate to Marie Gaudin, his childhood friend, how to skim a pebble on the sea; instead, he inadvertently struck her on the face. A few days later he was found lying on his back in the water, suddenly incapable of coordinating his swimming movements, and had to be fetched in from the sea. Ravel's biographers[20] claim that

[13] Madeleine Grey, 'Souvenirs d'une interprète', *La Revue musicale*, 19 (December 1938 [special issue]), 175–8: 177; 'il s'énerve, perd le fil, et, pressé d'en finir, enchaine la *coda* du *Final* à l'exposition du premier mouvement [...] cette mystification involontaire'.
[14] Marnat, *Maurice Ravel*, 640.
[15] Mercier, 'Biographie médicale', 67.
[16] Marnat, *Maurice Ravel*, 642–54.

[17] Arbie Orenstein, *Ravel: Man and Musician* (New York: Dover Publications, 1991), 102n.
[18] Bernard Mercier, 'La Maladie neurologique de Ravel', *Cahiers Maurice Ravel*, 5 (1990–2), 13–26: 20.
[19] Orenstein (ed.), *A Ravel Reader*, 314.
[20] Marnat, *Maurice Ravel*, 666; Orenstein, *Ravel*, 105.

these events occurred at Saint-Jean-de-Luz in the summer of 1933, but their assumptions are seemingly contradicted by a letter of 2 August 1933 which Ravel wrote from Le Touquet (a northern seaside resort on the Channel where he stayed in the villa of friends), to Gaudin:

> You won't see me this year at Saint-Jean, alas! Feeling rather washed-out for quite a long time, I continued nevertheless to work, but without any results. I had undertaken a pantomime: *Morgiane*, which is supposed to be performed next March at the Opéra. Increasingly tired, I went to see Vallery-Radot: blood-pressure: rather low. Blood test: the doctor was concerned about a rather large accumulation of urea. Now it's satisfactory. But the [cerebral] anemia continues. Medication: a bewildering host of drugs […] In 1 month all of the symptoms disappeared.[21]

Fortunately, in November 1933, he was able to conduct his *Boléro* and the Concerto in G in Paris, but in a concert that would prove to be his last public performance. On 30 January 1934, Vallery-Radot wrote to Jourdan-Morhange, asking her to convey to Edouard Ravel 'that I am very uneasy about his brother. I have had him undergo numerous examinations in order to be certain that there isn't any lesion whatsoever: there isn't; but he does indicate a state of intellectual fatigue which is very disturbing.'[22] And on 6 February 1934, Ravel finally agreed to be treated in a rest home called 'Mon repos' at Mont Pèlerin near Vevey in Switzerland, but he clearly did not improve since it took him eight days, painfully copying the characters from a dictionary, to write a letter of merely eight lines to his friend Maurice Delage, dated 22 March 1934.[23]

Following Ravel's return, Manuel Rosenthal, his favoured pupil, observed his lack of control of physical movements, his faulty eye movements which caused reading problems, his inability to write, and his speech difficulties which hindered communication,[24] in this way describing symptoms which, in the medical literature, are called dyspraxia, agraphia, and dysphasia. In order to assure the musical world that the composer was still creatively active, Rosenthal then proposed to orchestrate *Don Quichotte à Dulcinée* and did so under Ravel's supervision.[25] At a studio session to record the work in Paris in November 1934, Ravel 'made several remarks about wrong notes, tempi, and dynamics, both for the voice [baritone, Martial Singher] and the instruments [the Orchestra Colonne, conducted by Paul Paray]'.[26] Encouraged by the success of *Don Quichotte*, Rosenthal also orchestrated *Ronsard à son âme*, a song for voice and piano which Ravel had written in 1924.[27] After the

[21] Orenstein (ed.), *A Ravel Reader*, 316–17.
[22] *Ibid.*, 320.
[23] Jean Roy, 'Vingt-cinq lettres de Maurice Ravel à Maurice et Nelly Delage', *Cahiers Maurice Ravel*, 2 (1986), 13–40: 40.
[24] Marcel Marnat (ed.), *Ravel: souvenirs de Manuel Rosenthal* (Paris: Hazan, 1995), 184.
[25] Marnat (ed.), *Ravel: souvenirs*, 180–1.
[26] Orenstein, *Ravel*, 106.
[27] Marnat (ed.), *Ravel: souvenirs*, 182.

performance of this work by Martial Singher, with Piero Coppola conducting, Ravel and his sculptor friend Léon Leyritz set out, on 15 February 1935, on a trip to Spain and Morocco. The visit was at the instigation, and with the support, of Ida Rubinstein, who thought that an exotic journey would improve the composer's depressed mood. In August 1935 Ravel and Leyritz again travelled to Spain.

Across 1936–7, Ravel was finally cared for by his housekeeper Mme Revelot (some authors write her name as Reveleau, others as Révelot) at his house in Montfort-l'Amaury. According to Jourdan-Morhange, he made extensive walking tours in the nearby forest of Rambouillet and 'At this late time, despite his fatigue, he took me, with a surprisingly accurate memory, to places visited many years before.'[28] He also stayed at Levallois-Perret, just outside Paris, in the house of his brother Edouard where a studio was set up for him by Leyritz. During April–May 1936, Ravel took a cure in an institute at Lausanne where, according to the housekeeper of 'Mon port', the guesthouse where he stayed, he 'still has difficulty recalling proper nouns but given confidence, he talks about his travels or relates anecdotes about artists'.[29] In March 1937 he still managed to give advice to Jacques Février who was to play the Left Hand Concerto in Paris, while Madeleine Grey's recollection of the same year is also noteworthy:

> some months before his death [June 1937][30] he paid me a visit to hear me sing *Don Quichotte à Dulcinée*, with Francis Poulenc accompanying at the piano. When I had finished, I asked his advice. He looked absent and one could have thought that he had hardly been aware of what he had just heard. However, he made a very precise remark, rectifying a subtle liberty of metre that we, Poulenc and I, had allowed because we were happy with a breathing space of a semiquaver, not written down by Ravel.[31]

At concerts which he frequented in Paris, however, always in the company of friends, he 'seemed in another world, completely detached from things around him […] his blank expression was frightening'.[32] One day Jourdan-Morhange found him sitting silently and lonely on the balcony of his house,

[28] Hélène Jourdan-Morhange, 'Ravel à Montfort-l'Amaury', in Colette et al., *Maurice Ravel par quelques-uns de ses familiers* (Paris: Editions du tambourinaire, 1939), 163–9: 165. 'Dans les derniers temps, malgré sa fatigue, il me conduisait, avec une fidélité de mémoire surprenante, aux endroits prospectés bien des années auparavant.'

[29] Orenstein (ed.), *A Ravel Reader*, 324.

[30] Orenstein, *Ravel*, 108.

[31] Grey, 'Souvenirs d'une interprète', 178. 'Ravel était venu chez moi quelques mois avant sa mort pour que je lui chante *Don Quichotte à Dulcinée*, que Francis Poulenc m'accompagnait. Quand j'eus fini, je lui demandai son avis. Il paraissait absent et on aurait pu croire qu'il avait à peine eu conscience de ce qu'il venait d'entendre. Or, il me fit une observation très précise, rectifiant une infime liberté de mesure que, Poulenc et moi, nous étions permise, trouvant heureuse une respiration d'un quart de temps, non prévue par Ravel.'

[32] Norman Demuth, *Ravel* (London: J. M. Dent, 1947), 44.

and when she asked what he was doing he answered merely: 'I am waiting.'[33] '[H]e did not try to speak anymore, and, sitting between us,' Colette recalled, 'he yet gave the impression of somebody who, from one minute to the next, risks disintegrating';[34] he 'seize[d] the prongs of his fork' at a dinner, 'and gave me a look which seemed to hold all the world's distress', wrote Long;[35] Ravel's neighbour, the writer Jacques de Zogheb, noted that Ravel had great difficulty in opening the front door of his house.[36] Yet Ravel still showed insight, lamenting to Long: 'It is tragic what is happening to me,' and to Zogheb: 'Why has it happened to me? … Why?'[37]

However interesting all the symptoms noticed by his entourage may be, unfortunately these retrospective recollections do not chart either the exact chronology or the evolution of Ravel's disease. One year after the composer's death, Ravel's brother declared:

> four years passed after he [Ravel] had noticed the first sign of disease. We tried in vain all kinds of treatment. The most renowned physicians in the world were consulted. The poor patient was aware of the progression of his sufferings. Finally, 'we consulted Clovis Vincent. 'Medical treatment', he said to me, 'is useless. Surgically, there is a chance. It's up to you to decide.'[38]

Certificates, reports, and examinations by Ravel's physicians

The medical certificate of Dr Abel Desjardins concerning Ravel's condition after the taxi accident of October 1932 was published in 1992 by Bernard Mercier in the *Cahiers Maurice Ravel*.[39] Although, in Ravel's words, the accident was 'not very serious', it was not benign either. Desjardins wrote that he examined Ravel once he had returned to his hotel after medical attendance at the Beaujon clinic where two wounds had been sutured, one on the right eyebrow and another on the right side of the chin. He also had a superficial

[33] Jourdan-Morhange, *Ravel et nous*, 244: 'J'attends.'
[34] Colette, 'Un salon de musique en 1900', in Colette et al., *Maurice Ravel par quelques-uns de ses familiers*, 115–24: 123; 'il ne s'efforça plus guère de parler, et assis parmi nous il avait pourtant l'apparence d'un être qui, d'instant à l'autre, risque de se dissoudre'.
[35] Marguerite Long, *At the Piano with Ravel*, ed. Pierre Laumonier, trans. Olive Senior-Ellis (London: J. M. Dent, 1973), 115.
[36] Jourdan-Morhange, *Ravel et nous*, 250.
[37] Long, *At the Piano*, 116; Jourdan-Morhange, *Ravel et nous*, 251: 'Pourquoi est-ce arrivé à moi?… Pourquoi?'

[38] Edouard Ravel, interviewed in *L'Intransigeant* (2 January 1939), cited by Marcel Marnat, 'L'Image publique de Maurice Ravel 1920–1937', *Cahiers Maurice Ravel*, 3 (1987), 27–52: 50. 'Quatre années s'écoulèrent, depuis qu'il avait ressenti les premières atteintes du mal. Nous essayâmes en vain tous les traitements. Les plus illustres médecins du monde furent consultés. Le pauvre malade voyait ses souffrances augmenter. Enfin, nous nous adressâmes à Clovis Vincent. "Médicalement, me déclara celui-ci, il n'y a rien à faire. Chirurgicalement, il existe une chance. A vous de décider."'
[39] Mercier, 'La Maladie neurologique de Ravel', 13–26.

wound on the left side of his chin and a luxation (dislocation) of the nose. But Desjardins found more serious clinical signs in the chest region suggestive of a haemothorax (blood in the pleural cavity), although there were fractures neither of the ribs nor of the sternum (breastbone). He took Ravel to his own clinic where, after some days, his condition improved. Desjardins concluded that his patient could resume normal activity after a month; his report is dated 25 October 1932. Interestingly, however, most neurologists, especially Americans, were still convinced as late as 1999 that 'specifics of the taxi accident are lacking'.[40] In fact, Mercier had found Desjardins's certificate in the collection of Ravel's documentary records that Mme Taverne inherited from Ravel's brother, but publications such as the *Cahiers Maurice Ravel* are seldom in circulation outside France.

Another little-known report, mentioned only in Hans Heinz Stuckenschmidt's German biography, is Dr Michaud's description of Ravel's symptoms during his treatment at Vevey in 1934. It runs as follows: 'Insomnia, memory lapses, fatigue, concentration deficiencies, anxious condition, orthographic failure. Does not know any more how to write certain letters of the alphabet. He is stiff. Anxiety plays an important role in his discomfort. Continuously frightened. I tried to instil in him an indifference about his automatic reactions.'[41]

The observations and conclusions of Théophile Alajouanine (1890–1980), who followed Ravel for two years, were first published in English following a lecture this famous Parisian neurologist delivered for the Harveian Society in London on 17 March 1948. For decades this paper remained the only known medical document concerning Ravel. The composer had 'a Wernicke aphasia of moderate intensity, without any trace of paralysis, without hemianopia [*sic*; loss of vision affecting half the visual field], but with an ideomotor apractic [*sic*] component.' More specifically, Alajouanine observed a diffuse but moderate disturbance of Ravel's speech and writing, while his understanding of speech was generally better preserved. Ravel's writing was badly affected, largely resulting from his apraxia. Alajouanine also noticed a 'discrepancy' between the impossibility of 'musical expression' – both in writing and playing – and the yet relatively intact 'musical thinking'. Ravel could recognize melodies, even down to the precise rhythm and pitches, but in musical dictation he made many errors, possibly due to difficulty in naming items,

---

40   Robert J. Alonso and Robert M. Pascuzzi, 'Ravel's Neurological Illness', *Seminars in Neurology*, 19, suppl. 1 (1999), 53–7.

41   Hans Heinz Stuckenschmidt, *Maurice Ravel: Variationen über Person und Werk* (Frankfurt am Main: Suhrkamp Verlag, 1966), 296. 'Schlaflosigkeit, Gedächtnistrübung, Müdigkeit, Mangel an Konzentration, Angstzustand, orthographische Fehler. Weiss nicht mehr, wie man gewisse Buchstaben schreibt. Er ist starr. Die Angst spielt eine grosse Rolle in seinem Unbehagen. Beständliche Furchtgefühle. Ich versuchte, ihm zur Indifferenz betreffend die Automatismen zu bringen.'

since his ability to sing notes which were played for him remained fairly keen. His piano sight-reading was pitiful because, as well as reading difficulties, he had trouble finding the right keys, although playing scales and his own works was a little easier. Writing music was very difficult in dictation or when he tried to transcribe a composition, though it was better 'by heart'. Singing melodies from his own pieces was still possible; indeed, he claimed that he could hear melodies in his head. Faced with Ravel's loss of creativity, Alajouanine thus concluded:

> with a relatively preserved musical thinking that allows him to hear 'inside himself' a musical phrase, or even to sing a tuneful theme, to hear and to appreciate a performance, our composer cannot however express his thoughts by writing or playing them. Musical expression is in him grossly impaired. Accordingly, his artistic creation is completely destroyed […] with in addition an important apraxic component […] So one may see the importance of unaltered means of expression in artistic realization. To conceive is nothing, to express is all.[42]

Present-day knowledge about music and the brain

Alajouanine's observations on Ravel's case follow on from the clinical–anatomical discoveries concerning aphasia by Pierre Paul Broca (1824–80) and concerning agraphia by Joseph Jules Dejerine (1849–1917), from which emerged, at the end of the nineteenth century, the concept of hemispheric dominance (in right-handed people, linguistic functions are located in the left hemisphere). Later, some cases of expressive or perceptive amusia due to right temporo-parietal lesions suggested that musical functions were localized in the right hemisphere, and observations on aphasic musicians without amusia, such as Vissarion Shebalin,[43] Nino Sanzogno,[44] and Jean Langlais,[45] seemed to offer further proof. Indeed, these three famous artists were able to resume their musical activities. The problem was not so simple however, since cases of amusia due to a left-sided lesion were also described in subjects without aphasia. The occurrence of this double dissociation – amusia without aphasia and aphasia without amusia – therefore presumes a partial independence of the cerebral structures for these particular functions.

Moreover, musicians have cerebral characteristics (anatomical as well as functional) which distinguish them from non-musicians. For example, in 1961 the role of the two brain hemispheres in musical perception had

[42] Théophile Alajouanine, 'Aphasia and Artistic Realization', *Brain*, 71/3 (1948), 229–41: 239.

[43] A. R. Luria, L. S. Tsvetkova, and D. S. Futer, 'Aphasia in a Composer', *Journal of Neurological Sciences*, 2 (1965), 288–92.

[44] A. Basso and E. Capitani, 'Spared Musical Abilities in a Conductor with Global Aphasia and Ideomotor Apraxia', *Journal of Neurology, Neurosurgery, and Psychiatry*, 48 (1985), 407–12.

[45] J. L. Signoret, P. Van Eeckhout, M. Poncet, et al., 'Aphasie sans amusie chez un organiste aveugle', *Revue neurologique*, 143 (1987), 172–81.

been investigated with dichotic auditory testing of healthy subjects, showing involvement of the left hemisphere in temporal, sequential, and rhythmical discrimination; and of the right in tone pitch, melody, and harmony.[46] In 1974, however, another study with mono-aural stimulation established that the cerebral dominance for the recognition of melodies was located in the left in musicians, while right dominance was reconfirmed in non-musicians. Musical perception in musicians was thus argued to take place analytically in the left hemisphere, and in non-musicians holistically in the right.[47]

Modern neuropsychological, positron emission tomographic and functional nuclear magnetic resonance examinations which have compared normal subjects with patients afflicted by unilateral brain damage have, however, made clear that musical perception is dependent not upon the right hemisphere, but on neural networks in both hemispheres.[48] There is no centre for music in the brain because musical perception comes about as follows: the sound is propagated along the ascending auditory pathways via the brain-stem into the primary auditory cortex of the superior gyrus of the temporal lobe in both hemispheres. From there, components of the sound stimulus are transmitted to bordering association zones of the temporal lobe and to more remote cortical regions which are connected through neural networks corresponding with specific musical components. In normal individuals, the processing of melody, pitch, and timbre occurs mainly in the right hemisphere; rhythm and familiarity with tunes in the left. So the general theory of hemispheric differentiation (namely dominance) remains robust, although hemispheric interdependence also plays a role because the left hemisphere, which processes interval structure, can only perform this task when the right hemisphere is intact. Conversely, metre has no hemispheric lateralization. Subcortical (i.e. deeper) structures are equally involved in musical perception and performance: the thalamus in audiovisual aspects and the limbic system in emotional effects.

Functional imagery with positron emission scanning has even made it possible to see the brain 'at work', although this can be misleading (or cause oversimplification). In retrospect, when we add up all Ravel's clinical symptoms and signs, we may – in the light of positron emission findings about musicians playing a simple piano piece at sight with the right hand – speculate, as did Justine Sergent in 1993, about the type of brain lesions he had.[49] His verbal impairment (Wernicke aphasia and agraphia) would point to a lesion of the left superior temporal gyrus and inferior parietal lobe; his

46   D. Kimura, 'Left–Right Differences in the Perception of Melodies', *Quarterly Journal of Experimental Psychology*, 15 (1961), 156–65.

47   T. G. Bever and R. J. Chiarello, 'Cerebral Dominance in Musicians and Non-musicians', *Science*, 185 (1974), 537–9.

48   Baeck, 'The Neural Networks of Music', 451.

49   Justine Sergent, 'Music, the Brain, and Ravel', *Trends in Neurological Science*, 16 (1993), 168–72.

musical impairment (difficulty in sight-reading) would point to a lesion of the supramarginal gyrus, the posterior part of the superior parietal lobe, and the prefrontal cortex.

Even musical memory and musical imaging have been investigated with the new techniques. In one study, the test subjects had to compare the pitch of the first and last notes of a melody – which presupposes storage of the first note during a fixed time interval (short-term memory) – and it was found that in order to do so an interaction occurred between the associative hearing cortex on the right temporal gyrus and the frontal cortex.[50] In another experiment, the same team established that when a test subject hears a melody in his head without actual auditory stimulation – the phenomenon of musical imaging – another network is activated in which the frontotemporal cortex and the supplementary motor area are involved.[51] Having had the opportunity to study the case of a female piano teacher who was operated upon for a meningioma (a benign tumour) of the left lateral ventricle, Japanese neurologists claimed that they had found a rare case of pure musical agraphia – a rare case since musical agraphia mostly occurs together with aphasia – because the teacher could read and write single notes and musical signs, but her ability to write a melody was seriously impaired, the salient impairment being in notating rhythm rather than pitch.[52]

This latter case is certainly an interesting one, though only presenting one of the symptoms of Ravel (to whose case the authors did not refer). Had Ravel lived nowadays, neuroscientists would surely have competed for the privilege of examining him. But would Ravel have got better?

Conflicting witnesses about a fatal craniotomy

As Ravel's condition worsened in autumn 1937, his entourage sought the advice of a pioneering neurosurgeon, Thierry de Martel (1876–1940), who carried out numerous examinations but found that surgery would be of no help. Disappointed by this statement, Ravel's friends turned to Clovis Vincent (1878–1947), another neurosurgeon, who undertook the same radiographies[53] – a pneumo-encephalography whereby the ventricles of the brain hemispheres are filled with air in order to visualize radiologically the inner structures or a possible displacement of the brain – and, finally, decided to operate on Ravel's brain.

[50] R. Zatorre, A. Evans, and E. Meyer, 'Neural Mechanisms Underlying Melodic Perception and Memory for Pitch', *Journal of Neuroscience*, 14 (1994), 1908–19.
[51] R. J. Zatorre and A. R. Halpern, D. W. Perry, et al., 'Hearing in the Mind's Ear: A PET Investigation of Musical Imagery and Perception', *Journal of Cognitive Neuroscience*, 8 (1996), 29–46.
[52] A. Midorikawa and M. Kawamura, 'A Case of Musical Agraphia', *NeuroReport*, 13 (2000), 3053–7.
[53] Marnat (ed.), *Ravel: souvenirs*, 187.

Unfortunately, the radiological documents have been lost and, since Vincent's surgical protocol was not found for many years, dubious conclusions about the surgical procedure were drawn in the musicological, as well as the neurological, literature. Demuth wrote: 'A tumour on the brain was diagnosed [...] several treatments were tried, but to no avail [...] Eventually it was decided to operate.'[54] But Long was less affirmative in her memoirs, writing: 'Professor Clovis Vincent considered that it was better to try to do something on the chance of there being a tumour.' Moreover, she added: 'no tumour was found; all was lost'.[55] According to Roland-Manuel, Ravel's physicians had 'discarded the possibility of a tumour and arteriosclerosis and admitted that the patient [...] was suffering from a congenital illness affecting that part of the brain which is connected with the control of language. The illness, neutralized at first, finally overtook the motor mechanisms which put the conscious mind in touch with the outer world.'[56] Rosenthal was the only witness to reveal more of Vincent's reasons for operating: the neurosurgeon seemingly explained to Edouard Ravel, Delage, Roland-Manuel, and Rosenthal himself that 'Ravel was born with a slight deficiency in one of the cerebral hemispheres and the other had played its role very well until the moment when various accidents occurred.' After taking into consideration the taxi collision of 8 October 1932, the andropause (male menopause), and the abuse of tobacco and alcohol, Vincent continued: 'From now on, one of the hemispheres is, one might say, more depressed than it was before, and the other can no longer compensate.' He concluded, however, that: 'In the present state of science, there is no more than one chance in a million of reinflating the hemisphere which requires it.'[57] Apparently, therefore, Vincent did not operate on Ravel with the hypothesis of a tumour.

But one chance in a million seems no chance at all. No wonder that Long asserted in her memoirs: 'Many of us could testify that our friend would have rejected the idea of a surgical operation, preferring the worst [...] disintegration at the approach of death.' Underlining her conviction that a surgical procedure 'was not in accord[ance] with his [Ravel's] wishes', she added: 'When his beautiful [silver] hair was shaved, he begged again to be taken home, and a nurse who was helping could not restrain her tears at his despair.'[58] By contrast, Roland-Manuel related: 'I can still see Ravel, heroic

54   Demuth, *Ravel*, 43–4.
55   Long, *At the Piano*, 117.
56   Roland-Manuel, *Maurice Ravel*, trans. Cynthia Jolly (London: Dennis Dobson, 1947), 105.
57   Marnat (ed.), *Ravel: souvenirs*, 188–9. 'Ravel est né avec un des hémisphères cérébraux un peu déficient. L'autre a joué parfaitement son rôle jusqu'au moment

où sont survenus divers accidents [...] Désormais, l'un des deux hémisphères cérébraux est pour ainsi dire plus aplati qu'il ne l'a été jusque-là, or l'autre ne parvient plus à jouer son rôle compensateur. Dans l'état actuel de la science, il n'y a pas plus d'une chance sur un million d'arriver à "regonfler" l'hémisphère qui en a besoin.'
58   Long, *At the Piano*, 117.

until the bitter end, with a turban of white bandages, on the evening before the operation, laughing at the unsuspected likeness we thought he showed to Lawrence of Arabia,'[59] and according to his brother, Ravel had said on giving his consent on the evening before the intervention: 'If it is not too late…'[60] Igor Stravinsky recalled that Ravel said: 'They can do what they want with my cranium as long as the ether works,' but he was convinced that Ravel, on entering the clinic, knew that he was about to go to sleep for the last time,[61] and the memoirs of Rosenthal do not contradict him: 'Some days before the operation, his beautiful silvery hair had to be shaved. So as not to worry him too much in advance, his friends assured him that this was only necessary for another radiological examination. It was at this moment that he said: "Not at all: I know full well that they will cut off my head."'[62] In any event, reading all these different witness accounts, we must bear in mind that Long, Roland-Manuel, and Stravinsky possibly did not see Ravel on the same day, or at the same time, and that the attitude of the composer could have been ambivalent or changeable – a trait often encountered with desperate, incurable patients.

Finally, Vincent performed a craniotomy (an opening into the skull). Most of Ravel's biographers – Demuth, Jankélévitch, Long, Machabey, Petit, Roland-Manuel, Stuckenschmidt, and Tappolet[63] – are convinced that this was done on 19 December 1937. Additionally Marnat[64] and Orenstein[65] state that Ravel was admitted into the clinic on the rue Boileau on 17 December and that the intervention took place two days later. However, 19 December 1937 happened to be a Sunday, which would surely have been an unusual day to perform a non-urgent intervention, though Rosenthal seems to resolve the enigma. According to his recollections, the operation was planned for a Friday, but Vincent had to postpone it at the last minute because a child had been admitted who needed urgent surgery for a brain tumour. Ravel then left the clinic and spent the weekend with his friends the Delages at the nearby Villa de la Réunion and, therefore: 'It was on the following day, Monday,

---

[59] Roland-Manuel, *Maurice Ravel*, 107.
[60] Edouard Ravel, interviewed in *L'Intransigeant*: 'Pourvu que ce ne soit pas trop tard…'
[61] Igor Stravinsky and Robert Craft, *Conversations with Igor Stravinsky* (London: Faber and Faber, 1959), 62–3.
[62] Marnat (ed.), *Ravel: souvenirs*, 189–90. 'Quelques jours avant l'intervention, on dut raser sa belle chevelure argentée. Pour ne pas qu'il s'inquiète trop à l'avance, on l'assurait qu'il ne s'agissait que de faire une nouvelle radio. C'est à ce moment-là qu'il a dit: "Mais non: je sais bien qu'on va me couper cabèche."' Thus Ravel, who had served

during World War I, used the Moroccan infantryman expression 'couper cabèche', meaning to kill by decapitation.
[63] Demuth, *Ravel*, 44; Vladimir Jankélévitch, *Ravel* (Paris: Editions du Seuil, 1956), 186; Long, *At the Piano*, 117; Armand Machabey, *Maurice Ravel* (Paris: Richard-Masse, 1947), 30; Pierre Petit, *Ravel* (Paris: Hachette, 1970), 81; Roland-Manuel, *Maurice Ravel*, 106; Stuckenschmidt, *Maurice Ravel*, 305; Willy Tappolet, *Maurice Ravel: Leben und Werk* (Olten: Verlag Otto Walter, 1950), 166.
[64] Marnat, *Maurice Ravel*, 684.
[65] Orenstein, *Ravel*, 108.

that he underwent surgery.'[66] This Monday would be 20 December, but even though a Monday is more plausible than a Sunday, it is hard to follow the end of Rosenthal's account:

> Delage, reading a newspaper, noted that there was a Ravel Festival, directed by Albert Wolff at the Concerts Pasdeloup, [to be] broadcast on the radio [...] Germaine Martinelli appeared in the programme [...] singing *Shéhérazade* [...] The concert came to a close with the *Boléro*. And then, at the end, Ravel burst into laughter, slapping his thighs [...] hiccoughing: 'Ah! When I think what a good joke I have played on the musical world!'[67]

The problem is that it would appear from the Parisian newspapers, on the one hand, that there was no Ravel Festival on 19 December 1937 and, on the other, that while a Pasdeloup concert was broadcast on 12 December, it contained only one piece by Ravel: *La Valse*, at the end of the programme. The same Sunday, 12 December, Eugène Bigot conducted a Debussy–Ravel programme for the Concerts Lamoureux, including *Ma mère l'Oye*, *Shéhérazade*, and *La Valse* in the second half, but the soloist was Maria Branèze and the concert was not broadcast.[68] Although, as mentioned above, Long also considered 19 December as the date of the intervention, she referred nevertheless to 'twelve days of post-operative coma which preceded the end', during which 'Ida [Rubinstein] and I remained near our unfortunate friend'.[69] As Ravel died on 28 December, we must then return to considering 17 December for the intervention and this date appears to be consistent with that found on the surgical protocol.

Writing his biography of Ravel published in 1986, Marnat could only regret that Vincent's craniotomy protocol had been lost, but just the following year it was rediscovered. Vincent's protocol was sent to Robert Henson in 1988 by Professor J. Racadot,[70] and to the present author in 1996 by Dr Michèle Kujas of the Groupe Hospitalier Pitié-Salpêtrière in Paris. The protocol refers explicitly to 'Boileau 17 December 1937'. Confusingly enough, above the main typescript can be read a manuscript annotation: 'Wednesday 17 December 1937', though that date was in fact a Friday. While this small slip cannot be explained, we can at least be certain that the date of Ravel's craniotomy was Friday, 17 December 1937. By way of corroboration, Ravel's brother, Edouard, declared to the reporter

66 Marnat (ed.), *Ravel: souvenirs*, 190; 'C'est le lendemain, lundi, qu'il a été opéré.'
67 *Ibid.*, 190–1. 'Delage, consultant un journal, a découvert que, chez Pasdeloup, il y avait un Festival Ravel dirigé par Albert Wolff, retransmis à la radio [...] dans le programme, se produisait Germaine Martelli [...] elle chantait *Shéhérazade* [...] Le concert s'achevait avec le *Boléro*. Et là, à la fin, éclat de rire formidable de Ravel se tapant sur les cuisses [...] hoquetant: "Ah! Quand je pense quelle bonne blague j'ai jouée au monde musical!'
68 Erik Baeck, 'La Mort de Ravel', *Revue belge de musicologie*, 51 (1997), 187–93: 190.
69 Long, *At the Piano*, 32.
70 Robert A. Henson, 'Maurice Ravel's Illness: A Tragedy of Lost Creativity', *British Medical Journal*, 296 (1988), 1585–8: 1588.

for *L'Intransigeant* that 'The operation took place [at the] rue Boileau, 17 December.'[71]

As Vincent's protocol explains: having performed a 'right frontal bone flap; with frontotemporal basis' (Volet frontal droit; à base fronto-temporale), he found a 'slack brain, without actual softening in the area displayed. Gyri separated by oedema, but not atrophied' (Cerveau affaissé, sans aspect de ramollissement de la zone vue. Circonvolutions séparées par l'oedème, non atrophiées). He then tried to 'inflate' the right lateral ventricle with 20 cc. water but did not succeed despite 'multiple attempts'.[72] The protocol does not mention a tumour, and a biopsy was not taken. In addition, it contradicts Marnat's assertions of 'a depressed left hemisphere upon which a reinflation was attempted',[73] to say nothing of Orenstein who writes that Vincent 'succeeded in equalizing the levels of the cerebral hemispheres, one of which had become depressed'.[74]

The confusion in the musicological literature continues when Ravel's condition after the intervention is described. According to Roland-Manuel, 'The operation left him in a state of semi-unconsciousness which lasted a whole week. On Monday the 27th his life drew quietly to its end and he died without suffering in the small hours of the 28th December.'[75] Long's recollections are concordant: 'Ravel remained in a coma until his death.'[76] Hence, the composer did not reawaken after the intervention, although it was done without general anaesthesia as was customary in those days. But this view is in contradiction with Rosenthal's recollections: 'For 24 hours, we thought that the intervention had succeeded. He had spoken some words, he had been able to eat. He had also asked to see "a lady". We wondered who it could be. It was neither Mme Rubinstein, nor [Françoise] Meyer nor Long, but Mme Révelot, his housekeeper.'[77] And the declarations of Ravel's brother, Edouard, continue in the same direction: 'He entered into a kind of somnolence from which he did not come out until the following day, in order to speak some incoherent words. On the day after, somebody asked him, "Would you like to see your brother?" He answered

---

[71] Edouard Ravel, interviewed in *L'Intransigeant*: 'L'opération eut lieu rue Boileau, le 17 décembre.'

[72] Erik Baeck, 'Was Maurice Ravel's Illness a Corticobasal Degeneration?', *Clinical Neurology and Neurosurgery*, 98/1 (1996), 57–61. See too a facsimile of Vincent's protocol in Erik Baeck, 'The Terminal Illness and Last Compositions of Maurice Ravel', in Julien Bogousslavsky and François Boller (eds.), *Neurological Disorders in Famous Artists*, Frontiers of Neurology and Neuroscience, vol. XIX (Basel: Karger, 2005), 132–40: 135.

[73] Marnat, *Maurice Ravel*, 684; 'un hémisphère gauche affaissé sur lequel on tenta un regonflement'.

[74] Orenstein, *Ravel*, 108n.

[75] Roland-Manuel, *Maurice Ravel*, 107.

[76] Long, *At the Piano*, 117.

[77] Marnat (ed.), *Ravel: souvenirs*, 17. 'Pendant vingt-quatre heures, nous avions cru que l'opération avait réussi. Il avait dit quelques mots, avait pu s'alimenter. Alors, il a demandé à voir "une dame". Nous avons cherché qui ça pouvait être. Ce n'était pas Mme Rubinstein, ni Meyer, ni Long mais bien Mme Révelot, sa gouvernante.'

immediately: "Ah! I think so!" These were the last words that he spoke before falling asleep again.'[78] Interestingly, however, Rosenthal and Edouard Ravel did diverge on an important issue: while the former declared that 'he had been able to eat', the latter confided, 'We had hope: one after another, his functions seemed to resume. Except however, his deglutition [the action of swallowing]. He could no longer swallow, nor drink nor eat: he suffocated.'[79] These symptoms are noteworthy because they suggest that the surgical procedure provoked intracranial hypertension, followed by compression of the brainstem, which caused death.[80]

Various hypotheses on the nature of Ravel's illness

Ravel's terminal illness seems a diagnostic quagmire when we look over the list of hypotheses in the medical literature. Indeed, there will never be absolute certainty since – after the craniotomy from which Ravel died ten days later, on 28 December 1937 – no autopsy was undertaken. No doubt, Ravel's physicians had finally discerned that the symptoms, signs, and facts of his medical history pointed to a kind of pre-senile dementia, but the continuing fascination of neurologists with Ravel's decline has (in addition to his celebrity and artistic status) something to do with greater differentiation and classification of mental disorders such as Alzheimer's and Pick's disease than was the case in Alajouanine's days.

In 1966, Ravel's biographer Stuckenschmidt mentioned a statement by Alajouanine that Ravel had Pick's disease.[81] Neither the date nor the source of this statement was given in the original German edition of Stuckenschmidt's book, but the French translation specifies 3 July 1938.[82] Ten years later however, in 1948, Alajouanine declared in his Harveian lecture: 'The cause, though indefinite, belongs to the group of cerebral atrophies, there being a bilateral ventricular enlargement; but it is quite different from Pick's disease.'[83] It seems that Alajouanine changed his mind again in later years because in a personal communication to a Californian colleague he abandoned the theory of ventricular dilatation in favour of a cortical atrophy

---

[78] Edouard Ravel, interviewed in *L'Intransigeant*: 'Il tomba dans une espèce de somnolence d'où il ne devait sortir que le lendemain, pour prononcer quelques paroles incohérentes. Le surlendemain, quelqu'un lui demanda: "Voulez-vous voir votre frère?" Il répondit aussitôt: "Ah! je pense bien!" Ce furent là les derniers mots qu'il prononça avant de retomber dans le sommeil.'

[79] See again Marnat (ed.), *Ravel: souvenirs*, 17; Edouard Ravel in *L'Intransigeant*: 'Nous

eûmes un espoir: une à une, les fonctions semblaient se rétablir en lui. Sauf toutefois, la déglutition. Il ne pouvait plus avaler, ni boire, ni manger: il étouffait.'

[80] Baeck, 'La Mort de Ravel', 192.

[81] Stuckenschmidt, *Maurice Ravel*, 307.

[82] Hans Heinz Stuckenschmidt, *Ravel: variations sur l'homme et l'œuvre* (Paris: Editions J.-C. Lattès, 1981), 229.

[83] Alajouanine, 'Aphasia and Artistic Realization', 232.

similar to Pick's disease.[84] Moreover, Pick's disease is not always easy to distinguish from Alzheimer's when the patient is still alive, though it is suspected in dementia patients with local brain atrophy (proved in Ravel's days by pneumo-encephalography, and nowadays via brain scans) and impaired executive functions, but relatively preserved memory and visuo-spatial abilities. Currently neurologists claim that even merely on the basis of clinical manifestations, Pick's patients might be diagnosed: in addition to three of five clinical features (pre-senile onset, initial personality change, hyperorality, disinhibition, and roaming behaviour: all symptoms which Ravel presented), patients have tendencies toward decreased verbal output leading to mutism and reiterative speech disturbances (which Ravel also had).

Nevertheless, as recently as 1984, an American neurologist held the opinion that Ravel had Alzheimer's disease, citing 'amusia' among his symptoms.[85] Receiving immediate criticism from a colleague that he had used this term wrongly,[86] he replied boldly: 'Later on, he [Ravel] became unable to produce or comprehend music, even his own, hence my use of the term amusia.'[87] This American scholar was clearly not aware of Grey's recollection published in 1938, Alajouanine's paper published in 1948, or Singher's letter to Orenstein published in 1968. Moreover, Alzheimer's disease is hardly consistent with Ravel's relatively preserved memory, visuo-spatial skills, and insight, although a definite differential diagnosis between Pick's disease and Alzheimer's is only possible through a biopsy or autopsy.

The role of the taxi accident has also been the target of several theories, especially from authors who did not have access to all the medical documents. Traumatic sequelae have thus been proposed, among them whiplash[88] and chronic subdural haematoma,[89] but these hypotheses are also unlikely given Ravel's symptoms, Desjardins's certificate, Alajouanine's examination, and Vincent's protocol. Ravel did not complain of a stiff neck, dizziness or headache, nor did he lose consciousness as would be the case with whiplash; neither gait disturbances nor incontinence were noticed as would occur in normal pressure hydrocephalus, and his craniotomy did not show any signs of intracranial hypertension as in a chronic subdural haematoma (extravasation of blood between the skull and the brain). However, even Vincent took the role of the taxi accident into account as a possible factor in pointing up an underlying disease.

---

[84] R. C. Cytowic, 'Aphasia in Maurice Ravel', *Bulletin of the Los Angeles Neurological Society*, 41 (1976), 109–14.

[85] Donald J. Dalessio, 'Maurice Ravel and Alzheimer's Disease', *Journal of the American Medical Association*, 252 (1984), 3412–13.

[86] S. F. Wainapel, 'To the Editor', *Journal of the American Medical Association*, 253 (1985), 2962.

[87] Donald J. Dalessio, 'In Reply', *Journal of the American Medical Association*, 253 (1985), 2962.

[88] A. Otte, K. Audenaert, and K. Otte, 'Did Maurice Ravel Have a Whiplash Syndrome?' *Medical Science Monitor*, 9/5 (May 2003), LE [Letters to Editor] 9.

[89] F. Mahieux and A. Laurent, 'Les Dernières Années de Maurice Ravel: hypothèse diagnostique', *Encyclopédie Médico-Chirurgicale*, 2–17999 (Paris: Elsevier, 1988), 23–4.

It has already been mentioned that the best-known degenerative, senile brain diseases in Ravel's days were Alzheimer's and Pick's, but that many more conditions have been discovered in the intervening decades. Among the so-called non-Alzheimer disorders, conditions such as progressive aphasia, corticobasal degeneration, and frontotemporal dementia are now defined (classical Pick's disease being a specific form of frontotemporal dementia). Accordingly, Ravel's case has been reconsidered in the neurological literature.

Progressive aphasia was proposed as a diagnostic hypothesis in 1988,[90] although Alajouanine noted merely an 'aphasia of moderate intensity' and, on the contrary, 'an important apraxic component', the latter symptom not being congruent with the hypothesis. Equally, considering Ravel's dysexecutive syndrome with apraxia and aphasia, corticobasal degeneration was suggested in 1996,[91] although the typical asymmetrical Parkinsonian stiffness and tremor of this disease was lacking in Ravel's case, since Dr Michaud, who cared for Ravel in 'Mon repos', observed merely 'stiffness'.

Following the identification of hereditary frontotemporal dementia linked to chromosome 17, the question arose in 1999 of whether Ravel's terminal illness might have been hereditary.[92] In fact, Ravel worried that he would end up like his father whose condition he had described in November 1907: 'My father is weakening continually. His mental capacity is at its very lowest: he mixes up everything, and no longer knows where he is at times.'[93] But the mental deterioration of Ravel's father who died in 1908 at the age of 76 probably had a cerebro-vascular origin: Ravel had written on 28 July 1906 that a few weeks earlier 'he was stricken by a cerebral hemorrhage [...] It occurred while he was asleep.'[94]

Overall, the retrospective possible aetiology of Ravel's disease seemed to concentrate around such non-Alzheimer diseases as frontal lobe dementia, progressive aphasia, and corticobasal degeneration. And it appeared that they had commonalities: an overlap between clinical symptoms, macroscopic features of focal atrophy and underlying neuropathological changes, forming a spectrum of diseases which was termed 'Pick complex'. Although the term itself has had its opponents since its introduction in 1994, it was logical to conclude in 2004 that Ravel's disease might belong to this so-called 'Pick complex'.[95]

But progress in neuroscience never stops. Lately, developments in molecular neuropathology have led to protein-based classification systems for neurodegenerative disorders. One of these proteins is named 'tau-protein', and

90 Henson, 'Maurice Ravel's Illness'.
91 Baeck, 'Was Maurice Ravel's Neurological Illness a Corticobasal Degeneration?'
92 Alonso and Pascuzzi, 'Ravel's Neurological Illness'.
93 Orenstein, *Ravel*, 54.
94 Orenstein (ed.), *A Ravel Reader*, 84.
95 Baeck, 'The Terminal Illness and Last Compositions of Maurice Ravel', 136.

diseases such as corticobasal degeneration and frontotemporal dementia are called tauopathies because they have, as a common pathological feature (that is, a feature evident from microscopic and biochemical examination of brain tissue), the presence of intracellular accumulation of abnormal filaments of tau-protein. Ravel's case might have been one of these non-Alzheimer tauopathies.

Controversial opinions on Ravel's last compositions

There are some reports of patients who retained specific cognitive abilities despite becoming demented,[96] and of a trombonist with Alzheimer's disease who, although unable to insert the two sliding tubes of his instrument into one another, was still capable of playing notes and even short tunes when the assembled trombone was put to his lips.[97] Cases of frontotemporal dementia in which a change of musical taste occurred have also been described. One patient, a classical music lover, eventually listened to nothing other than pop music which he had formerly referred to as 'just noise'; another, who had shown little interest in any music apart from dance music before her illness, became a pop music enthusiast. Stopping short of affirming that pop music lovers have a frontal lobe dysfunction, these authors suggest nevertheless that some networks connected with musical perception and appreciation are damaged by lesions to the frontal and temporal cerebral cortex.[98]

Moreover, emergence of artistic talent has been noticed in patients who became visual artists in the early stages of frontotemporal dementia,[99] while conversely the freeing influence of frontotemporal dementia on an accomplished female painter has also been demonstrated.[100] As for the case of the famous painter Willem de Kooning (1904–97), who created new 'free, moving, abstract forms' in the 1980s when he showed symptoms of what was possibly Alzheimer's disease, there has been much debate over the relevance and the significance of his later works.[101] No wonder that some psychiatrists or

[96] W. W. Beatty, P. Winn, and R. L. Adams, 'Preserved Cognitive Skills in Dementia of the Alzheimer Type', *Archives of Neurology*, 51 (1994), 1040–6.

[97] W. W. Beatty, R. A. Brumback, and J. P. G. Vonsattel, 'Autopsy-proven Alzheimer Disease in a Patient with Dementia who Retained Musical Skill in Life', *Archives of Neurology*, 54 (1997), 1448.

[98] C. Geroldi, T. Metitieri, G. Binetti, et al., 'Pop Music and Frontotemporal Dementia', *Neurology*, 55 (2000), 1935–6.

[99] B. L. Miller, J. Cummings, F. Mishkin, et al., 'Emergence of Artistic Talent in Frontotemporal Dementia', *Neurology*, 51 (1998), 978–82.

[100] J. Chan Mell, S. M. Howard, and B. L. Miller, 'The Influence of Frontotemporal Dementia on an Accomplished Artist', *Neurology*, 60 (2003), 1707–10.

[101] C. H. Espinel, 'De Kooning's Late Colours and Forms: Dementia, Creativity, and the Healing Power of Art', *Lancet*, 347 (1996), 1096–8: 1097.

neurologists claim that Ravel's last compositions were influenced by the progression of his illness.

As early as 1975, the stereotype of the *Boléro* was put in the setting of Pick's disease;[102] in 1997, the 'throbbing rhythm of obsessive almost hallucinatory insistence' and the relentless repetitions of 'a single melody' were interpreted as a case of musical perseveration by another author, perseveration being in her view a striking feature of patients with frontotemporal atrophy.[103] What the authors of such theories seem to forget is, firstly, that mental and motor perseverations occur in the late phase of these diseases, whereas Ravel lived for another nine years after the completion of his *Boléro* and might have lived longer had he not undergone a craniotomy; secondly, that these patients are often not aware of their perseverations, whereas Ravel clearly described *Boléro* as: 'a monotone repetition imposed until discomfort, giving special attention to modifying the instrumentation at each recurrence'.[104] Besides, in an article of summer 1933 entitled 'Finding Tunes in Factories', Ravel wrote that he had found the inspiration for his *Boléro* in a factory.[105] The so-called perseveration is also intentionally and magisterially broken down at the end of the work following an unexpected modulation from C major to E major. Moreover, in Ravel's own words, *Boléro* is 'an experiment in a very special and limited direction [...] consisting wholly of "orchestral tissue without music" – of one long, very gradual crescendo'.[106] This experiment having been successfully realized, the main characteristics of the *Boléro* do not reappear in his subsequent works.

The provocative question of whether the Concerto for the Left Hand might have originated 'from the right brain' was first put forward in 1985,[107] and was taken up again in 2002. Arguing that, in the Left Hand Concerto, Ravel used a contrasting style and structure from that of the Concerto in G and that 'the right hemisphere is activated, above all, by the processing of timbres' whereas rhythm is associated mainly with the left, Luigi Amaducci and others claimed that Ravel had adopted differentiated orchestral timbres to avoid 'the difficulty of elaborating a complex structured theme' because a 'left hemisphere lesion may have modified [... his] music'.[108] Yet the slowly

[102] D. Kerner, 'Ravels Tod', *Münchener Medizinische Wochenschrift*, 117 (1975), 591–6.
[103] Eva M. Cybulska, '*Boléro* Unravelled: A Case of Musical Perseveration', *Psychiatric Bulletin*, 21 (1997), 576–7: 576.
[104] Emile Vuillermoz, 'L'Œuvre de Maurice Ravel', in Colette et al., *Maurice Ravel par quelques-uns de ses familiers*, 1–95: 89; 'une répétition monotone imposée jusqu'au malaise et le souci de modifier l'instrumentation à chaque reprise'.
[105] Maurice Ravel, 'Finding Tunes in Factories', *New Britain* (9 August 1933), 367.

[106] Michel-Dimitri Calvocoressi, 'M Ravel Discusses His Own Work', *Daily Telegraph* (11 July 1931). (In fact there are no actual crescendo markings; rather, the dynamics are terraced. [Ed.])
[107] L. A. Amaducci and A. Marini, 'The Ravel D Major Piano Concerto: For the Left Hand or From the Right Brain?', *Neurology*, 35, suppl. 1 (1985), 262–3.
[108] Luigi Amaducci, Enrico Grassi, and François Boller, 'Maurice Ravel and Right-Hemisphere Musical Creativity: Influence of Disease on His Last Musical Works?',

developing introduction of the Left Hand Concerto encompasses a grandiose climax of no less than 32 bars (up to Fig. 4); the melodic second subject of the work (Figs. 8–10) exhales an expansive lyricism; and the final cadence for the piano (Fig. 10), one of the most elaborate in Ravel's *œuvre*, combines them in a extraordinarily intricate manner with superb mastery. There is strictly speaking neither more timbre nor less rhythm (note, for example, the use of march and jazz traits) in the Left Hand Concerto than in the Concerto in G. Ravel's autograph manuscript of the Left Hand Concerto, as calligraphic as ever, showing no sign of dysgraphia – even on the last page dated 1930 – is ample proof that the composer was still at the height of his powers.[109]

Moreover, Ravel had always been fond of producing contrasting works. *Le Tombeau de Couperin* (1914–17, orchestrated 1919), for instance, was followed by *La Valse* (1919–20): the paired works embody complementary aspects of Ravel's artistic persona and may be seen as a prefiguration of the combined piano concertos. 'Planning the two piano concertos simultaneously was an interesting experience,' the composer declared in an interview with M.-D. Calvocoressi.[110] Yet Amaducci and his co-authors argued that the Concerto in G was 'conceived much earlier', deferring to Calvocoressi who later confusingly claimed the work as 'the belated materialization of a plan that ever since his youth he had kept in the back of his mind'.[111] But, at most, all that Ravel had used of the sketches from *Zaspiak-Bat* was possibly a brief theme, resembling a Basque folk melody, in the opening movement of the concerto.[112] Music scholars are in general agreement that the materialization of plans for the Concerto in G began shortly before Wittgenstein's commissioning of a Left Hand Concerto, and that the former was completed one year after the latter.

No doubt, the Left Hand Concerto has an idiosyncratic style, but this style was not conditioned by disease, rather by Wittgenstein's commission since Ravel found it absolutely 'essential', as he himself explained, 'to give the impression of a texture no thinner than that of a part written for both hands. For the same reason, I resorted to a style that is much nearer to that of the more solemn kind of traditional concerto.'[113]

Lastly, the two concertos were not Ravel's final compositions. Consequently, if the Left Hand Concerto showed features of a latent left-hemisphere impairment, then these supposed traits should be even more prominent in *Don*

European Journal of Neurology, 9/1 (2002), 75–82: 80.
[109] Manuscript in Robert Owen Lehman Collection, The Morgan Library, New York.
[110] Calvocoressi, 'M Ravel Discusses His Own Work'.
[111] Amaducci et al., 'Maurice Ravel and Right-Hemisphere Musical Creativity',

79; Michel-Dimitri Calvocoressi, 'Ravel, (Joseph) Maurice', in Eric Blom (ed.), *Grove's Dictionary of Music and Musicians*, fifth edition, 9 vols. (London: Macmillan, 1954), vol. VII, 55–63: 58.
[112] Orenstein, *Ravel*, 204.
[113] Calvocoressi, 'M Ravel Discusses His Own Work'.

Quichotte à Dulcinée, written during 1932–3. However, these three songs do not display melodic fragmentation, or any harmonic or rhythmic inconsistency. Yet, the supporters of the hypothesis that disease influenced Ravel's last works refer to the French musicologist René Chalupt who thought that the orchestration of *Don Quichotte* had been written 'by a friendly hand'.[114] The facts of the matter are that Ravel composed and completed these songs for voice and piano – on 6 April 1933 he wrote to David Diamond that he had just finished *Don Quichotte*[115] – and that Rosenthal's orchestration, which was made in 1934 under the composer's supervision, does not change anything of their musical content, structure, harmony, rhythm or melody. The realization, shortly afterwards, of the orchestration of *Ronsard à son âme*, a song for voice and piano which Ravel had composed in 1924, was to prove more demanding for Rosenthal, as he recalled in his memoirs, because the piano accompaniment, being confined in some bars to the left hand alone, was more rudimentary than that in *Don Quichotte*.[116]

Ravel still harboured plans for another ballet, *Morgiane*, of which only a few sketches were realized, as well as for a commemorative opera on Joan of Arc, though he admitted despairingly to Valentine Hugo in November 1933: 'I'll never do my *Jeanne d'Arc*, that opera is there, in my head, I hear it, but I'll never ever write it, it's finished, I can't write my music any more.'[117] And in July 1937, after attending a performance of *Daphnis*, he said to Jourdan-Morhange, weeping: 'I still have so much music in my head [...] I've said nothing, I still have everything to say.'[118] His brain disease had destroyed his creativity.

The specificity of Ravel's case within its artistic context

Ravel was not the only artist who lost his creativity due to a brain disorder. Friedrich Nietzsche (1844–1900) and Guy de Maupassant (1850–93) serve as tragic examples of writers who suffered the devastating effects of syphilitic brain infection, the so-called 'dementia paralytica' which finally caused their breakdown; the same fate befell musicians such as Robert Schumann (1810–56) and Hugo Wolf (1860–1903). The recent discovery and publication of Dr Franz Richarz's long-hidden disease history and autopsy report

[114]   René Chalupt and Marcelle Gerar, *Maurice Ravel au miroir de ses lettres* (Paris: R. Laffont, 1956), 249: 'c'est une main amie qui s'est chargée de cette tâche'.
[115]   Orenstein (ed.), *A Ravel Reader*, 316.
[116]   Marnat (ed.), *Ravel: souvenirs*, 180–1.
[117]   Valentine Hugo, 'Trois souvenirs sur Ravel', *La Revue musicale*, 210 (1952),

137–46: 145; 'je ne ferai jamais ma *Jeanne d'Arc*, cet opéra est là dans ma tête, je l'entends mais je ne l'écrirai plus jamais, c'est fini, je ne peux plus écrire ma musique'.
[118]   Jourdan-Morhange, 'Mon ami Ravel', 195; 'J'ai encore tant de musique dans la tête [...] Je n'ai rien dit, j'ai tout à dire encore.'

confirm definitively the syphilitic origin of Schumann's disease, while the cause of Wolf's has never been in doubt.[119] Interestingly, the handwriting of both composers remained unchanged for a long time, whereas their creative activity was destroyed early on in the course of their disease. Having hallucinations and delusions, and losing awareness of reality, both had to be cared for, and each died in an asylum.

Ravel, on the contrary, was perfectly and painfully aware of his decline: 'Why has it happened to me? … Why?' he sobbed.[120] It makes his case no less tragic than Schumann's and Wolf's (arguably much more so) and, doubtless, more so than that say of Aaron Copland (1900–90). Confronted around 1975 by Alzheimer's disease (although his physician could not make a definitive diagnosis), Copland found himself without fresh ideas for composition, saying 'it was exactly as if someone had simply turned off a faucet'. Just like Ravel, Copland wanted to write new works which never materialized, but he viewed this phenomenon with more composure. 'I must have expressed myself sufficiently,' he declared and, having neither apraxia nor aphasia, was at least able to substitute a conducting career for a time.[121] Unfortunately for the composer, pianist, and conductor Ravel, who said in tears 'I still have so much music in my head', life had lost its sense of purpose at the age of fifty-eight and death took away his human wrapping at sixty-two.

Across the intervening decades, numerous uncertainties, errors, and assumptions slipped into the musicological and neurological literature concerning Ravel's last compositions, his loss of creativity during the last four years of his life, his fatal illness, and his death. But scrutiny of contemporary witness accounts and medical documents, combined with knowledge of the neural networks of music and classification of pre-senile dementias, has served to enable a revision and reassessment of this situation. As a subsidiary element, comparison with other composers such as Schumann, Wolf, and Copland has helped to define Ravel's case. While most probably belonging to one of the so-called non-Alzheimer tauopathies, all retrospective diagnoses regarding 'le cas Ravel' remain, however, and will continue to remain, speculative.

---

[119] Bernhard R. Appel, *Robert Schumann in Endenich (1854–1856): Krankenakten, Briefzeugnisse und Zeitgenössische Berichte* [Schumann Forschungen, vol. XI] (Mainz: Schott, 2006).

[120] Jourdan-Morhange, *Ravel et nous*, 251.

[121] Howard Pollack, *Aaron Copland: The Life and Work of an Uncommon Man* (London: Faber and Faber, 2000), 516–17.

Select bibliography

Abbate, Carolyn, 'Outside Ravel's Tomb', *Journal of the American Musicological Society*, 52/3 (1999), 465–530.

Aguettant, Louis, *La Musique de piano: des origines à Ravel* (Paris: Albin Michel, 1954).

Alonso, Robert J., and Robert M. Pascuzzi, 'Ravel's Neurological Illness', *Seminars in Neurology*, 19, suppl. 1 (1999), 53–7.

Amaducci, Luigi, Enrico Grassi, and François Boller, 'Maurice Ravel and Right-Hemisphere Musical Creativity: Influence of Disease on His Last Musical Works?', *European Journal of Neurology*, 9 (2002), 75–82.

Aubert, Louis, 'Souvenir', *La Revue musicale*, 19 (December 1938 [special issue]), 206–7.

Baeck, Erik, 'Was Maurice Ravel's Illness a Corticobasal Degeneration?', *Clinical Neurology and Neurosurgery*, 98/1 (1996), 57–61.

'La Mort de Ravel', *Revue belge de musicologie*, 51 (1997), 187–93.

'The Terminal Illness and Last Compositions of Maurice Ravel', in Julien Bogousslavsky and François Boller (eds.), *Neurological Disorders in Famous Artists*, Frontiers of Neurology and Neuroscience, vol. XIX (Basle: Karger, 2005), 132–40.

Balliman, Raymond, '*L'Enfant et les sortilèges*' [review], *Lyrica* (February 1926), 693.

Baur, Steven, 'Ravel's "Russian" Period: Octatonicism in His Early Works, 1893–1908', *Journal of the American Musicological Society*, 52/3 (1999), 531–92.

Bhogal, Gurminder, 'Debussy's Arabesque and Ravel's *Daphnis et Chloé* (1912)', *Twentieth-Century Music*, 3/2 (2006), 171–99.

Bouchor, Jean, 'Chronique musicale: Maurice Ravel ou le Diable dans la Pagode', *La Rose rouge* (26 June 1919).

Brown, Julie A., 'Listening to Ravel, Watching *Un coeur en hiver*: Cinematic Subjectivity and the Music-Film', *Twentieth-Century Music*, 1/2 (2004), 253–75.

Bruhn, Siglind, *Images and Ideas in Modern French Piano Music: The Extra-Musical Subtext in Piano Works by Ravel, Debussy, and Messiaen* (Stuyvesant, NY: Pendragon Press, 1997).

Bruyr, José, 'Un entretien avec Maurice Ravel', *Le Guide du concert*, 18 (16 October 1931), 39–41.

'En Marge… d'un premier chapitre', *La Revue musicale*, 19 (December 1938 [special issue]), 279–80.

Calvocoressi, Michel-Dimitri, 'M Ravel Discusses His Own Work', *Daily Telegraph* (11 July 1931).

'Ravel, (Joseph) Maurice', in Eric Blom (ed.), *Grove's Dictionary of Music and Musicians*, fifth edition, 9 vols. (London: Macmillan, 1954), vol. VII, 55–63.

Carol-Bérard, '*L'Enfant et les sortilèges*' [review], *L'Epoque* (19 May 1939).

Chalupt, René, and Marcelle Gerar, *Maurice Ravel au miroir de ses lettres* (Paris: R. Laffont, 1956).

Colette, 'Un salon en 1900', in *Journal à rebours, Œuvres*, Claude Pichois (ed.), 4 vols. (Paris: Gallimard [Bibliothèque de la Pléiade], 1984–2001), vol. IV, 164–8.

  et al., *Maurice Ravel par quelques-uns de ses familiers* (Paris: Editions du tambourinaire, 1939).

Corneau, André, '*L'Enfant et les sortilèges*' [review], *Journal de Monaco* (24 March 1925), 4.

Cybulska, Eva M., '*Boléro* Unravelled: A Case of Musical Perseveration', *Psychiatric Bulletin*, 21 (1997), 576–7.

Dalessio, Donald J., 'Maurice Ravel and Alzheimer's Disease', *Journal of the American Medical Association*, 252 (1984), 3412–13.

Demuth, Norman, *Ravel* (London: J. M. Dent, 1947).

DeVoto, Mark, 'Harmony in the Chamber Music', in Deborah Mawer (ed.), *The Cambridge Companion to Ravel* (Cambridge University Press, 2000), 97–117.

Downes, Olin, 'Maurice Ravel, Man and Musician', *New York Times* (7 August 1927), X6.

  'Ravel in American Debut', *New York Times* (16 January 1928).

  'Mr Ravel Returns', *New York Times* (26 February 1928), section 8, 8.

Dunfee, Norman Vance, 'Maurice Ravel in America – 1928' (DMA dissertation, University of Missouri – Kansas City, 1980).

Frank, Nino, 'Maurice Ravel entre deux trains', *Candide* (5 May 1932).

Gautier, Eva, 'Reminiscences of Maurice Ravel', *New York Times* (16 January 1938).

Gonnard, Henri, 'Maurice Ravel, *Le Tombeau de Couperin*: approche analytique de la fugue', *Musurgia: analyse et pratique musicales*, 8/2 (2001), 49–58.

Goss, Madeleine, *Bolero: A Life of Maurice Ravel* (New York: Tudor Publishing Company, 1940).

Grey, Madeleine, 'Souvenirs d'une interprète', *La Revue musicale*, 19 (December 1938 [special issue]), 175–8.

Harwood, Gregory, 'Musical and Literary Satire in Ravel's *L'Enfant et les sortilèges*', *Opera Journal*, 29/1 (1996), 2–16.

Henson, Robert A., 'Maurice Ravel's Illness: A Tragedy of Lost Creativity', *British Medical Journal*, 296 (1988), 1585–8.

Hill, Edward Burlingame, 'Maurice Ravel', *Musical Quarterly*, 13/1 (1927), 130–46.

Hoerée, Arthur, 'Les Mélodies et l'œuvre lyrique', *La Revue musicale*, 6 (April 1925 [special issue]), 46–64.

Howat, Roy, 'Ravel and the Piano', in Deborah Mawer (ed.), *The Cambridge Companion to Ravel* (Cambridge University Press, 2000), 71–96.

  The Art of French Piano Music: Debussy, Ravel, Fauré, Chabrier (New Haven and London: Yale University Press, 2009).

Huebner, Steven, '*Laughter*: In Ravel's Time', *Cambridge Opera Journal*, 18 (2006), 225–46.

  'Maurice Ravel: Private Life, Public Works', in Jolanta T. Pekacz (ed.), *Musical Biography: Towards New Paradigms* (Aldershot: Ashgate, 2006), 69–87.

  'Ravel's Child: Magic and Moral Development', in Susan Boynton and Roe-Min Kok (eds.), *Musical Childhoods and the Cultures of Youth* (Middletown, CT: Wesleyan University Press, 2006), 69–88.

Hugo, Valentine, 'Trois souvenirs sur Ravel', *La Revue musicale*, 210 (1952), 137–46.

Ivry, Benjamin, *Maurice Ravel: A Life* (New York: Welcome Rain, 2000, reprinted 2003).

Jankélévitch, Vladimir, *Ravel* (Paris: Editions du Seuil, 1956); *Ravel*, trans. Margaret Crosland (Westport, CT: Greenwood Press, 1976); *Ravel*, ed. Jean-Michel Nectoux, third edition (Paris: Editions du Seuil, 1995).

Jourdan-Morhange, Hélène, 'Mon ami Ravel', *La Revue musicale*, 19 (December 1938 [special issue]), 192–7.

   Ravel et nous: l'homme, l'ami, le musicien (Geneva: Editions du milieu du monde, 1945).

Kaminsky, Peter, 'Of Princesses, Children, Dreams and Isomorphisms: Text–Music Transformation in Ravel's Vocal Works', *Music Analysis*, 19/1 (2000), 29–68.

   'Ravel's Late Music and the Problem of "Polytonality"', *Music Theory Spectrum*, 26/2 (2004), 237–64.

Kelly, Barbara L., 'Ravel, (Joseph) Maurice', in Deane L. Root (ed.), *Grove Music Online*: www.oxfordmusiconline.com/public/

Kerner, D., 'Ravels Tod', *Münchener Medizinische Wochenschrift*, 117 (1975), 591–6.

Kilpatrick, Emily, 'Into the Woods: Re-telling the Wartime Fairytales of Ravel', *Musical Times*, 149 (2008), 57–66.

   '"Jangling in Symmetrical Sounds": Maurice Ravel as Storyteller and Poet', *Journal of Music Research Online*, 1 (2009), 1–19: http://journal.mca.org.au.

   'The Carbonne Copy: Tracing the Première of *L'Heure espagnole*', *Revue de musicologie*, 95/1 (2009), 97–136.

Klingsor, Tristan, 'Maurice Ravel et le vers libre', *La Revue musicale*, 19 (December 1938 [special issue]), 121–3.

Kramer, Lawrence, 'Consuming the Exotic: Ravel's *Daphnis et Chloé*', in his *Classical Music and Postmodern Knowledge* (Berkeley: University of California Press, 1995), 201–25.

Langham Smith, Richard, 'Ravel's Operatic Spectacles: *L'Heure* and *L'Enfant*', in Deborah Mawer (ed.), *The Cambridge Companion to Ravel* (Cambridge University Press, 2000), 188–210.

   and Caroline Potter (eds.), *French Music since Berlioz* (Aldershot: Ashgate, 2006).

Larner, Gerald, *Maurice Ravel* (London: Phaidon Press, 1996).

Lassus, Marie-Pierre, 'Ravel l'enchanteur: structure poétique et structure musicale dans *L'Enfant et les sortilèges*', *Analyse musicale*, 26 (1992), 40–7.

Leong, Daphne, and David Korevaar, 'The Performer's Voice: Performance and Analysis in Ravel's *Concerto pour la main gauche*', *Music Theory Online*, 11/3 (2005): http://mto.societymusictheory.org/issues/.

Long, Marguerite, *Au piano avec Maurice Ravel* (Paris: Julliard, 1971); *At the Piano with Ravel*, ed. Pierre Laumonier, trans. Olive Senior-Ellis (London: J. M. Dent, 1973).

Machabey, Armand, *Maurice Ravel* (Paris: Richard-Masse, 1947).

Marnat, Marcel, *Maurice Ravel* (Paris: Fayard, 1986; second edition, 1995).

   'L'Image publique de Maurice Ravel 1920–1937', *Cahiers Maurice Ravel*, 3 (1987), 27–52.

   (ed.), *Ravel: souvenirs de Manuel Rosenthal* (Paris: Hazan, 1995).

Mawer, Deborah, 'Balanchine's *La Valse*: Meanings and Implications for Ravel Studies', *Opera Quarterly*, 22/1 (2006 ['Sound Moves' issue]), 90–116.

   The Ballets of Maurice Ravel: Creation and Interpretation (Aldershot: Ashgate, 2006).

Mawer, Deborah (ed.), *The Cambridge Companion to Ravel* (Cambridge University Press, 2000).

Mercier, Bernard, 'Biographie médicale de Maurice Ravel' (PhD dissertation, Université Paris Nord, 1991).

'La Maladie neurologique de Ravel', *Cahiers Maurice Ravel*, 5 (1990–2), 13–26.

Messiaen, Olivier, and Yvonne Loriod-Messiaen, *Ravel: analyse des œuvres pour piano de Maurice Ravel* (Paris: Durand, 2004).

Mirambel, André, 'L'Inspiration grecque dans l'œuvre de Ravel', *La Revue musicale*, 19 (December 1938 [special issue]), 112–18.

Morrison, Simon, 'The Origins of *Daphnis et Chloé* (1912)', *19th-Century Music*, 28/1 (2004), 50–76.

Nichols, Roger, *Ravel* (London: J. M. Dent, 1977).

The Harlequin Years: Music in Paris, 1917–1929 (London: Thames & Hudson; Berkeley and Los Angeles: University of California Press, 2002).

(ed.), *Ravel Remembered* (London: Faber and Faber; New York: Norton, 1987).

Orenstein, Arbie, '*L'Enfant et les sortilèges*: correspondance inédite de Ravel et Colette', *Revue de musicologie*, 52/2 (1966), 215–20.

Ravel: Man and Musician (New York: Columbia University Press, 1975; second edition, New York: Dover Publications, 1991).

(ed.), *Maurice Ravel: lettres, écrits, entretiens* (Paris: Flammarion, 1989); Eng. trans. as *A Ravel Reader: Correspondence, Articles, Interviews* (New York: Columbia University Press, 1990; reprinted [with minor corrections] New York: Dover Publications, 2003).

(ed.) 'La Correspondance de Maurice Ravel à Lucien Roger Garban. Première partie (1901–1918)', *Cahiers Maurice Ravel*, 7 (2000), 19–68.

(ed.) 'La Correspondance de Maurice Ravel à Lucien Roger Garban. Deuxième partie (1919–1934)', *Cahiers Maurice Ravel*, 8 (2004), 9–89.

Orledge, Robert, 'Evocations of Exoticism', in Deborah Mawer (ed.), *The Cambridge Companion to Ravel* (Cambridge University Press, 2000), 27–46.

Perlemuter, Vlado, and Hélène Jourdan-Morhange, *Ravel d'après Ravel*, fifth edition (Lausanne: du Cervin, 1970); *Ravel According to Ravel*, trans. Frances Tanner and ed. Harold Taylor (London: Kahn & Averill, 1970).

Perret, Carine, 'L'Adoption du jazz par Darius Milhaud et Maurice Ravel: l'esprit plus que la lettre', *Revue de musicologie*, 89/2 (2003), 311–47.

'Le Romantisme ravélien, un héritage choisi', *Musurgia*, 13/2 (2006), 17–32.

Petit, Pierre, *Ravel* (Paris: Hachette, 1970).

Potvin, Gilles, 'Maurice Ravel au Canada', in John Beckwith and Frederick A. Hall (eds.), *Musical Canada* (University of Toronto Press, 1988), 149–63.

Prod'homme, Jacques-Gabriel, 'Maurice Ravel (1875–1937)', *Le Courrier du centre* (8 January 1938).

Puri, Michael J., 'Dandy, Interrupted: Sublimation, Repression, and Self-Portraiture in Maurice Ravel's *Daphnis et Chloé* (1909–12)', *Journal of the American Musicological Society*, 60/2 (2007), 317–72.

Ravel, Maurice, 'Take Jazz Seriously!', *Musical Digest*, 13/3 (1928), 49, 51.

Contemporary Music, Rice Institute Pamphlet 15/2 (1928), 131–45.

'Mes souvenirs d'enfant paresseux', *La Petite Gironde* (12 July 1931), 1.

'Jazz – Democracy's Music!' [interview], *Rhythm* (August 1932).

'Finding Tunes in Factories', *New Britain* (9 August 1933), 367.

Roland-Manuel, *L'Enfant et les sortilèges* [review], *Revue Pleyel* (February 1926).
 'Une esquisse autobiographique de Maurice Ravel' [1928], *La Revue musicale*, 19 (December 1938 [special issue]), 17–23.
  A la gloire de… Ravel (Paris: Editions de la Nouvelle revue critique, 1938); retitled *Ravel* (Paris: Gallimard, 1948; reprinted Mémoire du livre, 2000); Eng. trans. as *Maurice Ravel*, trans. Cynthia Jolly (London: Dennis Dobson, 1947).
 'Lettres de Maurice Ravel et documents inédits', *Revue de musicologie*, 38 (1956), 49–53.
Rosen, Charles, 'Where Ravel Ends and Debussy Begins', *High Fidelity*, 9/5 (1959), 42–4 and 117–121.
Roy, Jean, 'Vingt-cinq lettres de Maurice Ravel à Maurice et Nelly Delage', *Cahiers Maurice Ravel*, 2 (1986), 13–40.
Sergent, Justine, 'Music, the Brain, and Ravel', *Trends in Neurological Science*, 16 (1993), 168–72.
Sordet, Dominique, 'Festival Maurice Ravel', *L'Action française* (22 January 1932).
Stuckenschmidt, Hans Heinz, *Maurice Ravel: Variationen über Person und Werk* (Frankfurt am Main: Suhrkamp Verlag, 1966); French trans. as *Ravel: variations sur l'homme et l'œuvre* (Paris: Editions J.-C. Lattès, 1981).
Suarès, André, 'Pour Ravel', *La Revue musicale*, 6 (April 1925 [special issue]), 3–8.
Tappolet, Willy, *Maurice Ravel: Leben und Werk* (Olten: Verlag Otto Walter, 1950).
Teboul, Jean-Claude (ed.), *Ostinato rigore: revue internationale d'études musicales*, 24 (2006): *Maurice Ravel*.
Vuillermoz, Emile, 'Le Style orchestral de Maurice Ravel', *La Revue musicale*, 6 (April 1925 [special issue]), 22–7.
Whitesell, Lloyd, 'Ravel's Way', in Sophie Fuller and Lloyd Whitesell (eds.), *Queer Episodes in Music and Modern Identity* (Urbana and Chicago: University of Illinois Press, 2002), 49–78.
Zank, Stephen, *Maurice Ravel: A Guide to Research* (New York: Routledge, 2005).

Index